THE FIRST LADIES
OF THE LAND!

Does the title always mean happiness?
Here's what it meant to a few—

Dolly Madison — More personal popularity than any other First Lady

Julia Grant—Such luxury as she had never imagined, and a fabulous White House wedding for her only daughter

Eleanor Roosevelt — An unequalled opportunity to help the underprivileged, both at home and abroad

Mamie Eisenhower — A home of her own for eight years, after 30 moves in 37 years of marriage.

Rachel Jackson—Undeserved slander and an untimely death

Peggy Taylor—Ill health, the life of a recluse and the death of her beloved husband after only 16 months in office

Jane Pierce—Her only child killed before her eyes in a train wreck on the way to the inauguration

Mary Todd Lincoln—False accusations, scandal, and finally an insane asylum

These are just a few of the stories—some amusing, some tragic—which highlight this warm, richly detailed chronicle of the Women in the White House.

AMERICA'S
FIRST LADIES

Christine Sadler

Illustrated

MB

A MACFADDEN BOOK

THIS IS A MACFADDEN ORIGINAL
NEVER BEFORE PUBLISHED IN BOOK FORM

A MACFADDEN BOOK

1st printing..........September, 1963
2nd printing............January, 1964

MACFADDEN BOOKS are published by
MACFADDEN-BARTELL CORPORATION
205 East 42nd Street, New York, New York, 10017

CONTENTS

FOREWORD

WHEN Jacqueline Bouvier Kennedy became America's thirty-first First Lady at the age of thirty-one, the tendency was to recall Martha Washington in her mobcaps and decide that the charming brunette with the bouffant hairdo was the youngest, most beautiful First Lady the country had ever known—and perhaps the only one with young children.

From the standpoint of beauty, there was no room for argument. The styles change with each generation and the shy Kennedy with the little-girl look truly is an enchantress who meets all the requirements of the mid-twentieth century. Rollicking Dolley Madison, who was inclined to overdo every-thing—even the rouge she wore—would seem terribly dated beside her. Elizabeth Monroe, who won the title of "la belle Americaine" from the Parisians, lacked personal warmth.

Mrs. Kennedy is actually the third youngest First Lady. Frances Folsom married President Grover Cleveland in the Blue Parlor before her twenty-second birthday and Julia Gardiner, "the Rose of Long Island," was a scant twenty-four when she became the second wife of President John Tyler. The average age of the wives of the Presidents (the actual wives, not the stand-in hostesses) has been a bit over forty-eight years. The oldest of all was the wife of "Old Tippe-canoe," William Henry Harrison. She was sixty-five when her husband became President. He was the first President to die in office, after only a month, and Anna Symmes Harrison, alone among the First Ladies, never came to Washington at all. She was ill out in Ohio. But she lived to see her grandsons go off to the Civil War; among them was Benjamin, who be-came our twenty-third President.

Frances Cleveland also surpassed Mrs. Kennedy on the young child front—although time may still rectify this. Two little girls were born to Mrs. Cleveland while she was First Lady and one of them, Esther (now living in England) was born in the White House. Edith Carow Roosevelt (Mrs. Teddy) brought five young children to the White House, as well as a sensational step-daughter named Alice, but the youngest of them was almost four at the time. Mary Todd Lincoln, the mother of Willie and Tad as well as of grown-up Robert, also had a young family. Mary at forty-two was a very young First Lady, although it is difficult at times to re-member it.

7

Nearly all administrations have known the laughter of young children, but usually it has been that of grandchildren. The first child born in the White House was the grandson of Thomas Jefferson. The latest one, the grandson of Woodrow Wilson.

Speaking of Jefferson, he was a widower of long standing when he became president. The country had no First Lady and got along quite well! Dolley Madison's husband was the fourth President but she was only the third First Lady. Andrew Jackson was a brand new widower when he became President. His Rachel was never First Lady in the White House, but only First Lady-elect. He buried her on the Christmas Eve after his election and stormed off to Washington to make his enemies pay for "murdering her" with campaign slanders. Jackson, the first President born in a log cabin, smashed the stranglehold of the East Coast to smithereens. Life in the White House would never be the same again—at least not until Jacqueline Kennedy came along. In many ways she is a throwback to the elegant "Ladies of the Revolution," who were there when the country was looking outward and learning to live with the rest of the world, rather than inward.

Washington, who spoke of "no entangling alliances," nevertheless set up the first protocol in this country with an eye to making a good impression on the older countries of Europe. Martha dressed as elegantly as the best of them among the early comers, although she did not speak a foreign language. Abigail Adams rushed to teach herself French when France joined in the American Revolution, though when she reached Paris she realized that her accent left much to be desired.

Jacqueline Kennedy's Bouvier forebears came to America to help Lafayette aid the Americans during their Revolution for freedom, and she knows three languages in addition to English. But this is no record, either. Lou Henry Hoover, perhaps the greatest scholar among the First Ladies, knew five languages well and several others in part. First Ladies did not need foreign languages so much in her day as they do now, but she talked Chinese "sotto voce" to her husband at White House parties.

All thirty-one First Ladies varied widely, but in large part they have been as wonderful as the country itself—with all its sectional differences evident. The wives of "the Ohio Presidents" are a saga in themselves. They were the first "new women," bent on education, temperance and votes for women. (Except that Abigail Adams, of course, wanted woman suffrage written into the Constitution and a First Lady from Ohio, Florence Harding, allowed alcohol to be served in the White House while Prohibition was the law of the land.)

Generalizations about First Ladies can be as hazardous as they are about the Presidents, but there does seem to be something different about the ones from beyond the Mississippi: Julia Grant, Lou Hoover, Bess Truman and Mamie Eisenhower.

First Ladies come from all social and economic strata. Perhaps Eliza Johnson from the mountains of Tennessee had the least chance for culture, but Abigail Fillmore from western New York did not have an easy time of it, either. Eliza and Abigail were both responsible for starting their husbands off on the road to education. Eliza, at sixteen, married younger than any other First Lady and Abigail Fillmore, older than her husband, kept teaching school after she married him.

The First Lady can have a great deal of influence, or she can have none at all. She can never do anything much about changing the country even if she wishes to, although Eleanor Roosevelt belied this. "Lemonade Lucy" Hayes refused to serve wines in the White House—and so did Sarah Childress Polk—but after their soirees and receptions Washingtonians went on to have their drinks elsewhere.

Some First Ladies "fight" the public for privacy—and who can blame them? Others ride with the tide and are happier. Julia Grant seems to have been the first First Lady who openly admitted that she liked the job. There have been others who acted as if they were imposed upon at every turn. The secret of Dolley Madison's phenomenal success was that she held no animosity toward any human being and her generosity knew no bounds. Grace Coolidge liked everybody and everybody in return liked her.

It's a tough job any way one looks at it and it can be murder for the First Lady who does not sympathize with her husband's career—politics. The First Lady is the only "public servant" who works for nothing. She has no salary nor is she elected, but there are always people eager to tell her exactly what she should do. Mamie Eisenhower was blamed for doing too little and Eleanor Roosevelt for doing too much. Supposedly the First Lady has some "set" duties, but what are they beyond entertaining her husband's contacts? If she chooses to go beyond that, as Mrs. Kennedy is doing in making the White House a great museum of American culture, the country is usually grateful. Abigail Fillmore was horrified that there was not even a Bible in the White House, and she started its first library. Congress was sympathetic and went along with the appropriations. The library was of no earthly use nor pleasure to some of the later comers. (Unfortunately, not all of our First Families have bothered to read so that it almost disappeared.) Mrs. Kennedy managed to have a law passed giving the White House museum status so that this cannot happen again. At least the books, if not wanted, cannot be sold at auction nor put in some government storehouse for the mice to nibble. Or at least that's the hope!

Margaret Taylor, the wife of Zachary, lived as a recluse in the White House and attended no function more public than Sunday School. Her daughter, Betty, took over the "set" duties, so-called, and when Zachary Taylor died from overexertion and eating the wrong food on a hot Fourth of July, it was news to some that he even had a wife. She is the only First Lady of whom there is no photograph nor portrait which satisfies the historians as being "real."

The whole bleak pre-Civil War period is crowded with First Ladies who reflected only the sickness of the country. Jane Pierce, who could faint on schedule and hated all thoughts of "dirty politics," was only a reflection of her times. How much influence she had in tearing her husband to pieces cannot be estimated because he—a Democrat from New Hampshire—already had more than he could handle as the Civil War came on. The record of Franklin Pierce would have been better, however, if his wife had cared at all about what happened to him, or had been able to understand even the remotest iota of what was going on. One sympathizes to the point of tears with the plight of Pierce, who found no bed made up for him at the White House and whose wife was being the complete invalid at a hotel in Baltimore because nobody dared bring her into Washington. Some First Ladies have indeed been a burden to their husbands.

On the other hand, many sympathized with McKinley because his wife was an epileptic and clung closer than a cocklebur, but he loved her clinging and would have been lost without it. He was able enough and devout enough, or both, to consider her no problem. Abraham Lincoln loved his wife when all others turned against her—but this tempestuous and talented woman was hounded into an insane asylum after his death. An everlasting bright summer's day is not guaranteed for any First Lady either by the Constitution or by tradition. If she loves her husband and vice versa the battle is half won, but being First Lady is no easy job.

It sounds like the most luxurious wife-spot in the country and it is—as well as the most glamorous. It has been estimated that it would take a personal income of $2,500,000 a year, tax free, to live as luxuriously as the President and his family not only can, but must. The White House at the moment is a well-run mansion of 132 rooms—depending on who is counting them. What's a closet to one administration can become a bedroom to the next. It is air-conditioned, in no danger of falling down, is valued at $25,000,000, has its own swimming pool and movie theater, and a built-in custodial staff of about seventy-five (Mamie Eisenhower thought she could help balance the national budget by cutting the staff, and so had fewer). The number of planes, ships, automobiles, and now helicopters at the President's disposal is limited only by the miles which he chooses to travel. But remember what happened to Mamie when she dared to ride in a government plane out to Elizabeth Arden's health farm in Arizona? Neither the White House nor any of its trappings belongs to a First Lady, and that can become most frustrating—as witnessed through the years.

Things are much better now than they were when the President had his offices on the so-called family bedroom floor and the offices began to take over every nook and cranny. The expansion of offices during the Civil War, for example, was so great that the Lincolns at times must have wondered where they were to sleep. Visitors came right into the spittoon-decorated front lobby, as to any hotel, and waited their turn to go up the steps and see Lincoln. Little Tad Lincoln, a pixie child, used to busy himself by being always on hand to give the callers preliminary interviews and once, as a way of raising money, he set up a concession in the lobby to sell refreshments. Mrs. Teddy Roosevelt was the first First Lady to get the offices out from under and to have a bedroom floor which was private. Cleveland outraged some of the public by buying a second home for himself and trying to honeymoon in semi-privacy.

The White House is Public Reservation Number One, a ward of the National Park Service. Tourists of today rush through it at the rate of about two million a year, every morning except Sundays (for reverence) and Mondays (for cleaning). When President Truman built his controversial balcony, it enabled the First Family for the first time in history to get out on "a porch" and glimpse what the weather was like before noon. It's quite a sight to see the White House staff take over behind the tourists, making every effort to sweep the tourists out by noon and to get the old place ready for a 12:30 luncheon for perhaps a hundred guests. Everything is vacuumed, the rugs go back down, the ropes are removed, the linens and silver and glassware and flowers go into place, the Marine Band (or some part of it) takes its position, and the show is on. If anyone catches a bit of dust on the stairway, it's the First Lady who is at fault, and nobody else!

The staff, increasingly good on the job, can be as impersonal as the Internal Revenue Service. At times each member of it seems to be living only until all the travail is over and he or she can write a book about what *actually* went on at the White House during *that* administration. Bess Truman

11

could not get hot biscuits in the White House until she brought her own cook from Independence, Missouri, and "Ike" could neither cook nor raid the icebox—two of his favorite diversions—until he built a kitchen for himself on the third floor. The staff is not perfect, although it at times acts as though it were. President Kennedy gets better service than President Pierce did, but the staff is on "hours" (plus retirement) although the First Lady knows no "hours."

If the President plays golf in the middle of the afternoon, that's bad. (After all, everybody in America works from nine until five!) If he is up all night talking to India and Pakistan and Berlin, that's only his job. The same applies to the First Lady. Jacqueline Kennedy worked very hard during her first year but her long vacation during the second summer was much resented, as well as misrepresented. The Washington *Post* said that she was away for three months, when in fact she was back conducting social functions at least twice during the interval. If she had closeted herself in the White House and done nothing at all perhaps nobody would have minded; but there she was off on water-skis over in Italy. Her "private" life is not private. Everybody keeps tabs, often inaccurately, but rather thoroughly. If she permits this sort of thing to bother her too much she's a goner, but if she goes ahead and makes her own contribution—with malice toward none and forbearance for all—she will probably remain as sensational as when she began.

Not since Eleanor Roosevelt has there been such interest in a First Lady. That Mrs. Kennedy wants to contribute to the cultural stream of America is obvious. She is not a sitter-downer. She must expect to be criticized, since neither she nor her critics are perfect, and she will, doubtlessly, make many mistakes. A full hundred percent of the country is never going to approve of her knees showing in each photograph, nor does everybody like her hairdo. This is only par for the course, however. If she does not care too much about something so trivial as arguments as to whether she wears a wig (and does she?) she will be a great First Lady. In fact, she already is. In her first years she has accomplished a great deal, and she has other plans in mind.

MARTHA CUSTIS WASHINGTON (1789-1797)

First in the Heart of the General

"TELL them it is Mrs. Washington who rides to join the General," a radiant little woman in a plum-colored cloak told her drivers as they neared Cambridge, Massachusetts, first Winter Headquarters of the Continental Army, on December 11, 1775.

A pretty and charming woman, Martha Washington, at forty-four, was on her first trip north of Annapolis, Maryland. It would be thirteen years before she became our first First Lady: the only one to serve wholly in the eighteenth century and before the present White House was built. Her full face by this time had started to collect the double chins known to generations of school children, but withal she retained the grace of an experienced horsewoman.

Coming as she did from the affluent background of early Tidewater Virginia, Martha loved to dance, was passable at cards, embroidered expertly, handled servants with finesse, played the harpsichord, knew about weaving, preserving, feeding guests, and filling a room with rose or herb scents. She ordered her finest dresses and furniture from England.

She departed from the norm to grind her own toothpowder from cuttle-fish bone. She was vain about her excellent teeth, pretty hands, and tiny feet. Her recipe book contained cooking recipes but was filled mostly with home remedies and with information concerning the best time to plant flowers. She was neat as a pin, an erect five-feet-two-inches tall, and had a stubborn streak which would stand her in good stead.

In addition to sixteen years of protected wedlock to Virginia's most popular military hero—a meticulous man who lavished attention on her and her children—Martha's life up to this time had included two other experiences of deep influence: a strictly disciplined childhood and an early marriage of almost seven years duration.

Thanks to a hardheaded mother, who descended from a line of clergymen, Martha underwent stiffer training than did many other little girls of the Tidewater area. She was the oldest of eight children. Often she was up at dawn studying her letters, rules on manners, and plantation crafts. To supervise a job well, thought her mother, Mrs. John Dandridge, one must know it backward and forward.

But Martha, an exuberant young miss, was not an eager scholar. She preferred hours on her pony to hours at her books, at the preserving kettle, or with a needle. But the Dandridge disciplines would come in handy and she would be most grateful for them. Some of her letters are still in existence and show that she had a graceful and informal style of writing, with spelling about par for her day. And her needlework has never been excelled by any other First Lady.

At seventeen Martha married Daniel Parke Custis, twenty years her senior and the catch of the Tidewater. This wealthy sophisticate showered his brown-eyed bride with emeralds and garnets, had her painted by Wollaston, and left her, age twenty-six, the most desirable widow in all Virginia. She had two small children, thousands of acres, fine houses (including one in old Williamsburg), 500 slaves, household silver later valued at $30,000, and pounds sterling with a cash-in value of about $100,000, as well as good credit with the Bank of England.

Her children had fortunes of their own. The little girl, Martha (Little Patt), died while still in her teens. The remaining child, handsome John Parke (Jacky) Custis, at twenty-one was considered the richest young man in Virginia. He and his pretty bride, Eleanor, of the Maryland Calverts, were with Martha as she neared Cambridge on this trip north. Using the elegant Washington coach-and-four, scarlet and white livery resplendent, the trio had been on the road for nearly a month.

It was a journey to change a life and this is what it did to Martha's. It took her right into the theater of the Revolutionary War and into the melting pot of public opinion. Because of this, when she became First Lady she could truthfully say:

"I have learned from experience that the great part of our happiness or misery depends on our dispositions and not on our circumstances. We carry the seeds of one or the other about with us in our minds wherever we go."

Her love for the General prompted the trip. He had left home on June 9 of that year to attend the Second Continental Congress in Philadelphia—and just kept going. In a hurried letter in mid-June he broke the news to "My dear Patsy" that Congress wanted him to command the military forces which would, if need be, fight the Mother Country all the way to freedom and as he saw the assignment, he might be away from home seven years!

Knowing how his Patsy would react, he next day dashed off another letter of love but of very cold comfort. She must know, he said, that his affection for her was so unalterable

14

that neither time nor distance could change it. Why, he could have more pleasure in her company in one month than he expected to find "abroad" should his stay turn out to be seven times seven years.

His biggest worry, her absent husband continued, would be about her.

"I shall feel no pain from the toil and danger of the campaign," he wrote. "My biggest unhappiness will flow from the uneasiness I know you will feel from being left alone. I therefore beg that you will summon your whole fortitude, and pass the time as agreeably as possible." This was what would relieve his mind more than anything, he continued.

"Nothing else will give me so much sincere satisfaction as to hear it from your own pen." As he well knew, Martha had a way of shifting the chores of letter writing to others. The General himself often wrote over her "M. Washington" signature. He wanted none of that this time and demanded to hear direct. He enclosed his will, writing that "the provisions made for you, in case of my death, will, I hope, be agreeable," and added that it would add greatly to his own uneasiness "to hear that you are dissatisfied or complaining. . . ."

Martha's reaction was to plead to be allowed to join him wherever he was, and in whatever danger. He considered this to be totally unfeasible, however, and she had almost despaired of winning him to her idea when the Tories gave her unexpected assistance in planning to capture and hold her as a valuable hostage worth more than her weight in psychological warfare. The General wrote a nephew, "I can hardly think that Lord Dunmore can act so low and unmannerly a part as to think of seizing Mrs. Washington by way of revenge upon me . . ."

Martha was in the Tidewater with relatives, presenting her new daughter-in-law, when she received word to join the General. Not waiting on ceremony, she piled her trunks and the bridal couple into the carriage and set out. Washington had written Joseph Reed of Philadelphia to meet her en route and send her north around Tory strongholds, but she beat the letter to Reed's by three days.

A Tory newspaper took advantage of her absence from Mount Vernon to write: "Mrs. Washington, being a warm loyalist, has separated from her husband . . . lives, much respected, in the city of New York."

None of this bothered Martha. She had joined the General.

She found him with his hands full and obviously needing her. She was someone to whom he could pour out his frustrations, if nothing else. He was, he said, "Imbarked on a tempestuous ocean, from which perhaps no friendly harbor is to be found." His army was almost powderless. The British were in Boston, and spies were everywhere. His pay-master was without funds. Reenlistments were almost nil, and the encampment swarmed with visitors.

His table expenses, as submitted to Congress, were run-ning about $1,000 a month—and the General never really enjoyed his guests. His wife was the diplomat on that front. She immediately assumed the "bookkeeping of hospitality" and became a screening wall for the many who sought to see the General. She had the knack of sending them away happy even if they did not talk with him personally.

Enlisted men and officers alike felt at home around Martha. There was no "side" to "Lady Washington," but only a feel-ing of warmth and correctness. As would be said a million times: "She created love and esteem." Ladies calling from Cambridge were surprised to find the General's wife in an apron, knitting or patching. Soon sewing societies became popular.

Her first Christmas at camp was oppressively gloomy, how-ever. The Colonies were in mourning more deeply, it seemed, than they were in rebellion. Congress had asked an end to merriment as well as to British imports. She thought a Twelfth Night Ball needed, but the idea was sternly vetoed by the General until she reminded him that it would be their seventeenth wedding anniversary. The dance helped morale —probably the General's as much as anybody's. He loved to dance, and subsequently all during the war, often under the bleakest of conditions, the occasional dance nights continued.

Under an orderly system which enabled anyone to drop in to see the General over a cup of coffee or at dinner, petty jealousies about rank seemed to lessen at headquarters. The sick received sympathy as well as coffee and medicine. Martha helped create an all's well atmosphere. As she wrote to a friend in Virginia: "Every person seems to be chearful and happy here . . . some days we have a number of cannon and shell from Boston and Bunkers Hill but it does not seem to surprise anyone but me. . . ."

On her way home to Virginia next spring, Martha decided to help insure her return the following winter by stopping in Philadelphia "to have the smallpox." Cases of the dread dis-ease had broken out in the Cambridge Camp and she feared that in case of an epidemic the General would make her stay home unless she was immune. To become immune in those days involved the awkward process of letting a doctor "give" you the disease and then spending several days in isolation while it ran its course. In a delightful eighteenth century document, John Hancock, President of the Continental Con-gress, wrote the General that "Mrs. Hancock would esteem it to have Mrs. Washington take the smallpox in her home."

Martha "took" it successfully in a Philadelphia inn, however, rather than be a bother.

The General was ill that autumn and delayed so long in sending for her that Martha threatened to start out on foot to Morristown, N. J., "if you can't find horses." When she arrived at a New Jersey inn, the wife of its keeper assumed that she was "Lady Washington's maid" until the General rushed in to wrap her in his long arms. Tiny Martha and her unimposing looks often had a hard time with first impressions. Also, during the summer she had become much more homespun.

In her carriage this time were samples from extra looms at Mount Vernon showing that fibers could be mixed and that ravelings from such materials as old chair bottoms could be made into "as good as new" cloth. She had much to show the ladies about making-do.

In all, Martha Washington made seven round trips to headquarters. Her husband wrote thank-yous to nearly everyone who befriended her on the way to and from Mt. Vernon, and on his expense account he entered the cost of it all at $4,000. Martha more than paid her way, however, and not in service alone. In the year 1780, she is credited with giving $24,000 to the freedom cause.

From Valley Forge, the low ebb in cold and frustration, she wrote her inquiring friend, Mercy Warren, in March of 1778: "The General is camped in what is called the Great Valley . . . Officers and men are chiefly in hutts, which they say is tolerable comfortable. The army is as healthy as can well be expected in general—the General's apartment is very small. He has had a log cabin bilt to dine in which has made our quarters much more tolerable than at first."

The General really did not get back to Mt. Vernon for nearly seven years. He stopped there in the autumn of 1781 on his way to the Battle of Yorktown. Martha gave a great feast for him and his victory-bound entourage. Jacky Custis, now the father of four small children, joined his stepfather as aide for this campaign and went on with him.

Yorktown was a victory overshadowed by personal tragedy for Martha. Jacky died of camp fever and thus the General's dear Patsy lost the last of her two children. The tragedy was personal for the General, too, and he left the scene of triumph to be with his stepson when he died at the home of Martha's sister near Williamsburg. Washington ever had been a loving stepfather and his own grief was such that he thought Martha, the real parent and perhaps an overly possessive one in the earlier years, would be so overwhelmed by Jacky's death that she would discard all thought of returning north with him for the winter encampment.

17

But his Patsy had grown stronger than he realized. Indeed she was returning to camp with him! Where else would she want to be? The General eased her sorrow somewhat by immediately arranging to take "to rear as my own" the two youngest of Jacky's four children: Eleanor (Nelly), less than two years of age, and George Washington (Little Wash) Parke Custis, then only a few months old. They would remain with their mother and two sisters, Eliza and Martha, until the Washingtons returned to Mt. Vernon. The General's wife was in camp with him at Newburgh, New York, when the last of the Revolutionary War prisoners were released in 1783.

Back home at Mt. Vernon, Martha turned her delighted attention to Nelly, then four, and Little Wash, a bouncing two. Her proudest boast to them always was that she had heard the opening and closing guns of most of the major campaigns of the long Revolution and "always marched home again in the spring." From the beginning she also impressed on them that "Your Grandpapa's thoughts are the most important things in the world."

The Potomac rolled placidly by as she taught Nelly the harpsichord, babied Little Wash, and entertained so many visitors that her husband claimed Mt. Vernon had become "a well resorted tavern."

Six years passed before Washington attended another political meeting of disturbing importance to Martha. She was as unprepared for his Presidency, in many ways, as for his commander-in-chiefship. Now fifty-seven years old, she was less inclined to uproot herself at a moment's notice. She questioned him: What is wrong with the Confederation of States that they now need a strong joint constitution and must have *you* again—and this time as President? What shall I pack? Is furniture furnished? Did you say four years?

The General dashed ahead without her, promising to send the carriage back. She missed his inaugural in New York on April 30, 1789, as well as the brilliant ball in both their honors. Most of all, she realized when she read the newspapers, she missed the General's triumphal entry across the Hudson river on a grand new barge built especially for the occasion, decked in red, white and blue and featuring everything in thirteens, in recognition of thirteen states *united* at last.

But Martha, aglow with pride, prepared "to march" again. Almost a month behind the General she journeyed up the Eastern seaboard, Nelly and Little Wash beside her, amid an unending serenade of church bells, fireworks, military escorts, speeches, and food.

In Baltimore she was served a great "collation," which included hot-house grapes, and the mayor noted with enthusiasm that she wore Made-in-America clothes. In Philadelphia the ovation was so great that she stood in the carriage and said a few words of thanks: her first and only public speech. How could she know that speeches by First Ladies would not be proper for another hundred years?

Best of all, the General had the barge brought out and he crossed the Hudson to meet her. She had a triumphal entry and an inaugural all her own. This was something no other First Lady has ever had. Not a man to leave things to chance, the General had sent a discreet notice to the newspapers that May 27 was the day she would arrive. The populace was out en masse. Thirteen guns boomed as she passed the Battery. It was June 8 before Martha caught her breath enough to write to her favorite niece, Fanny Washington, the following abbreviated account of her first days in her new role:

"My Dear Fanny: I have the pleasure to tell you that we had a very agreeable journey. I arrived in Philadelphia on fry day after I left you without the least accident to distress us. We were met by the city troops of Horses and conducted safe to Gray's Ferry, where a number of Ladies and gentlemen came to meet me and after a cold colation we preceded to town. I went to Mr. Morrises . . . the Children were very little of being sick.

"I set out on Monday with Mrs. Morris and her two daughters—and was met Wed. morning by the President . . . with fine barge you have seen so much said of in the papers with the same oarsmen that carried the P. to New York . . .

"Dear little Washington seemed to be lost in a maze at the great parade that was made for us all the way we came—the Governor of the state met me as soon as we landed and led me up to the House. The paper will tell you how I was complimented on my landing . . . The house is a very good one and is handsomely furnished all new for the General.

"I have been so much engaged since I came here that I never opened your box . . . but shall soon have time as most of the visits are at an end. I have not had one half hour to myself since the day of my arrival. My first care was to get the children to a good school, which they are both very much pleased at . . . Nelly shall begin musick next week. . . . She is a little wild creature and spends her time at the window looking at carriages, etc., passing by—which is new to her and very common for children to do.

"My hair is set and dressed every day and I have put on white muslin habits for the summer. You would I fear think me a good deal in fashion if you but could see me. . . . Give my love to Hariot and send me the measure of her foot. Believe me your most affectionate M. Washington."

The traffic problem may have been different, but the first

First Lady had learned what all her successors came to know. The wife of a President is on constant display and finds scant time for relatives and personal affairs. Martha's schedule was as full as that of any who came after her, and fuller than that of many, because Martha shirked no obligations.

Evidently she soon learned another thing that continues unchanging: the vying for attention, the currying favor, the meaningless compliments. At any rate she shortly wrote Mercy Warren: "Please do me the justice to realize that I care only for what comes from the heart." She did not want her old friend to think she was taken in by all the bouquets.

One person most eager to meet Martha was Abigail Adams, now a grandmother, too. Abigail's husband, John Adams, was Vice President, and in the elaborate social procedures set up, her place would be "always at Mrs. Washington's right." Mrs. Adams took her married daughter and rushed to call on the First Lady, and then dashed a glowing account off to her sister in Boston:

"She is plain in dress, but the plainness is the best of every article . . . Her hair is white, her teeth beautiful, her person short rather than otherwise. . . . Her manners are modest and unassuming dignified and feminine and not a tincture of hateur about her . . ." Abigail would defend Martha against all comers, always.

The General sometimes became "the P." in Martha's letters now. He knew his new job would involve much entertaining, and this he saw as part of his duty. But even before his wife's arrival, he realized he needed to bring the callers, dinners, and receptions into some kind of order if he was to get anything else done. He besought his Cabinet's aid, and Alexander Hamilton, a man almost as orderly-minded as he, was helpful in evolving a "protocol."

Washington would stick to this protocol, although many called it much too formal. Formality suited Washington's purposes, one of which was to make the brash new country respected at the courts abroad. He spent much of his own money and put great effort into proving that the brave new land called America could keep up with the European Joneses when it came to displaying good manners.

Martha often found his rules quite confining. At times, she confided to Fanny, she felt "more like a state prisoner than anything else" and complained that "I know nothing of what goes on in town." Also, she admitted to pen-pal Mercy Warren, she frequently thought herself a bit old. It was a shame, she said, that she enjoyed it so little, when a younger and gayer person might find it all rather enchanting. But she never let the General down. She followed his rules with verve and aplomb for eight long years, kept up the daily hair dressings, put on bright attire, spread her amiability in all directions. And always she exacted the courtesy due the wife of "the P."

Neither the President nor Martha could go out to private dinners after the rules of protocol were set. "The P." himself returned no calls made on him, but Martha returned all visits that the ladies made on her, and by the third day. Tobias Lear, the President's secretary, accompanied her and a liveried servant ran ahead to knock on doors and announce: "Madame, the wife of the President." A call lasted about half an hour, usually, including the cakes and tea.

Martha's evening to entertain the elite was "fryday" and only those in full dress were admitted. The ladies passed by Martha, who remained seated, to bow or curtsy (the American handshake was not then in vogue) and then find seats until the President came by to greet them. Subsequently everybody mingled and chatted over refreshments. It was a stately and elegant period and the guests were worthy of Watteau. The men wore powdered wigs and knee buckles. The ladies blossomed out in quilted pettiskirts and head plumes.

Official dinners were Tuesdays and Thursdays at four o'clock with but five minutes allowed the laggards. "I have a cook who asks not whether the guests are here but if the hour is," the President learned to say. Martha presided at these dinners even when it took three successive evenings to feed all members of the Pennsylvania legislature, as it did when the Washingtons entertained the lawmakers after the national capital moved to Philadelphia.

Also she must have favorably influenced the food. A Congressman who found the fare the thinnest of his memory before her arrival, soon regarded it the "best in town." History records only one occasion on which she was unable, even by means of good food, to save the evening. Senator William Maclay of Pennsylvania, reported the affair:

"It was a great dinner," he said, "the best of its kind I ever was at. The room, however, was disagreeably warm. First the soup; fish roasted and boiled, meats, sammon, fowl, etc. . . . The middle of the table was garnished the usual way with small images, flowers, etc . . . The desserts were apple pie, puddings, etc. . . . then ice cream, jellies, etc.; then water melons, musck melons, apples, peaches, etc. Not a health drank, scarcely a word said until the cloth was taken away . . . Mrs. Washington at last withdrew with the ladies. I thought that the men would now begin but the same stillness remained . . . The President rose, went upstairs to drink coffee; the company followed." End of evening!

Christmas and the Fourth of July were times for entertainment spectaculars in the Washington regime and everybody was included, full dress or no. The Fourth usually featured Revolutionary brigades from far and near. The cannon started at daybreak and everybody was fed, often from loaded tables under the trees.

Then the President's birthdays were added as regular dates for celebrations. The city of Philadelphia went wild on these occasions. The longer the Washingtons stayed in office, the greater their acclaim. No one has ever matched the General in awe and aura. Just to be in the same city with him was an event. Martha's dresses for these occasions were magnificent. Each year her satins and plumes became more colorful and her mobcaps starchier.

Washington loved the theater and attended often in New York and Philadelphia. He also took the children to the circus. Martha did not always participate in these "free evenings." As she wrote Fanny, she often became stubborn and did not go out when she could. Occasionally she and Abigail took the children on outings to see natural wonders like waterfalls and palisades. When Nelly grew up she often sang for Congressional dinners and one of her chores always was to see Grandmama to bed. After Nelly read her a psalm and played a hymn or two, they would reminisce about how peaceful things used to be at Mt. Vernon.

Grandmama grew tired as the years passed. She sometimes snapped a bit, perhaps because of her tight schedule. "You are late, Mr. Peale," she accused the artist one morning when he came to work on her portrait. "What's good enough for the General is good enough for his guest," she said sharply to Nelly when the young beauty wanted to fix her tresses before a beau arrived.

This was her motto always: the General comes first. "The General is always right," she assured a relative. Anything which benefited him was her pleasure. And she did a great deal to humanize the General among his associates and with the public. He owed her perhaps more than he knew.

She was sixty-five when Gilbert Stuart painted her most widely distributed portrait: full face and in the mobcap that came to be associated with old age. It does her an injustice. She was not *that* fat and not even her amiability shows. Eight years of state dinners may have added to her chins, but her deftness of spirit remained.

"They burn incense to her," Jefferson grumbled when he broke politically with the General, adding gratuitously that he attributed this to the goodness of her heart and not to the brilliance of her mind. Abigail Adams, loyal friend, rose to the defense. Mrs. Washington's accomplishments were

22

well known and her mind of great dignity always, Abigail shot back.

When the Washingtons went home at last to Mt. Vernon, it took several wagons to haul their household accumulation, which included a parrot and some canaries. Martha was so accustomed to running in high gear that she remained as busy as ever. The General frowned on her busy-ness and sent to New York for a housekeeper, the cost of same being declared unimportant.

She eluded him somewhat by reestablishing her training room for servants assigned to sewing and knitting, and spent hours in it daily. Visitors came from everywhere and received a welcome. Many of them wrote of the delightful old lady who entertained them.

After the General's death in December of 1799, Martha deliberately destroyed their letters to each other. Only two, caught in the recesses of her desk, escaped her fire. They were written by the General in 1775, and included the one in which he predicted he might be gone for seven years.

Congress asked Martha's permission to remove the General's body to a crypt in the Capitol when that structure was finished and also asked that she consent to be buried there, too. Although it was against her personal preference, she consented, saying that he had taught her never to oppose the public will. By the time the structure was finished, however, Martha also was dead (May, 1802) and relatives refused the removals. The Capitol crypts have remained empty. Both rest together at their beloved Mt. Vernon.

ABIGAIL SMITH ADAMS (1797-1801)

First in the White House

ABIGAIL ADAMS, a spicy intellectual from Braintree, Massachusetts, was fifty-six years of age and ending twenty-six years as a public wife when first she saw the muddy District of Columbia on Sunday, November 16, 1800. She arrived in early afternoon with an entourage of ten horses and nine people, after spending most of Saturday lost on the road from Baltimore.

Since Abigail always had taken a jaundiced view of having a special city built as a seat for the Federal government, she was not at all surprised to learn that the dreamers who planned it had forgotten to put up proper road signs. But it hurt her already sorely beset pride to have to be rescued Saturday night by Colonel Thomas Snowden, a hospitable Marylander who lived near Laurel. She had wanted to go to an inn with her large party but there was none nearby.

The truth is that the second First Lady, who often is called the brainiest of them all, at the moment found her life a shambles in all directions. Politically she already was a lame duck First Lady in that her husband, John Adams, would be a one-term President. She had picked up the voting returns along her way from New England and she wondered how in the world her irascible husband was taking them. He had preceded her to the new Federal city by several weeks.

Her main tenure as First Lady had been in Philadelphia and she noted as she passed through that city that the former executive mansion already had been turned into an inn. Her position was awkward and unprecedented. She would be First Lady only until next March, but in the meantime she must get the Presidential furniture, shipped ahead in early summer, in place and fix up a brand new home for all future First Ladies. Setting up housekeeping for other women could not have been an enviable job at best.

Just who would succeed John Adams, the Founding Father whom she loved with an ardor not outlined in the stern Puritan religion by which she lived, was not yet known. The votes were so inconclusive that Congress would have to decide between Thomas Jefferson and Aaron Burr. Abigail wondered what terrible sins so young a nation could possibly have committed to deserve either of these men.

Abigail must also have wondered how many votes, if any, she had lost for her husband. She was the first First Lady, but would not be the last, to be accused of meddling in state politics. "Madame President, but of a faction" was how Albert Gallatin, who would be in Jefferson's Cabinet, had described her. Abigail was not the silent type, nor was she given to compromises. She was outspokenly brilliant and many, including Jefferson, had through the years found her charming. Once he had sent her as a gift a dozen pairs of real silk stockings woven in a French monastery. She had mothered his youngest daughter, Maria, long ago in London and she had written home from France that he was "one of the choice ones of the earth."

She would have been less than feminine, however, if she had failed at this time to consider Jefferson too unspeakable for words. He had been Vice President to her husband and had let him down completely, in her opinion. Politics as practiced in America had in the election just passed been for the first time bitter and vitriolic.

And Abigail had personal problems, too. She had stopped in New York to visit her middle son, Charles, the attractive one who had been disowned by his father but never by her, and she had found him dying in poverty. She knew she would never see him again. She had one of his daughters, Susanna, a mite in a black dress, in the carriage with her as she drove south to face her few months in Washington.

As she probably expected, she found her husband gloomy and on the verge of resignation. Since he was not wanted again, he reasoned, why not get out now? But Abigail counseled against resignation most fervently. Charles Francis Adams, her grandson, would write that her influence on her husband nearly always was of this negative nature, and designed to prevent hasty indiscretions by one who was of an ardent and excitable temperament.

Abigail needed all the fortitude she could muster when she entered the green-timbered structure in which she must set up housekeeping. This building would later be known as the White House and eventually would be called beautiful but when Abigail first saw it, it was little more than a shell with only a few rooms here and there finished. Even the entrance steps and interior stairs were lacking. Workmen lived in the basement or in leantos pushed up against the outside. There were no bells with which to summon servants. She had to string her laundry in the big unfinished parlor, but she made the house function.

Much of the furniture shipped ahead had been damaged

in transit and some of the sofas and chairs had disappeared. Abigail's good china was partially smashed. But the determined First Lady intended to conquer the situation, even though White House grocery shopping had to be done in the little port city of Georgetown, where most of the District's three thousand inhabitants then lived. At times it took Abigail all day to get to Georgetown and back when returning her calls, but return them she did. Also she scheduled regular official dinners.

And by New Year's Day of 1801 she was ready for the first public reception ever held in the White House. All who ventured up the makeshift front steps that day witnessed the beginning of a White House tradition that would linger until well after World War I: a gay New Year's party at which the Marine Band always played and to which all in town were invited.

Guests were received in the upstairs oval room. By then some interior steps had been installed. The view down the river from this room was enhanced by glowing crimson curtains. Two mahogany sofas and twenty-two chairs, all upholstered in the crimson of Washington's day were in their places, as were end tables, a piano, a harp, and a guitar. A magnificent Aubusson rug brightened the floor and a huge wood fire roared up the chimney. The kitchen yielded up cakes and tarts, tea and coffee, curds and cream, punch and syllabub, and other goodies.

Abigail, in chic brocade, remained seated to receive her guests in the Federalist tradition. John Adams wore his powdered wig with bow in back, as well as his best black velvet suit, with silver buckles at his knees and on his slippers. All agreed that the "remarkable Adamses" initiated the new mansion with a very good party.

The First Lady's last official dinner, one for judges and their wives, was scheduled for February 3, and after it she said that she intended to rush home to Massachusetts and dry out her rheumatism, which had worsened in the Potomac climate and the damp house. But, in her heart, Abigail probably had no thought of leaving town until she knew who would be the next President.

Jefferson, finally voted the role of new President, called to say goodbye to the departing First Lady. Abigail had been the first American woman received at the Court of St. James and had there learned how to exude politeness that could chill to the bone. She received Jefferson with the utmost correctness but was coolly formal. However, the two would be friends again.

Her last official responsibility as First Lady completed, Abigail set out for Braintree, determined to keep her mind above politics. As it developed, this was impossible for her. Her husband stuck out his tenure of office until the morning of March 4 but he headed for home before the inaugural events and without congratulating the new President.

Just as Abigail left behind a workable plan for survival and entertaining, John Adams left on the record the beautiful words which now adorn the mantel of the White House State Dining Room:

"I pray heaven to bestow the best of blessings on this house, and all that shall hereafter inhabit it. May none but honest and wise men ever rule under this roof".

Abigail's life was a happier one before her husband became President. There is little indication that she enjoyed the chores that go with being First Lady, nor that she suffered the public gladly. Although she staunchly defended Washington against charges of too much formality and said there should be "more state" rather than less, many of the duties allotted to the womenfolk of officials irked her considerably, even when her husband was Vice President. She freely admitted in her letters that she soon learned to cut short her calls and callers by being otherwise engaged or not at home. She also called when she knew that her hostesses would be out.

Many of the receptions she had to give were to her exceedingly boring, as well as energy consuming and expensive. To succeed the rich Washington in the Presidency was not easy for a family which needed to watch its pennies and which evidently never saw any public relations value in any of the pageantry the first President had promoted. John Adams called the Vice Presidency the most insignificant job ever created and eight years in that spot no doubt took its toll of his spirit. He was not a popular president nor, apparently, did he wish to be. Abigail, who as First Lady sustained her husband and believed as he did, at the same time had the unfortunate facility for making his faults seem worse because she was in the picture, too. History in the end did not forget the great contributions to independence and liberty made by the first Adams, nor by his wife, Abigail, but this is not to say that they were public idols during their four years in the highest office.

Abigail, through her mother, Elizabeth Quincy Smith, was kin to fully half the elite of New England. Her father, William Smith, was a Congregationalist minister, like his father before him. He taught his second daughter, Abigail, her letters but other than that she for the most part educated herself and never attended school a day in her life. Her education was phenomenal—not only for her day but for now. She knew Shakespeare and Molière and apparently remembered every word she heard in long erudite sermons delivered on

Sundays. She knew the histories and writings of Greece and Rome, and also the nuances of world poetry.

She credited her maternal grandmother, Mrs. John Quincy, in whose home she was a favorite child visitor, with much of what she knew, but she also absorbed the books in the fine libraries of her father and a Boston aunt. Her grandfather, John Quincy, taught her a great deal about the boats in busy Boston Harbor, and he never shut her out when he had political callers. Abigail was a precocious little girl but sick a great deal, she said, and in the lonely days of her childhood she learned and learned.

When John Adams first saw her in the parsonage at Weymouth over which her father presided, he knew that she had the best and sauciest mind he had ever encountered in a girl. Her family considered her too fanciful and perhaps more given to books than to religion.

John Adams was planning to be a lawyer and law was not a highly credited profession in Abigail's family in those days. Her mother knew that almost any Quincy would have rated above an Adams in the seating at Harvard University, where the roll call was by social rating. John was fourteenth in a class of twenty-four. Her mother made them wait two years to marry.

Abigail was considered shy by her family, but the notes which she and John Adams exchanged during their enforced period of courtship were by no means shy. Her love for him was fierce and poetic from the beginning, and he responded by calling her "Miss Adorable." At one time she begged him to enumerate her faults. Well, certainly, she could not sing, he replied, and she blushed so easily that it laid an almost "insupportable constraint on (his) freedom of behavior". Other bad habits were "sitting with the leggs across," and of walking with her toes turned inward in parrot fashion. To all of which Miss Adorable replied: "A gentleman has no business to concern himself with the leggs of a lady."

Before she was quite twenty they were married by her father. With her red cloak flying in the wind, she rode off behind him on horseback to his nine and a half acre farm, to which her dowry would add an orchard and some meadowland. Foresighted Abigail already had planted some lilacs around the door of the cottage in which they would live.

By the time Adams went off to the first Continental Congress ten years later in 1774, they had four children: Abigail (Nabby), nine; John Quincy, seven; Charles, four, and Thomas Boylston, two. Unlike his rich friend, John Hancock, who took his wife with him to Philadelphia, John Adams had no money with which to take Abigail and the children and, anyway, the subject never came up. That he never would be back again to stay for long in their home until his Presidency ended, neither he nor Abigail knew at the time.

"I long to have you on the scene of action," she told him. "Don't worry about me. . . . I will become as good a farmeress as you are a statesman." "Fly to the woods if the British come nearer," he wrote her next year. "If they come here they will find a race of Amazons," she replied. And when the Battle of Bunkers Hill was in progress, Abigail grabbed young John Quincy by the hand and they raced to the top of their farm to watch it through spyglasses.

When the largest British fleet ever seen by Americans sailed into Boston harbor to punish the rebellious city, Abigail wrote her husband a letter that extended over several days. "I have just returned from Penn's Hill, where I have been sitting to hear the amazing roar of cannon from which I could see every shell which was thrown," she wrote in March of 1776, next day adding: "I hear we got possession of Dorchester Hill last night; four thousand men upon it today; lost but one man. The ships are all drawn around the town."

"I could not join today in the petitions of our worthy pastor for a reconciliation between our no longer parent state, but tyrant state, and these colonies," she wrote after church one Sunday. "Let us separate; they are unworthy to be our brethren." "I long to hear that you have declared an independency."

She went into Boston to hear the Declaration of Independence read. "In the new code of laws which I now assume will be needed," she urged in a missive to her husband in Philadelphia, "please give a thought to the ladies and see to it that it is put beyond the power of the 'viscious and the lawless' . . . to treat us with cruelty and indignity with impunity. Don't forget that all men would be tyrants if they could." But not her husband, she hastened to add. If the Founding Fathers had listened to Abigail they not only would have enfranchised their womenfolk while they were about their promotion of freedom, but they also would have stopped slavery, and done something about schools for girls.

In 1778, four years after Abigail had been left in charge of the homestead, Congress sent John Adams to France to strengthen the French alliance and find help elsewhere on the Continent for the struggling colonies. He wanted his oldest son, John Quincy, then eleven, to accompany him on the perilous wartime journey and Abigail consented.

Six months passed before she had word from husband or son, although she peppered the Atlantic with letters just as she had the road to Philadelphia. Then she received a noncommittal little missive saying all went well. "Have you

29

changed hearts with a Laplander that you can be so coldly heartless?" she demanded in reply, asking how her husband would like it if, after an unreasonable time, she wrote only that the children were well and "sent their duty." Please, he begged in quick return, she must realize that spies were everywhere. They would like nothing better than to publish a love letter by John Adams, he said!

The husband and son returned within eighteen months, but soon set out again for Europe. This time the second son, Charles, was permitted to make the journey, too. For this permission Abigail always would blame herself. Charles, unlike his older self-sufficient brother, John Quincy, was miserable when left to fend for himself on the Continent, and after many mishaps found his way home through Portugal.

No wife living through the long Revolutionary War possibly could have wanted it to end more than Abigail did. It seemed to go on forever.

"Who shall give me back time?" she would moan in her letters to a husband more removed from her than if he had been at home in the army. "Who shall compensate me for the years I cannot recall?. . . . Should I wish you less wise, that I might enjoy more happiness?" And another time she would write, "Alas, my dear, I am afflicted with a disease called the heartache, nor can any remedy be found in America. It must be collected in Holland, Petersburg, and Balboa."

She would write her husband of the deaths, the scarcities, the inflation on the home scene. "The cry for bread is painful beyond description. . . . Molasses is twenty dollars a gallon and sugar four dollars a pound." But she always ended her letters with love and trust. "In all places and situations know me to be ever, ever yours," was but one of her varied endings.

Part of his salary came through to her until she begged him please to stop it. Mere money was worthless in the last hard days of the Revolution. It would buy neither food nor shelter, and raiment was non-existent for very many. "Send me goods of any description," she wrote, "and maybe I can trade or barter them." Everybody had money; nobody had goods.

Abigail's flare for trading and investing would underwrite the comfort of the Adams couple in their old age, and she learned about percentages the hard way. Her husband always would prefer to invest his savings in farmland which, Abigail confided to her sister, probably never returned him more than one percent. But she knew better than to try to change him. At any rate, the Adamses, thanks in large part to Abigail, would have an income after the Presidency.

When John Adams was offered the chance to be the first American Minister to Great Britain, his wife begged him to come home and forget it. She had not laid eyes on him for three years and she was beginning to feel too old to cope with any more international affairs, she said. Their only daughter had been through a first romance but the father still wrote as if she were a very small child. Abigail wrote, "Give me the man I love. . . . I should have liked very well to have gone to France and resided there a year; but to think of going to England in a public character, and engaging at my time of life in scenes quite new, attended with dissipation, parade and nonsense—I am sure I should make an awkward figure."

But she was not to have her way. Abigail was only forty years of age when she and Nabby, then nineteen, joined John Adams in England in 1784, but she felt immeasurably older. The sons, Charles and Thomas Boylston, were left at home in school. She had but arrived in London when it was time for their oldest son, John Quincy, who had been at his father's side constantly, to return home to Harvard.

Abigail was the first American diplomatic wife to set out for foreign territories. She and Nabby sailed on the good ship "Active", and Abigail, naturally, recorded their sea voyage. John Quincy was a grown-up man of the world at seventeen when he showed up to greet her, and he located her without trouble although she had changed hotels to get a better bargain. Then, when her peripatetic husband arrived, he brought the delightful news that they were to go to France to stay several months while the diplomatic assignment to London was under negotiation.

Abigail was shocked by the worldly French but loved her months in a suburb outside Paris. Her self-taught French was none too good when it came to communicating, but with John Quincy, she and Nabby saw the sights, including naughty ballets and plays by Molière. She wrote her sister about the servants, the gardens, the birds she bought, her callers, her visits, and her sightseeing. Both Benjamin Franklin and Thomas Jefferson were in Paris at the time. She though Jefferson perfection itself but considered Franklin's taste in women a touch bizarre.

"To be out of fashion here," she wrote her sister, "is more criminal than to be seen in a state of nature, to which the Parisians are not averse. . . . They make a pleasure of life. To be 'triste' is an ailment of serious nature." She confided to Jefferson that she was more than a bit "triste" herself, however, when she had to embark for England.

She had to make a good showing in England as the wife of the first American Minister accepted there. She had her hair dressed professionally each day, set up housekeeping on fashionable Grosvenor Square, and prepared herself and

Nabby to be received at court by Queen Charlotte. For her debut in "the circles of the Queen," Abigail wore "white lutestring, covered with and full trimmed with white crepe, festooned with lilac ribbon and mock point lace." Her train was almost three yards in length.

"The Queen evidently was embarrassed when I was presented to her," Abigail wrote. "I had disagreeable feelings, too." Apparently there was no safe topic of conversation at the moment between the mother country and the so-lately colonies. None of this bothered Abigail too much. She was intrigued by the court procedure that required the royal couple and their daughters to make the full circle of two hundred persons with polite greetings for each one.

The King went to the right, the Queen and princesses to the left, Abigail wrote, and everyone was four hours standing. "Think of the task," she recorded in a letter to her sister. "One is obliged here to attend the circles, once a fortnight in summer but once a week the rest of the year. What renders it exceedingly expensive is that you cannot go twice the same season in the same dress, and you cannot make use of a court dress elsewhere."

She thought that in the future London might be a good diplomatic post but that at the "present salary and the temper of the British toward Americans, it is not too pleasant". She thoroughly enjoyed London itself, however, especially the Shakespearean plays.

Nabby became engaged to an American aide in the Ministry and was married in a large ceremony by the Bishop of St. Asaph.

When the Adamses returned home so that he could be Washington's Vice President, Abigail was a "lady of fashion," which is what Mrs. Washington called her. She was attractive to look at, small of stature, had pretty features, and she had remained pertly slender.

Despite her international wardrobe she remained Puritan and Yankee, however. She agreed with her husband that the people of Massachusetts were just a bit finer than other people, their religions more pure, their customs preferable to all others. Opinions of others were not always worthy of concern. Right was right.

Like Martha Washington before her, Abigail missed her husband's inauguration for President. His mother was too ill for her to leave her. The new President wrote her, "A solemn scene it was indeed, and it was made effective to me by the presence of the General, whose countenance was as serene and unclouded as the day. He seemed to me to enjoy a triumph over me. Methought I heard him say, 'I'm fairly out and you fairly in! See which of us will be happiest.'"

When she arrived in May he rode out twenty-five miles from Philadelphia to meet her and "there on the Banks of the Delaware, we spent the day, getting into the city at sunset . . ." she wrote her sister. Looking back, she thought it perhaps her happiest day as First Lady: a day of grace before starting her drawing rooms and before getting caught up in the politics of the next four years.

Like most First Ladies, and perhaps more vehemently than many, Abigail resented criticism of her husband, and it was her misfortune to be First Lady in a period marked by angry dissatisfactions and to be on the side which lost, at least temporarily.

The Adamses were the first First Family to have to accept public criticism and defeat at the polls and, however right or wrong they may have been politically, it is interesting to note that in the end they salvaged personal friendships without sacrificing their political beliefs. Most noteworthy of these old friendships was their relationship with Jefferson.

Abigail took the lead in bridging the way back to him, all unbeknown to her husband. When Jefferson's daughter, the lovely and fragile Maria whom Abigail had mothered so long ago in London, died, the former First Lady wrote the President a letter of condolence, admitting to him that it was "against my better judgment," but said she was writing to him in his role as father.

The President hastened to reply and to express puzzlement at what ever could have happened to chill the air between them. Abigail was having none of this sort of double talk from the wily Jefferson, however, and shot back a letter outlining her views that freedom for the press and for personal liberty did not cover freedom for irresponsibility and license. Also, she still could not agree with him, she said, and thought he would rue the day when he decided to cut national defense and rely on state militias. And, while she was about it, she let him know that she considered his removal of her son, John Quincy, from a minor government post rather inexcusable.

Jefferson in his next missive denied any knowledge of what had happened to John Quincy's job and defended his opening prison doors for those jailed for speaking and writing out of turn under the Alien and Sedition laws of the Adams administration.

Abigail ended the correspondence and showed the stack of letters to her startled husband. He noted on them that he had read same but had no comment. When Abigail died about a decade later, in 1818, at age seventy-three, Jefferson, by then an Ex-President himself, wrote Ex-President Adams a letter of condolence and the two old men corresponded until their deaths. After all, John Adams by now could afford to be generous because his son was doing so well in politics—and poor Jefferson had no son! Adams and Jefferson died on the same day: July 4, 1826, while John Quincy Adams was President.

FIRST YEARS WITHOUT A FIRST LADY
(1801-09)

THOMAS JEFFERSON and the country, too, apparently, rocked along quite well without a First Lady for the eight years beginning in March of 1801. The third President, however, did have to call on Dolley Madison, the wife of his Secretary of State, rather frequently to "assist with the ladies."

Jefferson was a widower of nineteen years standing when he moved into the President's house with his exotic flower plants, his fiddle, and his mockingbird so tame that it hopped up the stairs behind him to sing during his midday siesta.

He would have loved to have had his two children, Martha and Maria, with him all the time but they were very much married and busy with families of their own. Even if they had come, however, he would have run the household and planned the meals. His stature as gourmet among the Presidents has not been seriously challenged and some of his handed-down recipes still are in vogue at the White House today on special occasions.

Wives of the young federal city called on him en masse, but he did not yield in his determination to skip the "drawing rooms" expected by the ladies. His favorite form of entertaining was the small dinner, and he gave one almost every day at four o'clock and on Sunday, too, to the great displeasure of the clergy.

In his efforts to do away with all formality, Jefferson gave the death blow to bows for the President and his wife, and introduced the democratic handshake: that custom which has plagued First Ladies ever since and without a mastery of which a candidate might as well not announce for office. He kept Abigail's New Year's Day reception and also Washington's Fourth of July spectacle. These were the two occasions each year when everyone and his brother were more than welcome. Otherwise his entertaining, while not formal, was most select.

Both of Jefferson's sons-in-law, Thomas Mann Randolph and John Wayles Eppes, were in Congress at the time and lived mostly at the White House. Maria Eppes had that ethereal type of beauty of which Abigail Adams said "the experienced learn to look upon with dread because it betrays a physical organization too delicately fine to withstand the rough shocks of the world." Martha Randolph was very tall and almost the image of her father, red hair and all.

The sisters spent the winter of 1802-03 with their father in Washington and the next year Maria died, leaving two small children. After her death Jefferson insisted that Martha spend much more time with him. Her seventh child was the first baby born in the White House and was christened James Madison. Martha named all her sons for prominent Americans and her oldest one, Thomas Jefferson, would be the solace of his grandfather's old age. In addition to five sons, Martha also bore seven daughters. Thanks to Martha, Jefferson is today the President with by far the most living descendants.

Jefferson, who reared his daughters almost singlehandedly, was a doting and extravagant father and grandfather and he kept Dolley Madison busy shopping for them and keeping them in style. He was so grateful for Dolley's many services and liked her outgoing personality so well that he wanted her to be the next First Lady.

DOROTHY PAYNE TODD MADISON
(1809-1817)

An Extravaganza Born to Please

DASHING DOLLEY MADISON, whose White House receptions caused traffic jams on pioneer roads and rivers from 1809 until 1817, burst fullblown into Martha Washington's drawing rooms in Philadelphia in 1794, which was the year in which she married "the great little Madison," and she was enlivening the official social scene when the administration of James K. Polk ended in 1849. Her reign of personal popularity exceeded that of any other wife of any other President so far.

After the sedate formalities of the two former First Ladies and eight years of widower Jefferson, Dolley's freewheeling flamboyance struck a responsive chord in a country bursting at the seams with new territory, new states, and the new steamboat. Everything about the burgeoning land was bigger than life and splashed with daring—and so was Dolley. The extravagance of her hospitality was topped only by the sensationalism of her Parisian wardrobe, and her heart was as big and golden as the whole wide West, which seemed to be where all the new people were coming from.

Jefferson, the First President to court the West, left Dolley on a pinnacle and she courted everybody. He no doubt used the merit system when selecting her husband, his Secretary of State, to be the next President, but he also must have relished the thought of Dolley as First Lady. He loved her merriment and then too, he was indebted to her, as were all who ever came within Dolley's orbit. She could no more stop running errands and ingratiating herself by deeds like carrying covered dishes to the sick and giving whole live cows to the orphans—when other women were donating quarts of milk—than she could stifle her yen for the latest sleeve pattern.

Among other things, she shopped for nearly all the clothes worn by Jefferson's beloved granddaughters, including trousseaux for at least two of them; headed his drives, including one to raise money for the Lewis and Clark Expedition, and was his stand-in hostess when "ladies were present" at White House functions. He, who had insisted on walking to his own inaugural and then had lunch at the end of the boarding house table as usual, broke his rules about public display to attend Dolley's inauguration ball, the first ever held in Washington.

The ball was at "Mr. Long's Hotel on Capitol Hill" and it was staged by the Washington Dancing Assembly, which admitted an elite four hundred, several of them from neighboring Baltimore, only a full day's drive away if one had good horses and started early. The diplomatic corps was represented by an assortment of attaches and three full-fledged Ministers—the latter from England, France, and Denmark. Some of the dancers were from cities as far away as Boston and Charleston. All along the Eastern seaboard it was noted that as many as three stage coaches a day passed en route to Washington to see the Madisons come in.

Gold was Dolley's color, and she did the White House over accordingly. The faded red of earlier days was most bedraggled by now, in any event. Dolley threw it out, festooned the windows in bright yellow damask, bought new sofas and chairs in gold upholstery, put suns in goldleaf on decorative screens, and ordered a big noonday sun with shooting rays put above the mantel before which she stood to receive guests—and the more of them the merrier. In the midst of all this splendor, of course, Dolley herself was the most glorious sunburst of all and planned all her raiment to match the decor. If not in buffs and harmonizing yellow hues, she usually preferred to be in crimson, for its delightful contrast.

Dolley was a statuesque five-feet-nine inches tall even before she donned her sparkling high heels and put on her towering turbans. Usually her turbans were topped by flowers or plumes, but one eyewitness described a simpler variety which was quite startling enough. "I fear that it is the woman altogether whom I would wish you to see," wrote Mrs. Samuel Harrison Seaton, whose husband had just become editor of the *National Intelligencer* of Washington, D.C., and then Mrs. Seaton could not resist describing the turban of the occasion: "She wears a crimson cap that almost hides her forehead, but which becomes her extremely and reminds one of a crown from its brilliant appearance, contrasted with the white satin folds and her jetblack curls."

In addition to the curls, usually described as raven, Dolley had sparkling eyes of heavenly larkspur blue, and a complexion which resisted all blemishes. Just how beautiful she was remains a moot question, but when she was growing up in Philadelphia she had to be reminded: "Thou must hide thy face, Dolley. They stare at thee so."

She was forty years of age when she became First Lady, although she ordinarily called it thirty-six, and her friends declared that she looked no more than in her twenties. Her portraits, and Gilbert Stuart did at least six, show great loveliness. Personality and glamour were her strong points, however.

Dolley's "darling little husband," a term she used in great affection, was only five-feet-four inches tall and never weighed more than one hundred and twenty-five pounds. He could get lost in a crowd, it was said, and frequently did, by preference. He had both money and social prestige, in addition to his brainpower, and could not have cared less how much Dolley spent nor how many guests she had in to dinner just so long as he was spared the shop talk and did not have to watch to see who had what wines at dinner.

At times it seemed as if the Madisons were running two separate administrations—Dolley's from the drawing room and his from the library. But this was not true. Dolley's aims for the Madison regime were quite clear cut. She asked only that it be successful politically and brilliant socially. But where society ended and politics began was sometimes hard to figure. It could be that Dolley, just by being Dolley and never talking politics at all, influenced politics more than any other First Lady.

When she became First Lady her Wednesday night drawing rooms became the rendezvous for leaders of both political parties and it was definitely understood that at "Dolley's house" neither Federalist nor Republican was put on the spot as pro or con on anything more controversial than the latest book or the next horse race. Only once during her eight years did Congressmen boycott her receptions, and it almost broke her heart. They were mad at *him,* however, and not at *her.* It was during the angry period leading up to the War of 1812, and Madison had bought some bogus spy information which backfired into the "Henry papers" and infuriated the lawmakers regardless of their political persuasion. The freezeout was of short duration, though, and the receptions soon continued.

Dolley did innumerable good turns for the wives and children of Congressmen, and visited regularly on Capitol Hill, a coterie of leading ladies in tow, to chat in the corridors and pass the time of day. It is claimed that many a close vote was tipped in Madison's favor by the memories of Dolley's sunshine and favors. A few political students, among them James G. Blaine, said that but for Dolley her husband would have been a one-term President. "She saved the administration of her husband," Blaine said, "held him back from the extremes of Jeffersonianism."

Dolley had a phenomenal memory for names and personal information about the people she met, and apparently she was born with two built-in desires: to do kind deeds and to give parties. Due to her Quaker upbringing, she at times felt guilty about her love of gayety. She admitted to her sister, Anna, that she probably enjoyed "the routs all too well" and wrote of her dreams in which she still was a Quaker.

Dolley was born a Quaker, in North Carolina, to Virginia parents, but nothing about the simple and unadorned life ever appealed to her. Her maternal grandmother, Mrs. William Coles, who deplored what she considered to be the drab existence of her grandchildren, did not help matters any when she slipped little Dolley a pouch of heirloom jewelry to wear around her neck under her Quaker frocks as she walked to a small Virginia school.

Devout John Payne, her father, was among the first Virginia Quakers to feel so strongly about slavery that he freed his slaves, sold his profitable plantation, and took his family to live in the City of Brotherly Love, where he became a respected elder in the Society of Friends. That was in 1786 when Dolley, the second of his six children, already was a budding sixteen although she tried to remember it as "around eleven or twelve." Four years later she was married to John Todd, a promising young lawyer who died in the typhus epidemic of 1793, leaving Dolley a luscious widow with one small son. Dolley's father, the agrarian turned urban, lost much of his money but died happy about leaving his family in the good Quaker city of Philadelphia.

What John Payne could not have foreseen was that Philadelphia would become the country's second temporary Capital, and so be overrun with Virginians, many of them blood kin to his family. By the time Dolley was widowed and had returned home to live with her mother, her younger sister, Lucy, already had succumbed to the Virginia charm and had married no less than a nephew of the General himself, one George Steptoe Washington, and was living happily at Harewood, near what is now Charlestown, West Virginia.

Congressman James Madison, Jr., who at forty-three was considered to be a confirmed bachelor, spied the blossoming Widow Todd out walking one day. He did not rest until properly introduced by Aaron Burr, who knew the feminine field much better than Madison did and who also had been a lodger in the Payne home. Dolley sent a hurried note to her dearest friend, Eliza Lee: "Thou must come to me. Aaron Burr says that 'the great little Madison' has asked to be brought to see me this evening."

According to the grandniece, L. B. Cutts, who edited her "Memoirs and Letters," Dolley put on a mulberry-colored satin for this occasion, covered part of her curls with a demure Quaker cap, and had a mulberry scarf around her neck. Soon the unlikely romance was the talk of Philadelphia and the first First Lady, Martha Washington, herself took a hand, sending for Dolley to ask if they were engaged.

"If it is so," Martha said when Dolley stammered in hesitation, "do not be ashamed to confess it. . . . He will make you a good husband, and all the better for being so much older. We both approve of it . . ."

So in September of 1794, before she had been widowed quite a year, Dolley and bridal party went to her sister Lucy's home, Harewood, for the wedding ceremony. The future First Lady rode in an open barouche with her sister, Anna, a child of twelve, and her tiny son, Payne Todd, not yet three. Madison and several of their mutual friends drove or rode with them on the week-long trip in the autumn weather. Madison then took his bride for a visit to his father's estate, Montpelier. They were back in the capital in time for Martha's drawing rooms, where Dolley blossomed out in radiant finery.

Anna, the young sister, lived with Dolley, as did their mother part of the time. When Lucy was widowed, she also came to stay with Dolley, who by that time was First Lady. Lucy became the first bride in the still unfinished White House when she married Judge Thomas Todd of Kentucky, an Associate Justice of the U.S. Supreme Court. Anna by then was the wife of Congressman Richard Cutts from Maine. Both sisters were much in evidence at Dolley's parties.

Dolley loved house guests and a frequent one was Madame Patterson Bonaparte of Baltimore, the "divorced wife and widow of Jerome Bonaparte, King of Westphalia," and said to be the most beautiful woman in America. Her sensational international romance with a Bonaparte added an eclat to Dolley's drawing rooms. Mrs. Bonaparte kept a personal eye on the social training of young Payne Todd when he was sent to a Catholic school in Baltimore. The First Lady was delighted because she fully expected Payne to travel to the courts of Europe, and he did, although Dolley would live to regret her son's wastrel leanings.

As would be expected, Dolley's dinners were as lavish as her attire. Even before she moved into the White House, Mrs. Merry, the unmerry wife of the British Ambassador, had declared that Mrs. Madison's tables looked like feasts for harvest hands: an intended slur which Dolley turned to good public advantage by attributing the abundance to the richness of America, "where there is plenty for everyone."

As First Lady, Dolley hit on the popular idea of sending punch and cakes to her husband's office when he had diplomatic callers and of serving hot bouillon to her winter afternoon drop-in guests. She instituted all-female parties for Cabinet wives when their husbands had to be in long conferences and she held card parties with prizes. It was almost impossible to get away from Dolley's house without food or gifts—or both. She adored the visits of children and kept a pinafore closet so that no youngster would be sent home in a mussed apron, and she gave several high-style parties for her young nieces.

During the reelection year of 1812 Dolley's parties were at their greatest heights and the talk of the country. Mrs. Smith observed: "The drawing room—that center of attraction—affords opportunity of seeing all those whom fashion, fame, beauty, wealth or talent have rendered celebrated. It has this winter been in general much crowded. Seldom has the company been less than two or three hundred, and generally more. I cannot tell you what an interest is imparted to this assembly by the entrance of some celebrated person."

By modern measuring, Dolley's crowds seem tiny indeed but for her day they were overwhelming and they filled her White House parlors to overflowing. The "impossibly large" East Parlor was not yet in use, and so the custom of "standing and mingling" had to be brought into use. Not even the ladies had to sit, as formerly, and wait for the gentlemen to notice them. They stood and mingled, and the same freedom extended to Capitol Hill where, according to Mrs. Smith, who was not certain that she approved, the House of Representatives became "a lounging place for both sexes" and a spot at which acquaintances could be made as easily as at "public amusements." Dolley and her ladies also visited the Supreme Court, and Mrs. Smith was positive that she did not approve of this, since the Justices often paid more attention to the ladies, she felt, than to their legal briefs.

Kerchiefs which formerly concealed lovely bosoms, or at least played peek-a-boo with them, went into discard as the lowcut gowns of the early Empire period made their way to American shores, and rouge was a new daring. The rumor that the First Lady herself used rouge was firmly denied by Mrs. Seaton, who declared, "I myself saw her color come and go only last week. . . . She does not rouge."

It is a compliment to Dolley that in the midst of all her fine-feathered doings she kept several of her Quaker friends. She proposed a White House toast to one of them, saying, "Here's to the absence of thy broad brim, Friend . . ." and received the quick reply, "And here's to thy absent kerchief, Friend Dolley."

The political misfortune of the Madison administration was the War of 1812, which many segments of the country, particularly the New Englanders, considered to be thoroughly unjustified. Dolley would emerge from the war as the heroine who saved the big White House portrait of Washington as well as historic Cabinet papers including the Declaration of Independence. But not before she underwent the humiliating experience of having the White House burned over her head. Her sunburst furniture and much of her fabulous wardrobe went up in flames, too. Her last two years as First Lady would be spent in rented houses.

Knowing that the war with England, fought about freedom on the high seas, would cut off imports, Dolley hastened to lay in a supply of apparel from France. On one of the large shipments she had to pay a customs tax of $2,000, but that did not deter her from sending for another load before the fighting started. Her last supply arrived in May of 1812 on "The Hornet," which also brought the news that England refused to rescind the blockade decrees which were strangling American commerce. War was declared on June 18. Ironically, like so many things about this war, England by then had repealed the offensive decrees, but news was slower than the smoldering anger.

No one seemed to think that the British would attack Washington. Baltimore, with its fine harbor, yes, but not the little capital city. British Admiral Cockburn sent word that he would attend one of Dolley's receptions ere long, but none took him seriously. Not until James Monroe, the Secretary of State, mounted his horse and rode down into Maryland in August of 1814 to see a British fleet landing an army of four thousand veteran soldiers did anyone seem to worry, and by then it was too late. After the British passed Fort Washington on the lower Potomac, the exodus from the capital began. Militiamen and volunteers from surrounding states obviously were no defense. The President went into the field of action to see if troops could be rallied. Dolley stayed in the White House, which supposedly had a hundred guards around it.

Through two days of embattlement the First Lady packed many treasured documents. She went up on the roof and watched the oncoming British army through a spyglass. She wrote a running letter to her sister, and said:

"Two messengers, covered with dust, come to bid me fly . . . but here I mean to wait for him (the President) . . . Our kind friend Mr. Carroll has come to hasten my departure and is in very bad humor with me because I insist on waiting until the large picture of General Washington is secured, and it requires to be unscrewed from the wall . . . I have ordered the frame broken and the canvas taken out. . . ."

The portrait was not cut from the frame, as legend said, but removed intact, and not a minute too soon. Flames from the burning capital city lit the sky far into Virginia that night. The Capitol, the two Potomac bridges, the White

House, and most department buildings were ablaze. The Madisons, who met briefly on the Virginia side of the Potomac that night, were put into disguises to prevent their capture. And then came an unbelievable hurricane that doused the fire, and the British fled on to Baltimore.

Many people thought that the damage to Washington could not be repaired and that the federal city would not be rebuilt. Philadelphia invited the government to come back there. The Cabinet went into continuous session and quickly the decision was made to rebuild on the old foundations. The Madisons moved to nearby Octagon House and on February 15, 1815, had the public in to celebrate the Peace Treaty, signed before Christmas, and Andrew Jackson's great victory over the British at New Orleans in January.

Dolley was more popular than ever and her hold on the affections of Washingtonians was undiminished when she went to Montpelier at the end of her husband's two terms. He left the White House impaired in health. She nursed him until his death. Then she returned to Washington to live near the rebuilt White House. And was the city ever glad to see her. Life had been dull indeed without Dolley.

Dolley had heartaches in her later years. Her son ran through his fortune and hers, too. She pawned her silver spoons to help pay his debts. But in rusty black dress or whatever, Dolley's magic held. On New Year's Day almost as many came by to see her as called at the White House. She was on the ill-fated "Princeton" with President Tyler and his group when the new vessel blew up in the Potomac and she, naturally, helped nurse the victims.

She was an inveterate matchmaker and married one of her young cousins off to President Van Buren's son. President Jackson was so charmed with her that he persuaded Congress to buy additional Madison books and papers from her for $25,000. Already she had received $30,000 for an earlier supply.

She added sparkle to many a White House gathering and to her last one, when Sarah Polk was First Lady, she wore a new white satin gown, cut quite low, even though she was in her eighties. It would have pleased her to know that her funeral at old St. John's Episcopal Church, near the White House, drew the largest attendance that church had known. Dolley never let her public down—and her public always responded.

ELIZABETH KORTRIGHT MONROE (1817-25)

"La Belle Americaine"

ELIZABETH KORTRIGHT MONROE was sedately beautiful and had an air of reticence which would be called aloofness when she became First Lady succeeding Dolley Madison. Everything about Elizabeth's personality was in almost direct contrast to that of the colorful Dolley, and for long periods in her life she had managed to live almost unnoticed. For the wife of a man who had held more public offices than anybody else in the country, this ability was no mean feat in itself, but it would not help her to become a popular First Lady.

She was forty-eight years of age when her husband became President and she had lived in Washington as a Cabinet wife for seven years without, it was said, making either friends or enemies. "The Monroes are perfect strangers," wailed Margaret Bayard Smith, the capital city's most ardent note taker during the period and the one most often quoted, "not only to me but to all the citizens."

The story of Elizabeth is almost entirely the story of her husband, on whom she was unusually dependent. It was an arrangement which apparently suited him perfectly and which he perhaps had fostered. She was only seventeen when he married her in New York City on February 16, 1786, while he was a member of the Continental Congress. He was twenty-seven and a veteran of the Revolutionary War, with a scar to prove it, and had studied law under his idol and mentor, Thomas Jefferson. One of his Virginia colleagues in the Congress described Elizabeth as "the smiling little Venus" when she and her tall husband departed for a week-long honeymoon on the outer reaches of Long Island.

Elizabeth's father was Lawrence Kortright, a successful mercantile man who had other notably lovely daughters to his credit, and who was a Tory captain during the Revolution. Monroe adroitly concealed the Tory background from his relatives, writing them that his father-in-law had lost a considerable fortune during the war, and then he showed them Elizabeth as proof of his own good taste.

He devoted much time to making Elizabeth happy in Virginia when he returned there to continue his studies under

Jefferson. Perhaps it was Jefferson's way of planning the furnishing of Monticello, and the pleasure he had in running his own household, that influenced Monroe to do the same for Elizabeth.

At any rate, Monroe was the family front and planner and he was the one who selected the new furniture for the White House, the rebuilding of which was nearing completion when he took office. And Monroe was the one who set the social tone of his administrations.

It was on Monroe's first diplomatic assignment abroad that Elizabeth became a central character in a dashing and daring bit of international intrigue that was completely out of character for her but which she performed to perfection. It involved "storming" a prison and saving Madame Lafayette, the wife of America's favorite Frenchman, from the guillotine.

President Washington sent Monroe as Minister to France during the bloodiest days of the French Revolution, after it had become a civil war and had involved much of Europe. It had almost involved the New World, too, and there was still a chance that it could.

All Americans in Paris, particularly the Minister, were under strict orders from the Father of his Country to walk the tightrope of strict neutrality. Although Washington loved Lafayette like a son, he had been careful to make no overtures to the warring powers for Lafayette's release from the Prussian dungeon in which he, stripped of his properties, had been languishing for three years.

Many Americans felt no such self-restraint about the Lafayette family, however. Madame Lafayette and her two daughters were in La Force Prison in Paris. Already her mother, her grandmother, and her sister had died under the guillotine which threatened all members of the nobility and rumors that she would be next floated over Paris daily. A plan to save her was at least worth a try, the Americans thought.

It was a simple plan, if it worked, but it involved the use of United States insignia and needed the appearance of innocence which an impeccable and beautiful woman could supply. Elizabeth had won the title of "la belle Americaine" among the beauty-loving French and she spoke their language well. Her husband was not at all sure that her nerves were steely enough, but she was willing to try.

Dressed in her finest attire she drove to La Force Prison in the carriage of the American legation, and she had the driver whip it smartly around so that its United States insignia would be unmistakable.

The keeper and guards were astonished at the beautiful

sight, but not so much so that they failed to be Frenchily gallant. The keeper rushed to learn the business of "la belle Americaine" and was told that the wife of the American Minister was calling on Madame Lafayette, whose husband was so widely esteemed back home, and would it be possible to see her. "Why assuredly, Madame. Will you please wait in the reception room while we bring her?"

Poor Adrienne Lafayette thought the steps of the approaching guard were those of her executioner, and she was in tears during most of the short visit. But Elizabeth managed to whisper that the show of interest might do some good and, in a clearly audible voice, added that she would return for another visit quite shortly. Within a few days, however, the prisoner and her daughters were released. They were supplied with American passports which they used to join Lafayette in his prison. Adrienne would not consider going elsewhere.

President Washington, whatever he thought in his heart, did not join in America's applause but called Monroe home because he thought that his Minister in this and in other ways had overstepped neutrality. Monroe soon became Governor of Virginia. When Jefferson became President he sent Monroe back to France and then on other diplomatic assignments to England and to Spain. In all, the Monroes had almost a decade overseas. Their older daughter, Eliza, spent much of her girlhood in Madame Campan's School near Paris, where her closest friend was Napoleon's stepdaughter, Hortense. Monroe's much younger daughter, Maria, was born in France.

As a member of Madison's Cabinet the Monroes lived at 2017 Eye Street, Northwest, which today is the home of the Arts Club of Washington. Since the rebuilt White House still needed many finishing touches and a completely new set of furnishings, the Monroes continued to live quietly on Eye Street for some months after he became President. The inaugural reception was held there.

They lived much too quietly to please the women of Washington, who missed the daily round of activities initiated by Dolley. They were terribly upset when they learned that Mrs. Monroe intended to do no calling, either on a return basis or otherwise. The First Lady's health was none too robust but that was not the whole reason and, here again, Monroe was taking a tip from Jefferson and making the social customs fit his plans for the Presidency by cutting out those which he considered to be meaningless.

The older daughter, Eliza, now married to George Hay, prosecutor in the famous trial of Aaron Burr, and the mother of a daughter named Hortensia, came with her family to live with the Monroes and help the First Lady with the

47

social doings. She ran most of the events and won a reputation for being supremely haughty. None of this bothered Monroe, as he placed orders in France for White House furnishings and donned his old buff and blue uniform to make a good-will tour of the country. As "the Last of the Cocked Hats," he would travel far and wide binding up sectional wounds and reestablishing an oldtime feeling of national unity. The Era of Good Feeling which he created was much more important to him than squabbles on the social front. Whether Elizabeth shared in a feeling for what he was doing is doubtful but he became a most popular President. He deliberately turned to New England for his Secretary of State and named John Quincy Adams to the spot, putting him in line for the Presidency.

Monroe had thought to put many mahogany pieces of furniture back in the White House, since so many of the burned pieces had been of this wood, but the French merchants advised him that mahogany no longer was chic enough for even the simplest parlors and, knowing his tastes were good, they were taking the liberty of shipping him new lighter and gilded woods and knew that he would approve! He did, as it turned out. He liked French furniture personally and while in France had built up an excellent collection of it, buying at bargain prices from the impoverished nobility to whom bread came to mean more than heirlooms.

He had $30,000 from Congress with which to refurnish the mansion from top to bottom, still excluding the big East Parlor. Monroe soon saw that this was not enough. So, in a gesture of generosity which he later had cause to regret, he sold his best furniture, household linen, dishes, and silver to the government for what he had paid. The silver went for its weight rather than at antique or artistic values. The total bill to the government for his collection was $9,071.22½.

The White House was reopened for business with a New Year's Day reception in 1818, three and a third years after its burning. It was extremely beautiful, so the public thought.

As eventually has happened with almost all White House refurnishings and refurbishings, the cost of it all was questioned ·in Congress. Critical eyebrows were raised even at some of the cut rate prices on the inventory of Monroe's personal pieces. So the President in irritation bought his collection back. This left gaps in the furnishings at the end of his eight years, but it gave him some choice pieces for Oak Hill, the home which Jefferson designed for him, and where he and Elizabeth hoped to live when his Presidency ended.

Several pieces of furniture and many ornaments ordered by Monroe still grace the White House, however. Especially notable are the clocks, mirrors, and candelabra. Elaborate and beautiful Monroe table decorations are often used at State dinners today.

About the prettiest thing in the White House while the Monroes lived there, however, was not the furniture but their daughter, Maria, who at fourteen had the looks of a frolicksome Dresden figurine. Her parents considered her a mere child but she thought of herself as quite grown-up. Her mother's nephew, Samuel Lawrence Gouverneur, came to live with them as a junior secretary to the President and apparently Maria set her cap for him immediately.

No would-be bride ever had more delightful surroundings amid which to be part of a courtship, and Maria did become the first daughter of a President to have a White House wedding. She was almost seventeen when she and her cousin were married and her first son, named James Monroe, was born in the gleaming mansion.

Older sister Eliza was firmly in charge of the wedding arrangements, so they were no more lavish than her usual brand of entertaining. Very few guests were present for the ceremony and no White House reception was given afterward. Maria's wedding received the least fanfare ever accompanying that of a President's daughter, but it was a happy marriage and Monroe would live with Maria and her family after Elizabeth's death.

Eliza's haughtiness and the strict formalities of the Monroe regime put social chips on lots of shoulders and even involved the Secretary of State in a slight controversy over whether he should call on members of Congress, or they on him. Adams replied quite seriously that when he was a Senator nobody called on him and he assumed that everyone was "free to pursue the course of conduct dictated by his own sense of propriety."

As Monroe's national popularity increased the furore about protocol lessened and Elizabeth Monroe's receptions at the White House were well attended. Lafayette, by then a widower, came to make his legendary visit and this helped take the mind off lesser happenings. Also, Washington had an exciting new hero on the premises named Andrew Jackson.

Jackson, who had done a sort of repeat on his victory at the Battle of New Orleans by making short work of the Seminole War and making Florida safe for Americans, was now in the Senate. He had his wife, Rachel, with him in Washington for at least a year and he was feted everywhere. Rachel did not always go with him, preferring prayer meetings to parties, but she frequently attended Mrs. Monroe's at-homes and held a sort of continuing at-home herself by receiving a constant stream of callers in the parlor of their rooms at O'Neal's Inn.

When the eight Monroe years ended with a big party for John Quincy Adams, his successor, the Monroes went to live happy ever afterward at Oak Hill, near Leesburg, Virginia, which had been under construction during most of his Presidency. Unlike the other Virginia Presidents before him Monroe, the son of a carpenter, was not rich and took in promising students to study law under him.

They would not enjoy Oak Hill long. Elizabeth died there at age sixty-two, and he died a year later at Maria's home in New York City. Eventually, both would be buried at Richmond, the capital of the state of which he had been twice Governor.

It was a descendant of Monroe, Mrs. Rose Gouverneur Hoes, who began the collection of First Lady dresses now in the Smithsonian Institution. Another descendant, Laurence Gouverneur Hoes, heads the new James Monroe Library at Fredericksburg, Virginia, and hopes to find new material about his beautiful ancestress, Elizabeth.

LOUISA JOHNSON ADAMS (1825-1829)

"All Are Gone to Mrs. Adams'"

To LOUISA JOHNSON ADAMS, who married the oldest son of the second President, fell the delightful chore of making a parlor out of the vast East Room of the White House in which her mother-in-law had strung the family wash to dry twenty-four years earlier.

Louisa was the first First Lady with a foreign birthplace, having been born in London to a Maryland father and a British mother, and so far she is the only one to have a former First Lady for a mother-in-law. She had chic continental manners and a stylish air of great fragility. She grew silk worms as a hobby, painted water colors in the White House garden, wrote French verse, and played gay tunes on the harp.

She was twenty-three years of age at the time of her marriage to John Quincy Adams in London on June 26, 1797. The bridegroom was thirty. They had known each other since childhood. They had not been in love then, and alas, did not consider themselves to be so even at the time of the wedding. Both had been through unhappy first romances and thought of themselves as being on the rebound.

The future President had relinquished his heart's desire because he felt that he could not support her in a manner becoming to an Adams and Louisa, as she later would confide to her father-in-law, had undergone an experience that had left her without faith in the virtue of most men and made her determined never more "to build my house in the sand." But from the age of four she surely must have known that sturdy, self-reliant John Quincy never would be considered as shifting sand. There would come a day when she wished that he could shift a bit more easily, but then many public wives at times no doubt wish that.

John Quincy was eleven years of age and on his first trip to Europe with his father when he showed up at the Johnson home in Paris. The Johnsons were in France because of the Revolutionary War, Louisa's father having moved his family from London so that he could be openly pro-American. Joshua Johnson had represented Maryland and other colonial

51

tobacco interests in England for many years, but wanted no misunderstanding about where he stood in the colonies' war for freedom. Congress asked him to assume the task of bookkeeper for the accounts of Americans traveling abroad on official business at the time and his place in Paris became a clearing house for travel information and messages as well as for expense accounts. John Quincy was in and out of the place for the next several years, until he returned home at attend Harvard.

By the time of his marriage to Louisa he was a full-fledged diplomat. President Washington had assigned him to Portugal and now he was on his way to Berlin to be the first American representative at the royal Prussian court. He was merely stopping in London between assignments to be married—and sightsee. Lest this sound too grim a sendoff for a marriage which was to be more than successful, it should be noted here that on their fiftieth wedding anniversary the happily married husband of Louisa would write her a long poem of praise.

And after all, even in 1797 he was about to take her on a most glamorous honeymoon all the way to Berlin. His credentials were questioned along the way by border guards who never had heard of the new country which called itself the United States, but on they went—for their first four years of wedlock. By all accounts Louisa got along well at the Prussian court and he, as always would be true of him in foreign lands, was much respected for his learning and integrity.

When they returned to Massachusetts they had a son, who was named George Washington after their mutual hero. It was Louisa's first trip to America but since her uncle, Thomas Johnson, had signed the Declaration of Independence, she thought of herself as thoroughly Americanized. She had yet to learn of the Adams family, however, and to experience the workings of the American political system. She and Abigail Adams hit it off immediately, it appears, but John Adams at first thought her European education too effete for the new world. She won him over by refusing to change and became his favorite daughter-in-law.

Since Thomas Jefferson, then President, saw no need for an Adams anywhere in the government, Louisa's husband began to practice law in Boston—but not for long. The Federalists sent him to the United States Senate to vote against Mr. Jefferson and Louisa soon found herself in Washington. More surprising yet she and her husband were asked frequently to the White House to dine with the enemy and her Senator husband voted for several Jefferson measures, which did not at all please the voters who had sent him to Congress.

Louisa was so puzzled by the turn of events that she wrote her father-in-law asking why John Quincy should be criticized for voting as he thought best. John Adams assured her, perhaps with a chuckle, that the only answer for the wife of a man in politics was to delve deeply into the old fashioned philosophy of the Stoics, who refused to recognize pain and emotion, whatever the occasion. Louisa defended her "modern" education and said that she could not imagine herself becoming a Stoic. But she soon found herself back in Boston, because the Federalists recalled John Quincy.

When James Madison became President he asked John Quincy to become the first accredited American Minister to Russia. Louisa by now was the mother of three young sons, but mother-in-law Abigail, probably still remembering the long separation from her own husband, offered to keep the children so that Louisa could go along. The two older sons, George Washington and John, remained behind with Grandma, but Louisa took Charles Francis, who was only two, with her on the exciting journey to old St. Petersburg.

The Court of the Czars was by far the most splendid Louisa had ever seen. She mused that the number of diamonds worn to any court function could not be counted and could only be measured in bushels. The cost of living, unfortunately, was in line with the general splendor and the servant problem was endlessly involved. The Adamses found themselves in a rented house to which were attached a maître d'hotel, a cook with two scullions under him, a porter, two footmen, a mujik to make the fires, a coachman and postilion, a housemaid and a laundry maid. Many of these with family and children, who also seemed to be attached to the household. The poor American Minister had to feed all the retinue.

Czar Alexander, oddly enough, was a liberal minded monarch who found the American experiment in government fascinating and wished to further trade with the new country. He timed his morning walks and rides to coincide with those of Adams, to whom he liked to talk, and when the War of 1812 came along he offered to mediate the peace treaty. The American peace mission, including Dolley Madison's son, Payne Todd, came on to St. Petersburg, but the British delegates were not yet ready to call the war quits.

President Madison meantime offered Adams a place on the Supreme Court, but Louisa was expecting her fourth child and he turned it down rather than let her risk the long trip. The Adamses' only daughter was born, lived more than a year, and died in old Russia. When the peace mission reconvened in Ghent, Adams attended. Louisa and Charles Francis remained behind in St. Petersburg.

The Treaty of Ghent was finally signed on Christmas Eve, 1814, in time to be a Christmas gift by today's standards, but word of it did not reach America until after Andrew Jackson had won the greatest victory of the whole war, in New Orleans half a month later. After this Adams wrote Louisa to join him in Paris, telling her that their two older sons were coming and that the family would be together in his new post as Minister to the Court of St. James.

Louisa set out by carriage with her youngest son, now almost eight years of age, two servants, and assorted helpers hired for the trip. It was in the dead of winter and would have been a hazardous journey at best, but all Europe now was in a chaotic uproar caused by news that Napoleon had escaped from Elba. Stuck in snowdrifts, robbed, and nearly thrown in jail, Louisa and her little party pushed south and west. As they went into France the roads were clogged with veterans rushing to join their returning Emperor, and Louisa's Russian drivers decided they should hasten back home. But finally Louisa swept into Paris along with the veterans after having shouted "Vive L'Empereur" to the point of exhaustion.

No other First Lady would have such a thrilling and martial journey to look back upon, but Louisa was glad when her family reassembled in London.

As soon as James Monroe became President, he called the younger Adams home to be his Secretary of State and Louisa's days of foreign travel ended. After this Washington would be her permanent home. Washingtonians stood somewhat in awe of the John Quincy Adamses, however, because of their long sojourns at royal courts and also because of his ability to freeze the atmosphere. He frankly considered most Americans in public life to be only half educated and apparently he made them feel so.

He could be a charming guest, apparently, but Louisa thought him rather hopeless as a host. His diary is dotted with notations that Louisa had called him down for being gruff and curt to so-and-so, and later his sons would chime in with their mother. As a Cabinet wife, under the rules of Monroe, Louisa gave weekly parties on Tuesday evenings and returned calls made on her. She was considered to be "on the whole, a very pleasant and agreeable woman" as well as an attractive one. She gave very good parties and would have given more of them had her husband enjoyed them.

As it happened her most celebrated party was given before she reached the White House, when she as wife of the Secretary of State entertained for Senator Andrew Jackson on January 8, 1824, the ninth anniversary of the celebrated

Battle of New Orleans. Jackson was the most popular man in America at the time and John Quincy Adams had championed his actions against the Seminoles in Florida against all comers. (Their later hatred for each other was more than a year in the future.)

This was the party to which an almost unheard of one thousand people came, the wheels of their carriages rolling over the Washington streets at such a clip that those not invited complained of inability to sleep. And out of it grew the verse:

> "Wend you with the world tonight?
> Brown and fair, and wise and witty
> Laughing mouths and dimples pretty,
> Belles and matrons, maids and madams,
> All are gone to Mrs Adams'."

In the three-cornered race for the Presidency that autumn, Louisa rallied into the fray behind her husband's candidacy with numerous theater parties and public appearances. Margaret Bayard Smith, who was backing the third man, William H. Crawford, thought that Louisa overdid it somewhat but perhaps she was only jealous.

The months between the November elections in which Jackson received a majority of the popular votes but not enough to elect him, and the runoff in the House of Representatives, which chose her husband, must have been excruciating ones for Louisa. None can say that she, the foreign born, by that time had failed to see American politics in action, but her silkworms always would be more understandable to her.

Her hospitality as First Lady was warm and sincere and gracious but, since her husband found all social activities connected with his office oppressive, she did not get a chance to enjoy her parties much.

It was history repeating itself when Louisa fixed up the big East Parlor. Abigail had made the other rooms habitable for her successors, and Louisa got the parlor ready for Andrew Jackson's enjoyment of it. The bitter backwash from an angry political front seeped through the doors of the White House throughout her First Ladyship, but she tried not to let it bother her and she was non-political in her entertaining.

The three Adams sons, all grown by now, lived in the White House, as did one of Louisa's nieces named Mary Catherine Hellen. Mary Catherine and the middle Adams son, John, were married in the White House in 1828 and Louisa's first grandchild was born there. The baby was named Mary Louise Adams, but her fond grandfather called her "Looly" from the beginning and she brightened his last years in office.

Louisa no doubt was happy when it became time for another President to take over. Her husband ran a notice in the local papers to say that they were moving to another house, out on Meridian Hill, and that since this was rather far out they expected nobody to call on them on the inaugural day which ushered in Andrew Jackson.

Her so-called public life was not over. There would be seventeen more years of it, but from now on her husband would be in a job which he liked, and which gave him more freedom. Also it took the spotlight off her. After he left the White House John Quincy Adams was elected to the House of Representatives from his home district in Massachusetts and he served with great honor and distinction from 1831 until 1848—one of two ex-Presidents so far to become members of Congress.

Some accounts say that Louisa succumbed to melancholia in her later years, but it seems just as likely that she preferred the luxury and comfort of being able to live in the comparative seclusion then afforded a Congressman's wife and enjoying her harp and her grandchildren.

Her husband as a Congressman inevitably became involved in the slavery question, which would tear the country asunder, and frequently both his wife and his offspring tried to temper his uncompromising views on the subject. He thought slavery was wrong and he did not want to see it extended into new territories.

Louisa fussed about his clothes, thought he did not always look as well groomed as he should have. But life on the whole—winters in Washington, summers in New England—appears to have been pleasant enough personally, as well as remunerative to the country.

In Congress Adams became a living monument to individual integrity and died in harness on Capitol Hill on February 23, 1848, with the seventy-two-year-old Louisa, still lovely and still looking pleasingly fragile, by his side. He lingered for three days after suffering his second blow of paralysis at the age of eighty-one while on the floor of the House. He was bedded down in the office of the Speaker of the House of Representatives nearby. During this time, the House met and adjourned in whispers rather than jeopardize what chance he might have of recovery.

Louisa lived almost five years longer.

JACKSON AND HIS WOMEN FOLKS (1829-37)

WHEN Andrew Jackson, the fiery old warrior with the sentimental heart, stormed into Washington to become the first of the Frontier Presidents, he had been a widower for little more than a month. Not for a minute of that time did he doubt that the slanders loosed against his adored wife, Rachel, during his second campaign for the highest office had killed her.

"May God Almighty forgive her murderers, as I know she forgave them," he said. "I never can."

"In the presence of this dear saint I can and do forgive my enemies," he said in another blazing quote during her funeral. "But those vile wretches who have slandered *her* must look to God for mercy."

Rachel Donelson Jackson was sixty-one years of age when her husband was elected President in November of 1828 and they had been married for thirty-seven years. After the election she replied to congratulations with: "For Mr. Jackson's sake I am glad. For my own part I never wished it."

Rachel's favorite spot on earth was the beautiful and fruitful Jackson farm, the Hermitage, near Nashville, Tennessee, and the more she saw of other places, the more she loved her own home. Other places included New Orleans, where she deplored the "wicked luxury," although not enough to prevent her purchase of comfortable French beds and other fine furnishings for the Hermitage; Pensacola, where she influenced her husband, then military Governor of Florida, to decree that hereafter the Sabbath Day must be kept Holy —or at least quiet; and Washington, where she spent at least two winters and thought the principal sin there to be in "carding and running to parties."

In Washington she had learned from Mrs. Monroe, whose at-homes she attended, that the Presidency was most expensive. "Mr. Monroe is going out of office a poor man and much dissatisfied," she wrote home. Rachel herself was a budget-watcher and, although she liked and had good things around her and believed in living well, she was not the splashy spender which her husband was. Her management of the Hermitage during his many absences won his highest approval and he gave her credit for their solvency.

Rachel, who by religion and inclination saw no need to

court the spotlight, felt no personal elation at the thought of being First Lady, and conceivably dreaded it. "I'd rather be a doorkeeper in the House of the Lord than to live in that palace," she told numerous friends after the campaign ended.

But in the month after the election she began accumulating a suitable White House wardrobe, with the help of relatives and friends who were determined that the first First Lady from beyond the Appalachian Mountains must be arrayed magnificently.

She was resting in a Nashville inn between purchases, so the legends go, when she overheard women in an adjoining room give an almost total recap of all that had been said against her during the campaign and then top it off with the opinion that, really, would it not be just too bad to have a woman like that in the White House.

The First Lady-elect toppled moaningly from her chair in a heart attack and did not recover. Some of her relatives always thought that she did not want to recover.

"No, Emily, I'll never forget it!" she told the niece who would be hostess at the White House in her stead. "Listening to them, it seemed as if a veil was lifted and I saw myself, whom you have all guarded from outside criticism and surrounded with flattering delusions, as others see me, a poor old woman. I will not go to Washington, but stay here as often before in Mr. Jackson's absences."

And it shortly became clear to all except her disbelieving husband, who could not imagine life without her—and thought that surely he could *will* her well again—that Rachel truly would not go to Washington with him. Never leaving her side, he lost so much sleep and grieved so much that "He'll never live to get there either" became the word going out from the Hermitage.

He was the President-elect, the first of them to be born in a log cabin; the Robin Hood from beyond the mountains who was determined to show the East a thing or two—and did—but he could not bring his Rachel back to life. He buried her on Christmas Eve of 1828 in a corner of her acre-sized flower garden. The white dress which she had purchased for his inaugural festivities became her shroud.

Her funeral perhaps was the most spectacular one ever known in American political circles. More than ten thousand persons, or twice the population of Nashville at the time, made it to the Hermitage to be with their hero during his sorrow. It was estimated that perhaps three thousand of them walked over muddy roads to attend.

Old Hickory tarried at the Hermitage only long enough to put a Greek cupola tomb over Rachel's grave and to write an epitaph to "A being so gentle and virtuous slander might wound but could not dishonor." Then he charged off to Washington to clean out the scandalmongers. Everybody in Washington expected him to come in shooting from both hips, which, all things considered, might have been thoroughly justified.

On inaugural afternoon the White House was thrown open to the masses who streamed in from everywhere to whoop it up for Jackson. The pressure was so great that window panes were broken to furnish exits and tubs of beer were rushed to the lawn to stop the stampede. The new President himself made an escape through the kitchens.

And he still would have woman problems. Peggy O'Neal Timberlake Eaton, the wife of his Secretary of War, turned whole days of his administration into comic opera. Pretty Peggy was a local innkeeper's daughter who had a cutting tongue and a nasty reputation. No "good" woman of Washington wanted to be in the same town with her. Mrs. Monroe supposedly wrote her a note asking that she skip White House events to which the naval status of her first husband, Timberlake, gave her entrance. Then she became a Cabinet wife. It was too much to bear and Mrs. John C. Calhoun, wife of Jackson's Vice President, packed herself home to South Carolina rather than attempt the ordeal.

Emily Donelson, Rachel's favorite niece who was married to Andrew Jackson Donelson, Rachel's nephew and the President's favorite secretary, also despised Peggy. Emily, the White House hostess, refused smelling salts from Peggy when she was near fainting and deplored Uncle Jackson's sponsorship of Mrs. Eaton. To Emily it was equating Aunt Rachel's reputation with Peggy's—but as Uncle Jackson saw it anybody who would slander his Rachel would slander anybody. "She's as chaste as a virgin," Uncle Jackson told the Washington ministers whom he ordered to the White House to upbraid them for their remarks about Peggy.

Only someone as wily and worldly as Martin Van Buren, the Secretary of State, could have solved Uncle Jackson's Peggy problems. It made him President and probably should have. In a set of maneuvers as complicated and disguised as anything in history, he worked it so that John Eaton was sent to Spain as Ambassador. Peggy became a great favorite at the Spanish court and lived to run away with her granddaughter's music teacher. A woman more unlike Rachel never lived.

Rachel, whose middle name should have been Piety, was born in Virginia to Colonel John Donelson, a member of Virginia's House of Burgesses. Donelson led a flotilla of flatboats by the river route to bring the first settlers in 1780 to what is now Nashville. The trip was a saga in itself and is made much of in Teddy Roosevelt's "Winning of the West." Rachel was twelve years of age at the time, a merry brown-eyed lass who, legend has it, helped keep the log on her father's "Good Boat Adventure." The log, not as complete as one would wish, is said to be the only written record of such a thrust westward.

The promised land was as gorgeous as everybody promised, but the first year's crops were flooded and, to lessen the burden of getting through the winter, Donelson and some others took their families to somewhat older blockhouse settlements in nearby Kentucky. There Rachel met and before she was sixteen married Lewis Robards. It was an unhappy union from the beginning and any grooves in the roads today probably were caused by one or two of Rachel's brothers going to bring her home, or Robards following right behind to take her back again.

Andy Jackson had it easier. He rode a fine horse over the mountains from the Carolinas, his law books piled on another fine horse. He and his great friend, John Overton, boarded with the Widow Donelson. (Rachel's father was killed, supposedly by the Indians, on one of his trips back to Virginia.) Rachel came home on one of her safaris and when Robards came for her she refused to return with him. So he stayed a while and they lived briefly in the area. Meantime Andy and Overton had moved from the Donelsons. When Robards left this time he said that he was petitioning the State of Virginia (of which Kentucky then was a part) for a divorce. Then he sent word that his petition was granted and Rachel went to Natchez, Mississippi, to be with relatives (she was kin to nearly everybody in an area which would become several states) while she pondered her sorrows.

Red-headed Jackson, hearing the divorce news, took out down the Natchez Trace to marry her—and did. Although a lawyer, he never checked Robards' papers. He and Rachel had been happily married for more than two years when they were bombshelled by the news that Robards had *not* obtained a divorce but only permission to apply for one in the courts of Kentucky. He was doing so and naming Jackson as the co-respondent! It caused much frontier snickering when he and Rachel had to undergo a second red-faced wedding. So the campaign stories about Rachel being a bigamist were for a time literally true. But nonetheless they were as false as any words ever spoken in reflecting Rachel's character.

Eleven years after the second wedding ceremony Jackson shot and killed young Charles Dickinson in a duel brought on by the recurring subject. Dickinson, at a horserace, overheard Rachel brag about one of Jackson's horses leaving another far behind. "Yes," muttered Dickinson, "about as far out of sight as Mrs. Jackson left her husband when she ran away with the General." It was repeated and one thing led to another. Rachel pleaded with her husband to ignore the remark and thought that she had his promise not to fire whatever happened as he and his friends rode off to Kentucky—where duels were legal—to have it out with the crack shot of the area. Jackson came home wounded and as Rachel nursed him back to life she became more pious than ever. He built her a church on the property so that she and her Presbyterian neighbors would not need to take the long trip into Nashville.

She remained a spirited and energetic woman, by all accounts, and was never a nonentity. She kept house for the General and his increasing circle. Her kindness, generosity and hospitality were famous. Beautiful in her youth, she remained a handsome woman despite her increasing number of chins. Jackson wore a miniature of her around his neck during his Presidency, placing it on his bedside table at night.

A noted portrait of Rachel was done long after her death and given to the White House in 1942. It was by Howard Chandler Christy, who was authorized by the Tennessee legislature to paint her "as she must have been," so that the folklore about Rachel being an old crone who sat by the chimney smoking a corncob pipe might be dispelled forever. It is ravishing but bears a marked resemblance to the miniature and to another portrait done during her life by Ralph E. W. Earle. For a woman who never was in the White House as a First Lady, the wife of Jackson influenced more pages of history than many First Ladies ever do.

WIDOWER VAN BUREN'S TERM (1837-1841)

His Daughter-in-Law Matched the Gold Spoons

MARTIN VAN BUREN, the sophisticated New Yorker who
followed rugged Andrew Jackson into the Presidency, was a
widower and had been so for eighteen years when he moved
into the White House. Else he might not have been able to
make the move. If Hannah Hoes, the winsome Dutch cousin
to whom he was married for twelve years and who bore him
four sons, had lived until he became Secretary of State in the
Jackson cabinet she—like many other official wives in Washington—might have disapproved of her husband's being nice
to Peggy Eaton. That might have hampered his freedom in
maneuvering the beautiful troublemaker out of the country.

But as it turned out he stuck by Jackson throughout the
"Battle of the Petticoats" and the embattled old warrior re-
turned the favor by sticking by him and sponsoring him for
President.

When Van Buren and his sons, all grown, moved into the
White House there was not a woman anywhere on their horizon, and the new President began a cleanup campaign to
ready the place for his type of living. Jackson had lived
lavishly in the old mansion but in a free-for-all atmosphere
rent by a constant stream of relatives and visitors.

Van Buren auctioned off furniture which he considered to
be rickety or outmoded and spent $25,000 to make the place
more chic for the small perfect dinners which were his entertainment specialty. Also, he unlocked the gold spoons
acquired during President Monroe's day in a plan to use them
much more frequently. He made his oldest son, Abraham,
who had attended West Point, his private secretary and he
named the third son, Martin, Jr., Abraham's assistant. The
second son, John, called "Our Prince John" by Whig newspapers because he once had dined with British royalty, was a
social ornament and well schooled in political intricacies as
was Smith, the youngest son. Soon the Van Buren White
House was noted for its selective polish and the perfection of
its intimate dinners.

Aging Dolley Madison, who lived less than a block away,
watched the womanless proceedings with foreboding. Dolley,
a matchmaker at heart, naturally believed that every White

House needs a wife and while she had no hopes of getting the urbane widower President married off, she ached for a chance to break up the merry bachelorhood of the four sons. And the chance came when one of her gorgeous young cousins showed up from South Carolina.

Angelica Singleton, the breathtaking cousin, was enough to turn any man's head and Cousin Dolley earmarked her for a Van Buren son: just which one she was willing to leave to fate. Angelica really was visiting her uncle and aunt, Senator and Mrs. William C. Preston, and would have met the Van Burens in the normal course of events, but Dolley wanted better than that. As a former resident of the White House she knew how distracting crowds could be and she arranged to take Angelica calling when she knew the sons would be at leisure.

Angelica was the daughter and granddaughter of wealthy Carolina aristocrats and was herself the finished product of Madame Greland's Seminary in Philadelphia. She and the oldest son were married in November of Van Buren's second year in office and for the New Year's Day Reception of 1839 the President proudly had his lovely daughter-in-law beside him when he received his guests.

In the spring of the same year the couple went abroad on an extended honeymoon spent mostly in London where Angelica's uncle, Andrew Stevenson, was the American minister. Mrs. Stevenson saw to it that the beautiful Angelica was presented to Queen Victoria and met all the proper royalty.

It was a triumphant pilgrimage and young Angelica came back with three plumes to wear in her hair and a dress of royal blue velvet with a skirt ten yards full. At the first opportunity she wore the regal attire at a White House reception and remained seated to receive her guests. It created quite a controversy, but all who bowed before Angelica knew that they never had seen a more beautiful or charming young girl, nor one with a sweeter smile.

The perfect bliss of the dazzling young beauty who enjoyed White House hostessing was marred by the death of her baby girl, born in the historic mansion, who lived only two hours. After the Van Buren term ended, Angelica and her husband resided for many years in New York City, where she bore three sons and where her home became noted for its elegant hospitality. "Up to the time of her death, in 1878, she was a lady upon whom it was a pleasure to look, . . . considerate of others, sweet in disposition, and gracious in speech."

ANNA SYMMES HARRISON
(March 4-April 4, 1841)

First Lady in Absentia

ANNA SYMMES HARRISON never came to Washington during the short time her husband was President. She was ill at their home in North Bend, Ohio, when the sixty-eight-year-old William Henry Harrison started off for his inaugural and the doctor forbade her traveling the mountain roads until much warmer weather. She was still ill when she received word of his death, which happened exactly a month after he took office.

If she had been with him, he might have worn an overcoat, tempered down his inaugural festivities, and lived longer. March 4, 1841, was a very cold and stormy day in the capital city. Harrison stood in the open to make the longest inaugural speech on record. It lasted an hour and forty-five minutes. Harrison had been in town for days, celebrating every step of the way, and after the big parade featuring cider barrels and log cabins was over, he went to all three inaugural balls. His had been the jazziest campaign so far on record—the granddaddy of all the public-relationed splendors to come later—and the old Indian fighter still was keeping up the show for the populace.

Filling in for the ailing wife at the White House were a widowed daughter-in-law, Jane Findlay Irwin Harrison, and the latter's aunt, Mrs. James Findlay, a seventy-three-year-old social arbiter from Cincinnati. Two of Jane's teen-aged sons and possibly other relatives were also on the scene. Mrs. Findlay had the seat of honor at the dining table. A few mornings before his cold turned into pneumonia, the President slung a market basket over his arm and went out to look for groceries.

Anna Harrison was sixty-six years of age at the time of her husband's death and would live to be almost eighty-nine, not dying until 1864 after she had seen her grandsons, including Benjamin, who would become President, go off to fight in the Civil War. She had thought her husband more than a bit silly to consider the Presidency at his age, but she would have made an interesting First Lady had circumstances permitted her to serve.

She was born in New Jersey during the first year of the Revolutionary War. Her father, John Cleves Symmes, later a judge, was in the American army and when her mother died he came home and disguised himself in a British uniform to take four-year-old Anna through the lines to her maternal grandparents on outer Long Island. After the war Judge Symmes went West to Ohio and at one time, it was said, held titles to almost a hundred thousand acres of western land.

Anna attended Clinton Academy at East Hampton, Long Island, and then went to Isabella Graham's finishing school in New York City. Her father returned East to remarry, and then Anna traveled West with her stepmother and a caravan of settlers going to live on some of her father's acreage. She was a pretty young lady with dark hair and eyes, a full mouth and a dimpled chin.

Young Captain William Henry Harrison recently had come to Ohio to command Fort Washington and wanted to marry Anna the minute he saw her. The judge wanted more than an army salary for his daughter, however, and refused his consent. One day when the judge was away from home Anna walked out of the house and married the captain.

The couple built their own four-room log house and nine years later, in 1804, when the captain was Governor of the Indiana Territory, he designed a governor's mansion for them at Vincennes. It was of brick, two and a half stories high, with four great chimneys and eighteen-inch-thick walls. The upper stories extended outward for defense purposes. There was a lookout station on the roof and a powder magazine in the cellar, but nonetheless Harrison made it look as much like his ancestral home, Beverly, in Virginia as possible. The Harrisons lived well for the area, but they did not accumulate much in the way of worldly goods—except children.

Anna bore ten children, six sons and four daughters, in rapid succession. Only six of them were still living when she became First Lady, however. For much of the time there was a tutor living with the Harrisons, teaching their children, and also the other children of the settlement. Preachers who came that way stayed with the Harrisons, too, and always the family was interested in helping start schools, churches and libraries.

In 1811 Harrison defeated the Indians in a battle at Tippecanoe on the Wabash river in Indiana—and also won a nickname. In the War of 1812 he won so many battles that he became a major general. When finally he defeated the great Indian chief Tecumseh, Harrison was ready to resign from the army, and did so in 1814.

Anna's father had left her three thousand acres of land at North Bend. The Harrisons moved their original log house down the river to this spot, covered it with clapboard and kept adding ells until it had twenty-two rooms, all of them in use by family and guests. Their country hospitality was fabulous, with fifty visitors for dinner nearly every Sunday. In the course of a year three hundred hams were consumed at their groaning tables. Farmer Harrison was elected to Congress, then to the Ohio Senate, and next to the United States Senate for three years; but there never seemed to be enough cash to go around.

When son William went to Transylvania College in Kentucky in 1820, his mother wrote him that she wished she had some money to send him. "But I will get your Pa to send you some from Cincinnati, if it should be but little. . . . God bless and protect you, dear son."

The third son, Scott, gave up his ambitions to become a doctor and became the one who held the acres together and looked after his mother in her widowhood. His reward was that his son, Benjamin, became President.

Congress granted Anna $25,000, or a full year's salary for a President in those days, at the death of her husband, and this custom was followed for needy widows of Presidents for many years before a regular pension system for widowed First Ladies was initiated.

Anna was a beloved matriarch in her area, noted for her conversational ability and aid to good causes. She kept up with the news and deplored the approach of the Civil War, but was happy that her grandsons were fighting against the cause of slavery.

LETITIA CHRISTIAN TYLER . . The Mother of Seven
(April 6, 1841–September 10, 1842)

JULIA GARDINER TYLER . . . . The Mother of Seven
(June 26, 1844–March 4, 1845)

ARISTOCRATIC John Tyler, who eventually would father four-teen children, brought two wives to the White House during his less than four years there, and his administration became the greatest family affair of all time. In his partial term as President, the Executive Mansion witnessed a daughter's wedding, the births of two grandchildren, the death of a First Lady, and the coming of a new one as a bride.

No one, including Tyler himself, expected that he would be President. "Old Tippecanoe and Tyler, Too" sounded good in the campaign slogans of 1840, but the two men on the win-ning ticket had nothing in common except Virginia as a birthplace. Tyler's beliefs ran counter to those of the Whigs, who elected him, on all major issues and he became the Presi-dent without a party until, as he quipped, his second wife gave him a magnificent one to celebrate his major victory in office —the annexation of Texas.

As Vice President, which was the job he wanted, dashing Tyler expected to live on in old Williamsburg, go on with his law practice, and journey up to Washington only for the ses-sions of Congress. His dreams of such peaceful coexistence with the Whigs were shattered by loud knocks on his hand-some door at five o'clock on the morning of April 5, 1841. Daniel Webster's son, accompanied by the chief clerk of the Senate, had ridden a day and night to bring him news of Har-rison's death. Tyler and his two oldest sons, Robert and John, Jr., left with the messengers immediately and the five men were in the capital city by daybreak the next morning.

Ladies of the Tyler household would follow later in the month after they had assembled wardrobes and closed the family home. Their move was complicated by the fact that the new First Lady, lovely Letitia Christian Tyler, was a victim of paralysis and had lived mostly in a wheel chair for three years. She was fifty years of age and, according to her daughter-in-law, Priscilla:

"She must have been very beautiful in her youth, for she is beautiful now in her declining years and wretched health. Her skin is as smooth and soft as a baby's; she has sweet, loving black eyes, and her features are delicately moulded; besides this, her feet and hands are perfect; and she is gentle and graceful in her movements, with a most peculiar air of native refinement about everything she says and does. She is the most entirely unselfish person you can imagine. . . ."

In her own home she had continued to regulate "all the household affairs, and all so quietly that you can't tell when she does it." In the White House, however, she lived quietly in her own suite, attended by her daughters and avoiding excitement, and she would make only one semi-public appearance.

She was the mother of seven children. Her two older daughters were married and in homes of their own. The eldest son, Robert, and his wife, Priscilla, and their infant daughter lived with the Tylers. John, Jr., was married and also would live with the family in the White House. The two single daughters were Elizabeth, a seventeen-year-old belle who would marry in the White House, and Alice, a child of fourteen. Then there was the youngest son, Tazewell, only ten.

Tyler asked Priscilla, then twenty-four-years old, to assume the duties of White House hostess. Lively and witty, the charming Priscilla conferred regularly with family-friend Dolley Madison, who lived nearby, and also took tips on White House protocol from Daniel Webster, the Secretary of State.

Although often called a failure politically, the Tyler administration was a real success socially. Politics was never discussed with guests and invitations went out on an unbiased basis. Unfailing courtesy and hospitality were extended to holders of all shades of political opinion. Congressmen who voted against Tyler still could have a friendly time at the White House.

Priscilla had lived with the Tylers ever since her marriage three years before, and was delighted that Robert now would have a job in the Land Office that paid him $1,500 a year. To befit her new dignity, she wrote her sisters that she had bought among other things "a pearl-colored silk that would set you crazy," especially when worn with pink roses in the hair and a corsage of the same flowers. For her calls on the ladies of Washington she had a most elegant "white chip bonnet trimmed with moss rose buds."

Priscilla was the daughter of British tragedian, Thomas A.

Cooper, who married a New York society belle, Mary Fairlie —much against the wishes of her prominent mother—and who became a favorite matinee idol throughout America in the 1820's and 30's. As happens to all handsome Hamlets sooner or later, Cooper's star and income waned and, after her mother's death, talented Priscilla toured in plays with her father.

She was playing Desdemona in Richmond, Virginia, when Robert first saw her. The audience gave her a standing ovation, and the smitten Robert stood the longest of all. They were married at the Cooper home in Bristol, Pennsylvania, with John Tyler and John, Jr., in attendance, and Priscilla loved all the Tylers as her very own.

At the bi-weekly receptions and monthly public levees Priscilla and young Elizabeth Tyler often received together, with no thought of rivalry, and they often walked together on pleasant days with Priscilla's daughter Mary Fairlie between them. Much of the time, however, Elizabeth attended her mother and Priscilla did the honors alone.

She had so looked forward to the first official dinner at which she would be the only woman. When the night came, her daughter was ill and poor Priscilla was miserable the whole evening. She liked the Cabinet dinners best of all, because Webster sat at her right. They became friends after she fainted dead away at one of the very first such affairs.

She described the embarrassment in a letter to her sisters: ". . . . at the moment the ices were being put on the table, everybody in good humor, and all going 'merry as a marriage bell', what should I do but grow deathly pale, and, for the first time in my life, fall back in a fainting fit! Mr. Webster . . . picked me up . . . in his arms . . . and Mr. Tyler (Robert), with his usual impetuosity, deluged us both with ice-water, ruining my lovely new dress, and, I am afraid, producing a decided coolness between himself and the Secretary of State. . . ."

Priscilla's second daughter was born in the White House later that spring and christened Letitia Christian for the invalid First Lady, whose health grew steadily worse. The First Lady had been able to attend Elizabeth's wedding to William Waller in the East Room in late January, her only semi-public appearance in the White House. She died there in September, 1842, the first of three First Ladies who would die while their husbands were President.

To help break the gloom that followed her death, Priscilla celebrated Mary Fairlie's third birthday with a brilliant costume party for the young elite of Washington in early 1843. Dolley Madison was the only adult invited to participate, but a contingent of Cabinet members and diplomats came to have a look and to hear the laughter.

Napoleon's aide de camp, Count Henri Bertrand, came visiting that year while the President was in Virginia and Priscilla decided to invite two hundred "of the very prettiest girls and nicest people I could collect" to dinner to meet him and his party. "No party ever went off better. . . It is so easy to entertain at other people's expense," Priscilla wrote her sisters.

When Priscilla used the phrase "at other people's expense" she revealed what had been on her mind for some time now. Although her husband was holding his first job, he had not yet begun the practice of law, and they had lived with his parents all their married life. After one particularly gay White House party, she had written her sister that all she could think of when she noted the jewels worn by the Russian Ambassador's wife was that they would have financed a good education for Mary Fairlie. She wanted to leave the White House and move to Philadelphia, where her husband could launch himself in the legal profession.

Her chance to get away came sooner than she had dared hope and in the lovely shape of Julia Gardiner, a New York belle, who soon became Tyler's second wife. Julia was the daughter of wealthy David Gardiner from Gardiner's Island, off Long Island, and was a beauty with a flair for the unusual and the daring. She was only twenty-three when the President met her but already she had made a hit at European courts and had permitted a colored lithograph of herself to be used in a New York store advertisement. It was titled "The Rose of Long Island" and in it she carried on her lovely arm a purse with the placard: "I'll purchase at Bogert and Mecamly's. . . Their goods are beautiful and astonishingly cheap."

An olive-skinned brunette with clear gray eyes, Julia came to Washington with her father for the social season of 1843. She was immediately taken with the elegant ease of the President's conversation, the melody of his voice and his grace of manner, and he found her enchanting. Viewing the difference in their ages, Julia felt that they should not make marriage plans, but Priscilla, knowing how the handsome Tyler men wooed in poetry and song, never doubted the outcome. Priscilla was expecting her third child and her husband agreed that if she were willing to live in lodgings while he studied day and night to pass the bar exam and then to take her uncertain chances on his success, then so was he. And with no regrets, they moved to Philadelphia.

The wedding of the President and Julia was hastened by a tragic disaster in which her father, David Gardiner, and the Secretary of the Navy, Thomas Walker Gilmer, were among those killed. About four hundred guests, including President Tyler, his Cabinet, and the diplomatic corps and, of course, Dolley Madison, were on the U.S.S. *Princeton*, the first propeller-driven warship, for a Potomac cruise during which the firing of a new gun, called the "Peacemaker," would be demonstrated. All went well, including the gun, until on the return trip when it was decided to give the "Peacemaker" another firing. The President, below deck talking to Julia, declined to come up for the show, remarking that he was better engaged. The gun exploded and those nearest it were killed.

Four months later, in June of 1844, she and the fifty-four-year-old Tyler were married in New York City. It was the first time that any President had married while in office and the public avidly read everything written about the romance and wedding. Ex-President John Quincy Adams, who saw little good in the Tyler administration from beginning to end, confided to his diary that the age difference would make them laughing stocks. But he could not have been more wrong.

Julia was First Lady for only eight months but they were glamorous ones indeed and the marriage was an exceedingly happy one. She hero-worshipped him, thought his speeches the greatest ever made, and espoused all his political causes. After his term ended she added seven more children to the rolls and made Tyler the greatest daddy among the Presidents.

Entertainment during her tenure was as lavish and gay and regal as any the White House had known. Twelve maids of honor, six on either side and all dressed alike, frequently received with the First Lady, who often sat on a slightly raised platform before the south windows of the Blue Room. Her headdress often resembled a crown, and one such reportedly was made of bugles, although mostly they were of plumes. There was some criticism of such "copying from royalty" but, no doubt about it, the Tyler administration which began in deep gloom and political weakness ended in a brilliant blaze of social success as well as in political victory.

Tyler's great desire for his administration was to bring Texas into the Union, an idea unpopular with Whigs and others who feared and opposed the addition of any territory which permitted slavery. He insisted that his championship was not sectional but good for the country as a whole and that the monopoly on cotton thus obtained would give the nation a needed economic advantage over Great Britain.

Since Texas was an independent nation, the annexation was accomplished in treaty form, which involved negotiations between the two countries and then a ratification of the treaty by two-thirds of the votes in the Senate. It took him months and months and failure after failure to finally insure the votes needed and in the doing of it, as Julia's son would later write, he toppled four political giants of the period: Henry Clay, Martin Van Buren, Thomas H. Benton and Francis P. Blair, editor of the *Globe*.

Julia leaped into the fray most heartily and when the final Congress of his term assembled, she thought that her husband's message to it was the finest bit of prose ever written. "Oh, if it only will have the effect of admitting Texas!" she wrote.

Texas was admitted and in the month before the term ended Julia gave a grand ball to celebrate Tyler's victory. More than two thousand guests came. The quadrille and the polka were danced in the big East Room to music by the Marine Band. She had instructed the band to play "Hail to the Chief" the moment her husband appeared: an innovation immediately adopted for use on future occasions to signal the arrival of the President in office.

Tyler gave Julia "the immortal gold pen" with which he had signed the necessary annexation papers and she wore it hung from a chain around her neck all through the inaugural ceremonies for James Knox Polk.

When he left the White House Tyler took Julia to Sherwood Forest, a place he had purchased for her on the James river. Their home there was a comparatively simple frame house set amid forests and gardens covering eleven hundred acres but they added so many connecting ells and additions to the structure that it became known as the deepest frame house in the country. From front door to back it extended three hundred feet.

Virginians wondered how the sophisticated city girl would take to the simple country life. The answer was that she loved it. They had a magnificent rowboat called the *Pocahontas* in which they visited neighbors across the river and also a handsome carriage for calls on their side of the James. And life on the James did not prove to be too simple. When Julia's sister visited her one winter eight balls, eleven dinners, and uncounted teas were given in her honor.

Julia came back to Washington with her husband in 1861 for a Peace Conference which, it was hoped, might forestall the North-South conflict. It did not, and she threw her lot with the Confederacy along with his. He was elected to the Confederate Congress and was in Richmond ready to serve when he died in 1862. No notice was taken of his death by the government in Washington.

Other Presidential families and descendants suffered during the Civil War, but the Tylers perhaps more than the others. There were so many of them. Jaunty Priscilla and Robert, who had considered that they were getting along quite well, were caught in an angry outcry against anybody named Tyler and hurriedly had to leave their home in Pennsylvania as the storm gathered. They ended up in Alabama. Elizabeth Tyler Coleman, in a charming biography of her relative, Priscilla Cooper Tyler, tells how Priscilla never managed to have much money of her own, but remained always undaunted.

Julia lived to see one of her sons, Lyon Gardiner Tyler, become president of William and Mary College, the alma mater of his father and grandfather, and this Mr. Tyler lived to see Williamsburg—for which the Tylers had given their "middle plantation"—restored by the Rockefellers. Sherwood Forest still remains in the family.

Julia suffered so many pecuniary losses that in 1879 shortly after she came back to live in Washington she petitioned Congress for a pension. One for $3,000 annually was immediately granted. Three years later when Congress granted pensions of $5,000 annually to Lucretia Garfield and Sarah Polk, Julia's was raised to the same amount, and thereafter the $5,000 annuity was available for all widows of Presidents. (In 1958 the amount was raised again, to the $10,000 annually which it is today.)

The eighth First Lady, the adored young wife of the fatherly Tyler, outlived her husband by twenty-seven years and died in Richmond in 1889 at the age of sixty-nine.

SARAH CHILDRESS POLK (1845-1849)

She Stopped the Refreshments

RUGGED old Sam Houston once said in exasperation and perhaps after he had imbibed a dram too much that the only fault with James Knox Polk, the President who literally worked himself to death, was that he was "addicted to the drinking of plain water." Some felt much the same way about Polk's handsome wife, Sarah. Her disciplined goodness was apt to bore and then to irritate lesser mortals.

She was vivid to look at—a real Spanish-beauty type with the air of a high-born donna, and her dresses were of magnificent fabrics in gorgeous colors—but in personality she was determined to be colorless. She was gracious, democratic, affable, and pulled no conversational bloopers. She was well-educated and some have said that in some respects she was a better politician than her husband, but ladies of her day did not discuss politics—not if they were real ladies. Sarah Polk, with her belief in the non-controversial, would not have discussed it anyway. Her conversation, at which she was considered quite good, ran to exclamatory sentences such as, "Sir, I've never known it otherwise!" and to little come-ons such as, "How so, Sir?"

If she had been less good to look at, said one writer of the day, she might have been considered the epitome of stuffiness. But she was a much esteemed First Lady and, although many a Washingtonian groaned at the Presbyterian ground rules by which she ran the White House, her high principles received the approval of the general public. The truth seems to have been that she was just what she seemed to be: a stunning looking and perfectly satisfied with herself woman, born without a shred of need for excitement in her pretty make-up.

Polk, at forty-nine, was the youngest President to date and Sarah, at forty-one, ranked with Dolley Madison in youthful bloom. Sarah was no drawback to her husband's dark-horse nomination. Quite the contrary. During her husband's fourteen years in Congress, three of them as Speaker of the House of Representatives, Sarah had been with him in Washington every winter except one and had more than held her own

74

among the fixture wives such as Mrs. John C. Calhoun and Mrs. Henry Clay. She was much admired and respected among the politicians who would select her husband as the non-controversial candidate to run against Henry Clay, the popular Whig who for so long had wanted to be President. But by 1844 Clay had been compromising for too long! The uneasy public at least knew where Polk stood and believed that he would stay hitched.

He wanted the boundaries of the country extended to the Pacific Ocean, with clear title to the territory, and he was willing to fight Mexico to gain it.

Polk believed that unremitting toil could cinch almost anything. He made his Cabinet sign an agreement that its members would stay totally on the job, not have their eyes on any other office and would forsake vacations. In return he promised that he would do the same and, furthermore, that he would not seek reelection. Despite doctors' advice, he lived up to his promises and had only one short enforced rest during his four years in office. He worked around the clock—and so did Sarah.

She was his confidential secretary, the first working-wife First Lady. A few other First Ladies have promoted their husbands' programs and were assets on the political and amount-of-work-done levels, but the stately Sarah was in the inner sanctum editing speeches and helping write them, clipping and filing, marking paragraphs and columns so that her husband could go right on working at night. She sifted his correspondence and truly did know what was going on. The Polks had no children to engage her attention and they relied on each other, and saw eye to eye.

There is no hint of her changing his opinions. She was just a helping hand, like any good secretary. She was not a policy maker. But possibly she influenced him to go speak at the women's rights convention in Seneca Falls, New York, in 1848—an item always mentioned in his biography. But there is no indication that Sarah was an exponent of women's rights —or ever felt any need to be.

Her character was one of utter rectitude, by conservative Presbyterian standards, and with no deviations. She stopped the serving of wine at the White House, did not permit dancing nor card playing in the mansion, and when the crowds at her receptions grew too large she cut out refreshments in general. Not even a cookie! It could have been called stinginess, since Polk was one of the few early Presidents to leave office with earned cash in his pocket, but it probably was just her way.

Without either food or personality, a party can fall mighty flat and Sarah's did before she learned to call in Dolley Madison, by then an old lady in a rusty black dress but still the grand dame of Washington. When President Polk entered the East Parlor with Dolley on his arm, the crowd felt that it was getting its due. Neither age nor poverty could dull the excitement of Dolley's personality.

After the Polks' New Year's Day reception the cream of the crowd went on to Dolley's where there was always something to drink and eat, whatever the condition of her pocketbook. When Congress bought some more of her late husband's books Dolley splurged on white satin to brighten Sarah's parlor. Sarah did not know how to be outgoing—and Dolley could not help being so. One of Dolley's civic ventures during this period was raising money for completion of the Washington Monument, which President Polk dedicated.

Sarah was born in the lovely little shade-tree town of Murfreesboro, Tennessee, in 1803, into a well-to-do family whose head, Captain Joel Childress, believed enough in education to send her to one of the best schools of the day: the Moravian Institute in Salem, North Carolina, established and run by religious refugees from Moravia.

She and Polk married on New Year's Day in 1824 when he was a member of the Tennessee State legislature. He went to Congress the following year and eventually became Speaker of the House of Representatives. After fourteen years in Congress he was elected Governor of Tennessee. Sarah presided over the state mansion with great poise and graciousness.

It was said of her that she lived above the warring factions of politics and was respected by politicians holding all shades of political opinion. Apparently that was her great gift. It may have made her a bit dull conversationally and personally but it was still a great gift for a politician's wife. And other politicians noted and valued it.

There were two inaugural balls when Polk took office and he and the First Lady attended one of them for a brief while. It was well understood that they did not dance and, out of deference, the dancing stopped during their visit. Sarah wore a gorgeous blue ball dress to this event. It is in the collection of dresses of First Ladies at the Smithsonian Institution, still fresh in color and now back in style.

When Sarah abolished dancing and other light amusements from the White House during her stay, it met with wide approval from both the newspapers and the public. Her press was very good indeed and also rather remarkable for her day, when women received scant notice in the newspapers. The writer of a letter to the Nashville *Union*, who said that even the advocates of frivolous pastimes would respect her, proved to be correct. They might have wished for more gaiety

76

in the White House occasionally but they respected Sarah's sincerity and honesty and found their gaiety elsewhere.

Polk kept his word and refused to run for reelection. The Polks' departure from Washington and their trip home was a scene of ovation and triumph. Nashville gave them a great homecoming. They had purchased a large house on a commanding hill very near the State Capitol and after they had enlarged it somewhat and put it in complete order their plan was to take a European tour. The Ex-President had already engaged a courier who could speak French and German to go with them. But he was so tired that he was unable to throw off a slight illness. He died in June, after having left office in March. His last words were: "I love you, Sarah, for all eternity. I love you."

Laura Holloway wrote that "the death of her husband was the only affliction of Mrs. Polk's life. It had been invariably calm, cheerful, and happy. . . . The sympathizing attention paid to her grief was universal."

The Ex-President's study, on the second floor of their Nashville home and looking toward the State Capitol, was kept just as he left it. Sarah made Polk Place into a museum piece over which she presided for forty-two years after his death. She survived her husband for more years than any other First Lady ever has. She adopted a namesake niece who lived with her. On each New Year's Day the State Legislature called on her in a body, as did many other groups which met in Nashville. No distinguished visitors came through Nashville without calling on Polk's widow.

All during the Civil War Sarah lived on in her noncontroversial world, holding herself above the conflict and attending church regularly. Nashville, being in a border state, was occupied by both sides on different occasions. The state government fled but not Sarah. At Polk Place she received dashing General Beauregard, who wore the gray, and later on she received dashing General Sherman, who wore the blue. Her relatives were with the South and perhaps her heart was, too, but as the widow of a former President she refused to take sides, and none questioned her right to do so. Probably she prayed for both sides as she knelt in the First Presbyterian Church. She was almost eighty-eight when she died in 1891.

MARGARET SMITH TAYLOR
(March 4, 1849–July 9, 1850)

She Declined the Honors

IF she could have managed it, sixty-year-old Margaret Smith Taylor would have poured wax into the ears of her husband, "Old Rough and Ready," to shut out the siren Whig song of 1848 which lured him to the Presidency. She considered it absurd for him to listen to the tune even for a moment. Just home from the Mexican War and loaded with honors, he was now ready, she maintained, to enjoy the happy retirement to which they both had looked forward for so many years.

She pleaded with him to no avail, and then with God— with the same results. Zachary Taylor laughingly told how she prayed several times a day that Henry Clay—or anyone other than her husband—would get the nomination, and then she prayed against his election. But to her it was no laughing matter.

She remembered "Old Tippecanoe" as well as the Whigs did, and with much more concern. The Whigs remembered that they had won the Presidency with an old Indian fighter, but she remembered that William Henry Harrison had lived only briefly thereafter. Her husband was nearing sixty-five, and in her opinion he had been a victim of "government politics" during much of his military career, in that promotions which she felt he merited went to others. Now that he had won national acclaim she could not understand why he would stoop to politics and forfeit his peaceful future.

But Zachary Taylor had his reasons. All during the War with Mexico he had been on a tightrope and, as he wrote to his son-in-law after winning the Presidency: "My election has no doubt astonished those in power, who resorted to every measure to break me down as far as they could do so, when (I was) in a foreign country in front of the enemy, and to destroy me by the vilest slanders. . . ." Men more politically astute than Zachary Taylor had expected to walk off with the honors of this war, but they could not top Taylor's magnificent success on the battlefield nor touch his popularity among the soldiers he had led to victory. He would have been less than human to turn thumbs down on the chance for total vindication for all his unsung years in the service.

For forty years his wife, Peggy, who grew up in the comfort of a Calvert County, Maryland, home, had followed her military man to outposts from the Canadian border to Tampa Bay and then to Baton Rouge, Louisiana, from whence he went off to Mexico. Her six children were born in four different states and territories, and her oldest grandson, John Taylor Wood, was the first white child born in Minnesota. Rather than relinquish the company of her husband, she had relinquished her children for long periods to relatives and to Eastern schools. Two of her five daughters had died in infancy and the other three—two of them much against their parents' wishes—all married military officers. But only the oldest, Ann, duplicated the pillar-to-post existence of her mother. For the only son, Richard, who was the youngest child, the Taylors had managed four years of study abroad and a Yale graduation.

When Taylor was assigned to help quell the Seminoles of Florida, Peggy made the newspapers by going along as usual, despite the chance of extermination. But as she saw it that chance was part of her job as a military man's wife. She lived through the Seminole Battle of Okee-Chobee, and then proposed to take her stand in a Spanish cottage at Baton Rouge on a rise above the Mississippi. She worried about her rough and ready husband and about the delicate health of their son, Richard, but once the Mexican War was over, she thought she need never worry again about her husband.

Her daughter, Ann, and Ann's children were with her during much of the Mexican War. So was her youngest daughter, Elizabeth, a scant twenty-two years old and unmarried, but in love with Colonel William Wallace Smith Bliss. This would be one military marriage for their daughters that the Taylors would not oppose. Colonel Bliss was so estimable that he was know as "Perfect Bliss." He and Betty married in 1848, the year in which her father won the Presidency. Colonel Bliss would be his father-in-law's secretary at the White House and Betty would be his hostess there. Mrs. Taylor absolutely declined the honor of presiding at the mansion.

Only reluctantly did Mrs. Taylor consent to go to Washington at all and she made it clear that she would join in no official festivities whatsoever. If Betty wanted to act as her father's hostess, fine and good, but she herself would live in her own quarters and do as she pleased.

One of the few people received by Mrs. Taylor in the White House was, by odd coincidence, the wife of Mrs. Taylor's former son-in-law, Senator Jefferson Davis of Mississippi. Davis, as a young lieutenant under Taylor, had fallen in love with the middle Taylor daughter, the lovely Sarah Knox Taylor, and when parental consent was not forthcoming he and Knox had eloped to marry at the home of her relatives in Kentucky. The tragedy of this elopement was that the young couple fell ill of malaria and three months after the marriage beautiful Knox was dead, before her father had spoken a word of forgiveness.

Nine years later Davis, still unforgiven, married an unusual and dramatic girl named Varina—who later would be the First Lady of the Confederacy—and came to Congress. When the Mexican War came along Davis resigned his Congressional seat and left Varina behind to go join his ex-father-in-law. The general needed his gallant and distinguished help at the Battle of Buena Vista, and it was there that all was forgiven. Davis then returned to Congress and Varina was one of the capital's most stylish hostesses when the Taylors came to the White House. Although always jealous of the memory of Knox, Varina was quick to defend Margaret Taylor as a charming and well read lady. The Davises went often to the White House for family dinners, and these the recluse First Lady attended.

At the inaugural ball for Taylor in 1849 Betty wore a simple white dress with a single rose in her dark hair and was quite the belle. It was remarked at the time that her simplicity was more pleasing than the diamonds and satins worn by other celebrities. Her dress in the Smithsonian collection is not the white dance dress, but a "walking dress" in colorful plaid grenadine; the last dress in the collection to have been made totally by hand. The sewing machine was just coming into vogue at the time.

Little if any notice was taken of Margaret Taylor's absence from the inaugural festivities. When Old Rough and Ready died after sixteen months in office, it was news to some that he had a wife, let alone one in the White House, although she had attended church regularly at St. John's Episcopal Church just across Lafayette Square and had received her relatives and a few close friends in her own quarters.

Whether she gardened at the White House is not known, but it was noted that the dahlias and roses looked uncommonly well during the autumn of her tenancy. She and her husband became life members of the American Sunday School Union and on his second hot Fourth of July in office, the President and his wife together listened to Baptist Sunday School children in a concert of patriotic hymns before he left without her for a program at the Washington monument. Over heated, he came home to drink ice water and milk, and eat cherries. He became ill.

Five days later, on July 9, 1850, President Zachary Taylor died, and his wife considered that the Presidency killed him. She accompanied the Blisses home and never referred to the

White House again—nor was it ever mentioned in her presence. She died two years later.

Among all the First Ladies she is the only one of whom there is no photograph, engraving or portrait that is accepted by her descendants. Nor is there one that satisfies Holman Hamilton, the Taylor biographer, as a probable likeness.

ABIGAIL FILLMORE (July 10, 1850-March 3, 1853)

She Started the White House Library

ABIGAIL POWERS FILLMORE, wife of the handsome Vice President, succeeded Margaret Taylor as First Lady. Abigail, being five feet six inches tall, was not considered attractive by her era's standards, but a photograph of her made on the south portico of the White House indicates that by today's ideas she would have measured up quite well. She had been a schoolteacher and was the first First Lady to have held a paying job before her husband became President.

Mrs. Fillmore was one of two First Ladies responsible for much of their husbands' education. As Abigail Powers she was a twenty-year-old teacher when Millard Fillmore, then 18, became a pupil in one of her classes. He had served out an apprenticeship to a wool carder and cloth maker and was eager to become an educated man. Miss Powers sympathized with this ambition and she encouraged him, becoming both his teacher and his inspiration.

Abigail was born in Saratoga County, New York, the daughter of an itinerant Baptist preacher. When he died her courageous mother took her and her younger brother to Cayuga County, New York, closer to the frontier, in the belief that her limited funds would stretch more if she lived farther from an urban area. Abigail was sixteen when she began teaching in the summers so as to pay her tuition in school during the winters.

Young Fillmore decided he wanted to be a lawyer, and that required a long struggle. Abigail waited and taught for seven years before they were married in 1826. Their first small home in East Aurora, New York, was built entirely by his own hands. Abigail continued to teach until her husband was elected to the state assembly several years later. Then, in another pull on his bootstraps, he sought a legal connection in the thriving little city of Buffalo.

When Fillmore came to Congress from the Buffalo district in 1833 his wife was the mother of a five-year-old son and an infant daughter. She was happy to live in Washington where she could attend lectures and take piano lessons. Abigail was fifty-two years old when she became First Lady in July of 1850, and her pretty daughter, Mary Abigail, was eighteen. The daughter, who aspired to be a teacher like her mother, could play both piano and harp. The young girl often helped her mother dispense White House hospitality.

The First Lady had a weak knee which acted up during the long periods of standing required at receptions, so that she often stayed in bed in the mornings to rest her knee for the events later in the day and evening. She used this time to teach herself French.

It did not take the former schoolteacher long to see that the White House had no books—not even a Bible nor a dictionary. She asked Congress to let her have $5,000 so that she could start a library. Most of the first books acquired went into the upstairs oval room, where Mary Abigail had her harp and piano and where she and her mother frequently played duets for informal visitors.

The White House during this administration also obtained a newfangled iron range for the kitchen and it was more of a problem than the library. The President had to visit the Patent Office and look at the description to learn how it was operated. The White House cook went into a tizzy when he had to use the range instead of the large fireplace in which he had prepared state dinners for many years. There were some newspaper editorials against the invention, the belief being that meats could not be cooked except in direct contact with the embers. And why waste money on such a foolish contraption?

Congress was more lenient on the money front with this First Family than with many others, not only because Fillmore had been popular in Congress, but also because, after Taylor's death, the newspapers had put on a real crusade to prove that the White House with its damp cellars and many inconveniences was a death trap when it came to malaria and sundry other ailments. The Fillmores had running water installed without even asking Congress for it!

Even so, the White House was not too comfortable a home as was indicated by the President when he asked his old law partner, Solomon G. Haven of Buffalo, to bring his wife and come down for the Christmas season of 1850 to "this temple of inconvenience."

There was no thought of Fillmore running for election as President in his own right. He and his wife planned a long deferred trip to Europe to celebrate their rise together and to fulfill Abigail's unquenchable desire to travel and to learn. Their trunks were packed early and moved to the Willard Hotel so there would be no delay in getting away after the inauguration of Franklin Pierce.

The next First Lady would be Jane Pierce, but on the eve

83

of the inauguration, her only son died and she was unable to be at the swearing-in. To help the incoming President, Abigail Fillmore volunteered her aid with the inaugural festivities. Again March 4 was bitterly cold and the overtired Abigail stood too long on the windswept portico of the Capitol talking with William Makepeace Thackeray, Washington Irving and others. She contracted pneumonia.

Abigail Fillmore never left Washington alive. She died March 30 at the Willard Hotel, amid her trunks packed for that trip to Europe. Another chapter in the sad saga was that her daughter, Mary Abigail, died in a cholera epidemic the following year.

JANE APPLETON PIERCE (1853-57)

"The Shadow in the White House"

SATURDAY, June 5, 1852, was a lovely day in Boston. Franklin A. Pierce took his fragile and flowerlike wife for a morning carriage ride all the way to Cambridge, for a tour around peaceful Mt. Auburn Cemetery. They were heading back to the city when up galloped a horseman with the news that Pierce had won the Democratic nomination for the Presidency. Jane promptly fainted, which is just what her husband had feared and expected might happen.

Pierce was prepared for the startling announcement but he knew that his invalid wife—Jeanie, as he called her—had not the remotest idea that his friends, with his knowledge, had been working hard and long for his candidacy. She had been visiting her prominent relatives in Boston, while at their home in Concord, New Hampshire, Pierce followed reports from the deadlocked Democratic Convention in Baltimore. As the days wore on, Pierce saw that he, the darkhorse candidate and the most popular Democrat in New England, might win. He rushed to be with Jane when she heard the convention's verdict.

Jane not only loathed and despised politics, but feared it and all its trappings. Pierce was in the U.S. House of Representatives when she married him but, as part of what she considered to be her wifely duty, she started immediately to woo him away from the political path. The Washington climate did not agree with her at all and she regarded his political friends as most uncouth. The Pierces' first son died as an infant and she linked the death to political office.

Nevertheless the magnetic and convivial Pierce continued his rapid rise and he was in the United States Senate when their two other sons were born. At the very young age of thirty-four, however, he resigned from the Senate in order to make peace with his wife and to make a happy home life for them in Concord, where he became a successful lawyer. Even when his good friend, James K. Polk, became President and offered him the Attorney Generalship in the Cabinet, Pierce turned it down with the explanation that it would be detrimental to his wife's health for him to accept.

Another of the sons died, but the youngest, Benjamin, was a healthy, bright lad of eleven when his father received the Presidential nomination. One reason that Pierce had dared to seek the office without telling Jeanie was that he believed his success would mean a great deal to Bennie's future, for more than most couples the Pierces had built their lives around their surviving son. Also, Pierce believed that Jane would rally to the cause once she recovered from the initial shock.

Jane did rally, superbly, and took great pride in the overwhelmingly successful results that carried Pierce into office as the youngest man so far elected President. A more congenial family than the President-elect, the prospective First Lady, and young Bennie would have been hard to find anywhere in the country as they boarded the train in Boston the morning of January 6, 1853.

As the train pulled out, Bennie was talking a mile a minute and, as usual, had the full attention of his parents. Suddenly without any warning beyond a slight jolt, the car in which they were riding became uncoupled and toppled into a ravine. The parents escaped from the wreck with minor scratches, but literally before their eyes their beloved Bennie was crushed to death. It was a tragedy which shocked the nation and from which Jane never recovered.

There are indications that Bennie's father never was the same again, either, although the most crushing part of his personal sorrow well may have been the loss of his wife's support. She saw the death of Bennie as an act of God—designed to free her husband for a full-time political career. God must have thought that Bennie would have been a burden to his father, she reasoned, and took him away so that the father could give all his time to the Presidency.

This tragic loss of an only child would have been deep grief for any normal family, but to the family life of the Pierces it was a killing blow, for it added another burden of guilt on the husband who already felt guilty about what his political aspirations were "doing to Jeanie," since she disapproved of them so thoroughly. He had not won after all. As always with Jeanie, he lost. He entered the White House alone—probably the loneliest of all the Presidents.

Within the space of a few days he had lost Bennie, rapport with his wife, his self-confidence, his ability to lead, and perhaps his will to succeed, says his biographer, Roy Franklin Nichols. The spark went out and Pierce became known as one of the most ineffectual of all Presidents. Pierce in the White House, many have said, was not the dashing Pierce who never lost an election.

Just why Pierce married the disapproving lovely who kept him waiting six years for her answer appears to have had three explanations. He loved her and she was beautiful. He was ambitious and she represented a position in life, socially and intellectually, toward which he aspired. And his great personal friend, Nathaniel Hawthorne, had made a success of his marriage to the invalid among the Peabody sisters. Invalidism was no barrier to marriage in those days and, in fact, having a female invalid in the family was in many ways a status symbol. A woman too refined and delicate to face the winds of life at times became a precious and desired burden!

Pierce lacked the imagination to rouse his Jeanie from her concern with her health; or perhaps she really was an incurable and always suffering invalid. He was vulnerable, too, in his background, which was fine by many standards, but not by those of the Puritan hierarchy in which Jane grew up. He enjoyed having a drink with the boys in the back room before he went home in the evening. A tendency toward drink ran in his mother's family and he may have been as ashamed of it as Jane was.

Pierce was born in Hillsborough, New Hampshire. His father had been a militia general in the Revolutionary War and became Governor of his state. He sent his son, Franklin, to Bowdoin College, where he was a brilliant student and where he became friends with Jane's brother-in-law, one of his teachers.

The Pierce family was outgoing and political. But Jane's family was infinitely more estimable. Her father, the Reverend Jesse Appleton, had been president of Bowdoin College and no mere President of the United States ever ranked this high in Jane's estimation. The Reverend Appleton worked and prayed himself into an early grave. He cut down on his food so that he would not need to exercise and he allowed himself only about four hours of sleep nightly so that he could devote more time to his theological students. He died of consumption, leaving a widow and six children. Jane was thirteen at the time and already tubercular.

The widow went with her children to live with her mother, "the formidable Madame Means," an aristocrat and a model for correct behavior in Amherst, Massachusetts. Jane was given a careful and thorough education, but she took no walks in the sun. Even the pious have said that the Reverend Appleton felt a morbid responsibility toward his students and Jane could always find the morbid side of the street on which to walk.

The Means family did not approve of Pierce as a suitor, nor did they like his politics. All the "best people" were or had been Federalists. Nevertheless he wooed and won Jeanie and if he ever blamed her for any of his problems, it is not on the record.

After Bennie's death it was out of the question for Jane to go to Washintgon for the inaugural period. She and Abby Kent Means, a long-time friend who had married Jane's uncle, came as far south as Baltimore and rested there until late in March of 1853.

On March 2, two days before the inaugural, Pierce went to Baltimore for the night. He found his wife in a pitiable condition. One of her relatives had been there and had told her that Pierce, far from being drafted for the Presidency, had worked hard to get the nomination. She moaned out this new information and supposedly rehashed what had happened to Bennie as a result of his political ambition.

He left early next morning without saying goodby. Poor Jane had a lock of Bennie's hair which she had intended to give him to wear in a locket around his neck when he took the oath of office but she neglected to give him the token, which at least would have signified a crumb of forgiveness.

The inaugural ball was cancelled in the national mourning period for Bennie, but the inaugural address, given without notes, was widely admired, and great crowds called at the White House in the afternoon to pay their respects to the new President. When the last of them left that night, President Pierce and his secretary, Sidney Webster, made their first trip to the upstairs family quarters. Everything was in great disarray, no housekeeping arrangements having been made, but they found mattresses and fell on to them exhausted.

In addition to Jane's prostration and kindly Abigail Fillmore's death at the Willard Hotel from pneumonia contracted on the windy inaugural day, Pierce also was without a Vice President. Rufus King, too ill to reach Washington, had been permitted to take the oath of office in Cuba and in mid-April he died at his home in Alabama on his way to the capital city. Before the summer was well under way, the President himself developed malaria. The punishments must have seemed unending.

The President managed to secure a New Hampshire hotelkeeper and his wife to take over the running of the White House. On March 11 he went to Baltimore to be with Jane on her forty-seventh birthday. He learned that she was much better both in health and in spirits. It was decided that within a short time she could be moved to the White House, and she and Mrs. Means came to Washington at the end of March.

The newspapers of the day show that the President did most of the social honors alone at first. By New Year's Day of 1855, however, Jane was able to receive with her husband at the annual reception and some of the diaries of the day recorded her as having received at smaller affairs earlier. Virginia Clay-Clopton, wife of a Senator, who wrote *A Belle of the Fifties,* recalled that the First Lady received with her husband late in his first year in office. Jane at the time was clad in black velvet and wore diamonds. Mrs. Clay-Clopton noted that they accentuated her natural pallor. "To us who knew her, the stricken heart was none the less apparent hidden under such brave and jewelled apparel," she wrote.

Jane wore black during all her days as First Lady and hers is the only black dress in the Smithsonian collection. The sympathy with her grief and invalidism was universal and Mrs. Clay-Clopton, who often accompanied her on carriage rides, was only one of many who found her charming.

At informal White House dinners she was described as an intelligent and attentive listener. Mrs. Robert E. Lee, who lived just across the Potomac, wrote in a private letter: "I have known many of the ladies of the White House, none more truly excellent than the afflicted wife of President Pierce. Her health was a bar to any great effort on her part to meet the expectations of the public in her high position but she was a refined, extremely religious and well educated lady."

Always at state dinners during the Pierce administration, a bouquet of camellia japonicas from the White House green-house, wired into an elaborate paper lace collar, was at the plate of each guest. It was a style-setting note and "for an entire season the japonica was the only flower seen at the houses of the fashionable or mixing in the toilettes of the belles," wrote Mrs. Clay-Clopton, who also noted that while White House entertaining remained sober and starkly simple, that done in the homes of rich Senators and by the diplomatic corps "made ample mends for it." Jane became known as "the shadow in the White House," but life in Washington was overall gay and expensive and becoming more so.

The Friday afternoon receptions at which the First Lady began receiving regularly, with the aid of Mrs. Means, were beautifully and quietly done and Jane was always gracious. The decorum of these parties was highly esteemed by the old residents of the capital city and they attended them in large numbers.

Pierce's own state of New Hampshire turned against him, and in the mid-term Congressional elections, the Democrats lost more seats in Congress than he had brought in with him. His Cabinet was a warring and ambitious one, and sectional sores grew ever more tender. Biographer Nichols, who grieved for his subject's lost leadership qualities, said that the times called for "daring and ruthlessness" in the Presidency but that Pierce, defeated personally, never regained the traits which had made him so popular when elected President. Nonetheless, he did the gallant thing and, knowing that there was no chance of his running again, pitched in and helped elect another Democrat, Buchanan.

Ironically enough, when the time for Buchanan's inaugural came, the Washington climate was more suited to Jane's condition than the harsher one of New Hampshire, and the Pierces visited around in the area until balmier days. Then Pierce, who had saved almost half his salary, took his Jeanie on two years of wanderings in Europe.

Abby Means had died the summer before the Pierces left the White House, and Jane took along on her travels a most treasured gift from her most treasured friend: a small box with locks of hair from the three Pierce sons and also locks from Jane's dead mother and sister. The Ex-First Lady could not shake the melancholy in which she had lived for so many years. Her husband was devotedly attentive and remained so when they returned home to Concord to live.

She died in 1863, during the Civil War, and Hawthorne came to be with Pierce in the sad days of the wintry burial ceremonies.

OUR ONLY LIFELONG BACHELOR (1857-61)

And His Violet-eyed Niece

ALTHOUGH two bachelors have been elected President, only the first of them decided to remain that way. He was tall and ambassadorial James Buchanan of Pennsylvania, and when he was running for the high office in 1856 his political advisers went into numerous huddles to discuss whether his state of single blessedness would help or hurt his election prospects. The decision was to take no chances but have it both ways.

For those who loved the sad romantic stories which were so popular at the time, the campaign literature told of his engagement in young manhood to a beautiful young girl who died before the wedding. For those who might have thought that by the age of sixty-five, which he was when elected, he should have mastered his sorrow and begun to look forward, there were rumors that he yet would marry Sarah Polk, the handsome widow of the President under whom he had been Secretary of State.

His hostess all along, however, was his truly lovely niece, Harriet Lane. Harriet was twenty-nine, a statuesque blond with violet eyes. She was the daughter of Buchanan's sister, Jane, and when her parents died she, at the age of nine, selected Uncle James to be her guardian. He supervised her education and took her with him to the Court of St. James when he was Ambassador to England. Her decorum and graces were admired by Queen Victoria and when the Ambassador took her with him on a visit to Oxford, the scholarly British lads knew that they rarely, if ever, had seen a more beautiful young lady.

It is interesting that her blooming good health received more campaign attention than her training and beauty. But it was quite logical, for in that bleak pre-Civil War period only Sarah Polk and Harriet Lane could not lay claim to at least a touch of invalidism. Some of the country by 1856 must have been growing disillusioned with the increasing numbers of what Bess Furman in *White House Profile* called the "languishing and reluctant women" who for so long had inhabited the Executive Mansion. It was time for a change—

and Harriet Lane was a good one. During the difficult four years immediately preceding the war, she served with charm and level-headed distinction.

Buchanan, a man with elegant leanings, sought to reestablish the social prestige of the White House, which was at a low ebb. Buchanan's inaugural ball was elaborate and designed to dispel the gloom of the Pierce administration. Five thousand revelers danced the night away in a specially built structure and between the reels they consumed "twelve hundred gallons of ice cream plus four hundred gallons of oysters, five hundred quarts of chicken salad, five hundred quarts of jelly, sixty saddles of mutton, and thousands of dollars worth of wine." All this in addition to a four-foot cake featuring the thirty-one states of the about-to-be-dissolved union.

Harriet, for all her years among celebrities and royalty, was warm, sincere, and kindly. She worked hard and practiced household thrift. Babies all over the country were named for her and many a song was dedicated to her.

One of her special contributions to the White House was to enlarge the old conservatory into a bright new west wing where visitors could promenade and lounge among the orange and lemon trees, and the camellias, on public reception days.

The highlight social event of the administration was the visit of the Prince of Wales, who was to become King Edward VII. He was only nineteen, but the newspapers of the day made it a romance between him and Harriet. It was the first visit of British royalty to American shores since the Revolutionary War, and the country went wild when he traveled to Mount Vernon to put a wreath on Washington's tomb and to plant a tree on the grounds. The visit was down river aboard the cutter *Harriet Lane* and there was dancing en route to music by the Marine Band. Supper was served on the way back.

When Buchanan was going out of office Harriet did an especially kind and thoughtful thing for the incoming Presidential family. Remembering how bleak it was when she came to the White House after her uncle's noon inaugural and found no food on hand, she had the staff prepare a good meal to be held in readiness for the Abraham Lincolns.

Harriet did not marry until after the Civil War and was thirty-six when she became the bride of Henry Elliot Johnston, a well-to-do business man of Baltimore, in 1866. It was a happy marriage and she became the mother of two handsome sons. But in the course of a comparatively short time her uncle, her husband, and her two sons all died.

She then returned to live quietly in Washington and spent much time traveling abroad collecting paintings. The bulk of her fortune she left to Johns Hopkins Hospital in Baltimore to found a wing in memory of her sons and to be dedicated to the medical treatment of all children without regard to race, creed, or financial circumstances. The Harriet Lane Wing still flourishes and has benefitted many thousands of children.

She left her painting collection to the Smithsonian Institution and it forms the nucleus of the National Collection of Fine Arts. It has been honored with a room of its own called the Harriet Lane Johnston Room. Her wedding dress, displayed in the Smithsonian collection of gowns worn by First Ladies and hostesses in the White House, elicits constant admiration as perhaps the most beautiful of them all.

MARY TODD LINCOLN (1861-April 15, 1865)

With Malice from Nearly Everybody

"Miss Todd, I want to dance with you in the worst way," the tallest and most unusual looking member of the cotillion committee told the newest girl in town. "And he certainly did," laughed the petite and bubbly newcomer as she viewed the damage to her footwear later on that evening in December of 1839.

The scene was Springfield, the muddy little capital of Illinois, where the frontier merged with roads going on West, and the characters were Abraham Lincoln, the railsplitter who became President, and Mary Todd, the Lexington, Kentucky, belle who soon made up her mind to marry him. She had her problems with marriage-shy Abe Lincoln, but three years later—after a broken engagement and a showdown with her relatives—she got him to the altar.

That he ever regretted it there is no logical reason to believe, just as there is none for doubting that he loved her almost immediately at the time they met, continued to do so during the time their engagement was off, and certainly did so more than a quarter of a century later when he was shot while holding her hand during a performance at old Ford's Theater in Washington.

As Lincoln's wife, Mary became the most maligned First Lady in American history, and after his untimely death she was the object of a hate campaign so unremitting that it helped send her briefly to an insane asylum and then into self-exile in Europe for most of her last years.

Only in recent times has anyone sought to do much about clearing Mary's record of charges that ranged from high treason and hatred of her husband to stinginess with White House food and personal extravagance. Her guilt was so set in the public mind that in the late 1860's and throughout the seventies it was thought kind to say, "Poor woman. Wasn't it the worst part of her tragedy that the bullet which killed him did not kill her, too?"

Of all the crosses Mary had to bear, being of the temperament she was, the attacks on her love for her husband and his

94

for her—all made after his death—were perhaps the hardest on her and the most devastating.

Back in 1839, as they danced at the holiday ball, he was almost thirty years of age and she was just twenty-one. He was six feet four inches tall and she could stand under his outstretched arm. They were "the long and the short of it," as he years later would tell crowds along the way to his Presidential inaugural.

Lincoln had ridden into Springfield in 1837 to practice law in the office of Mary's cousin, and she had arrived on the eve of the cotillion to make her home with her oldest sister, Mrs. Ninian W. Edwards. Mrs. Edwards had married the son of the Governor of Illinois while that state was still a territory and was one of the area's most prominent matrons. She considered herself to be something of a mother stand-in for all three of her sisters, two of whom already had married quite well-to-do men met in the fine Edwards parlor. It was expected that Mary, so witty and pretty, would do likewise.

All four sisters and their only brother, Elihu, were the children of Robert Todd by his first wife, after whose death he remarried and fathered another group of nine children. Mary was seven when her mother died and she spent much of her childhood in boarding schools in Kentucky. She went to preparatory school at Ward's Academy and then entered select Mentelle's Academy where she was a star student, majoring in French and literature. She took the lead in school plays. She had tried the move to Illinois once before and then had shocked the Edwardses a bit by returning home to Kentucky for two years of graduate work at Ward's. Mary always had a mind of her own.

She also had dancing blue eyes with long dark lashes, fleeting dimples, an abundance of light brown hair, and lovely hands and arms of which she was exceedingly proud. She usually kept her hands and arms in motion to attract attention to them while talking. Most of all she had a vivid and original personality. Her gift of mimicry almost equaled Lincoln's own. According to her sister, she "could make a Bishop forget his prayers," and one of her many admirers called her "the very creature of excitement."

Both she and Lincoln, by mundane standards, were on the unusual side. He never had met anyone like the vivacious Miss Todd, who knew so much about literature. And certainly she had met no one like him, a man whose thoughts ranged the mountain tops of potential achievement, but who was still so gentle and amusing.

Soon A. Lincoln was monopolizing the horsehair sofa in the Edwards parlor, wooing the entertaining Mary. They read poetry by the yard, especially that of Bobby Burns, his favorite. They recited Shakespeare and reread his plays, among which Mary preferred the tragedies. They swapped stories of their earlier experiences. Both loved to laugh and they shared the same sense of the ridiculous. Geography fascinated them and both had always longed to see Niagara Falls. He told her of rafting on the Mississippi and of the terrain he saw during the Black Hawk War. They talked of the Oregon Territory, and at one time seriously discussed moving there.

She told him of Kentucky, the state in which both were born: she in the fine brick house of an aristocratic family which had been there for three generations and he in the log cabin of an itinerant who soon went on to Indiana and then to the newer lands of Illinois. She told him of her little half-sister, Emilie, her favorite in her father's second family, who later would become Lincoln's favorite, too—causing them no end of heartaches during the Civil War. (All five of Robert Todd's first family remained loyal to the Union but all the second family, including the beloved Emilie, sided with the Confederacy.)

Lincoln especially liked Mary's stories of Mammy Sally, the Negro nurse who kept the large Todd brood in hand by professing to know a jaybird which went to hell each Saturday night and reported directly to the devil on all their misdoings. All four of the Lincoln boys would come to know this jaybird quite well.

Mary and Lincoln also shared another major interest: politics. Both were Whigs and ardent supporters of Henry Clay. Mary had been outspokenly Whig since she was fourteen and had cut a childhood chum from her list for daring to be an Andrew Jackson fan. She esteemed public officeholding and put a high value on Lincoln's having been elected to the Illinois state legislature and his ambitions to go to Congress.

Among her coterie of Springfield friends Mary was exceedingly popular and considered to be dashingly daring. While walking home from town one day she grew so tired of the mud that she hitched a ride on a dray wagon. Her companion on the occasion, pretty Mercy Levering, could not bring herself to such unwomanly action and trudged on alone in the ooze. Mary's friends made up a poem about the escapade and Lincoln once dated another event by recalling that it was on "the day Mary rode the dray."

Lincoln was almost involved in a duel when he covered up for a deft bit of her political verse run anonymously in the local newspaper and aimed at one of his political competitors. The victim demanded satisfaction and Lincoln, knowing he was no shot, selected broadswords as the weapons, believing that with his long arms he just might win. This turned the matter into a joke and the duel never came off.

Less than a year after they met, Mary and Lincoln were engaged to marry. Mary's father had no objection, but the Edwardses and her other sisters hit the ceiling, maintaining that Lincoln was a nonentity, could not support a wife, and had no future. Surely Mary with all her charms and talents would not throw herself away on such an unpromising man! Mary would, though, and most happily—except that Lincoln found himself agreeing with the Edwardses. The more he thought about it, the more he agreed. He was at least $1,500 in debt and at best made about $1,000 a year. When would he ever be able to buy Mary the things he would like her to have?

Also, Lincoln was basically afraid of marriage and always had been. He and his good friend, Joshua Speed, something of a ladies' man, had often grown morbidly philosophical on the subject of marriage. But Lincoln had been engaged once before and had escaped the altar only because he was such a laggard suitor. The other girl was not Ann Rutledge, but a Kentucky girl named Mary Owens, the sister of one of Lincoln's friends, Mrs. Bennett Abell, of New Salem, Illinois. Lincoln had met Mary in 1833 when she came to visit her sister, and later when Mrs. Abell was going to Kentucky to see her family, Lincoln suggested that she bring her sister back with her as he would like to marry her.

". . . . I was most confoundedly well pleased with the project," Lincoln admitted later. "I had seen the said sister some three years before, thought her intelligent and agreeable. . . ." But Lincoln was not so pleased with Miss Owens when they met again. He wrote that she had grown so fat that "A kind of notion ran through my head that nothing could have commenced at the size of infancy and reached her bulk in less than thirty-five or forty years." She really was only twenty-eight at the time. Lincoln conceded that he still admired her mind, but he wanted to talk her out of the engagement and used the excuse that he was too poor to make her happy. She admired him but did not love him anyway, her descendants said. And she could not have liked his wooing technique!

Once when he and Miss Owens were out horseback riding with some other couples and came to a creek, the other swains attentively helped their girls across, but Lincoln rode on ahead leaving Miss Owens and her horse to ford the stream unaided. Lincoln did not have to break the engagement. Miss Owens did, which was just what he wanted although he had said all along that he would make good his word and marry her. "I want in all cases to do right; and particularly so, in all cases with women . . ." he said at the time.

Lincoln's wooing technique suited Mary Todd very well,

however, and there is no evidence that he grew tired of her or ceased to think of her with love during the broken engagement. He did not stand her up at the altar after the wedding cake was baked, as was written after his death. Mary evidently left the final decision up to him, and when he had made it, he would have preferred to write her a letter explaining it, but Joshua Speed made him go in person.

Mary cried when he told her and he took her on his knees to comfort her, much as one would a child. Indeed there would always be something of the precocious child in Mary's makeup. He later called her "my child wife" in endearment. Mary's sister said that she told him that while she released him, she "would hold the question open—had not changed her mind, but felt as always." Mary, who knew of Lincoln's brooding moods, spoke to a friend of the time "when Hamlet will be himself again."

Lincoln took to his bed after the broken engagement and mooned around for months, but for almost two years he and Mary went their separate ways. He dropped out of Springfield society and she kept up a merry front. But she wrote in letters to close friends of interminable days, which was not like her, and not even a trip to Missouri to see new scenery cheered her too much. Among her beaux during the interim was Stephen A. Douglas, with whom Lincoln would have the famed political debates. The Edwardses heartily approved of Douglas. He had background, money, and, they felt sure, a brilliant future. Whether he proposed to Mary is uncertain, but Mary is on record that she did not love him. Also, he was a Democrat and Mary was not wishy-washy about being a Whig. Eventually Douglas would marry one of Dolley Madison's beautiful nieces and would dance with Mary Todd Lincoln in Washington on the night of Lincoln's inaugural ball.

At last Providence took a hand in the lagging romance. Mrs. Simeon, wife of the editor of the Sagamon *Journal*, brought the estranged ones face to face at her house, without letting either know the other was to be there—and the engagement was on again. This time Lincoln and Mary planned to wed without letting the Edwardses know. He bought the wedding band, had "Love is Eternal" engraved inside, and engaged the minister for November 4. That morning he ran into Ninian Edwards on the street and felt it only gentlemanly to say, "Mary and I are getting married today."

Mrs. Edwards insisted that the ceremony be in her parlor. A bakery cake was obtained in a hurry, but there was no time to plan a wedding reception and invite guests. Mrs. Ninian Edwards did not approve any more than she had originally, but little sister was wed under her roof in the room where the courtship with Lincoln first flourished.

The happy newlyweds went to live at Globe Tavern at four dollars a week. This would save money so that his debts could be paid sooner and, too, it would prevent Mary being alone while he was away riding his long legal circuit. He piled more work on himself to get ahead quicker and to get Mary a carriage like her sisters had. The carriage was mentioned frequently as his idea of a status symbol and when someone wanted to borrow the one he finally obtained he said: "Only two things I won't loan, my wife and my carriage."

Their first son, named Robert Todd for Mary's father, was born in the tavern, and then the Lincolns had to go househunting whether able to afford the luxury or not. They paid $1,500 for a one-and-a-half-story house within walking distance of his office. Then while he was off on the circuit, Mary had the roof raised to make it the two-story house it is today. She spent $1,000. Lincoln thought it hilarious of her —once he had recovered from the shock!

Lincoln refused to be bothered about family finances or money in general, saying that he had never had enough of it to worry about. He never knew how much his income really was, and the Lincolns apparently did not try to operate on a budget. Mary had free access to his pocket change and she had charge accounts at the stores. In an effort to push their fortunes ahead, Mary did try quite strenuously to save in some ways, but then she would have spurts of giddy extravagance. She believed in keeping up with the Joneses on fronts that to her mattered—and did not at all mind the hard work necessary to make it possible.

She was a spic and span housekeeper and an excellent seamstress. She not only made Lincoln's shirts but ironed them, too. Thanks to her sewing, their children dressed as well as any in town. Dress always was important to Mary, but it took her a long time to break Lincoln of the habit of answering the door in his shirt sleeves. Lincoln paid a neighbor boy to bring in stovewood when he was not at home, and occasionally Mary had a girl in to help her.

Her economies consisted of working harder and doing without until she could afford quality, and in small things like not having fires in all the rooms. Her outbursts of spending ran to things like the new story for their house and buying a new carpet and seat pads for their church pew when she noticed that a nearby worshiper had them. On one occasion in church she saw that the then Governor's daughter wore a much prettier hat than her little sister, Emilie, who was visiting the Lincolns at the time. That was just the kind of challenge to which Mary would rally. Nobody was going to outdress her sister. And out she went to buy Emilie the most expensive hat in town. Lincoln was much amused.

It would have been better in the long run if Lincoln had taken a hand in the family spending and had been more frank with her about his own. At times he cancelled out her economies by donating twice as much to some cause or event as he told her; sometimes he slipped a bit extra to workmen after Mary had paid them. Irrationality about money was the thing that sent Mary briefly to the asylum years later.

Mary wanted to prove to her disapproving sisters that Lincoln was coming up in the world, just as she had predicted, and she became adept at adding chic touches at the psychological moment to impress them. She was proud of her economies and when she learned belatedly that Lincoln split legal fees with his junior law partner, William H. Herndon, she was furious. She disliked Herndon, an admitted agnostic. Also she regarded him as a graceless man with scant ability, and considered it shocking that he made as much as her talented husband. She let Herndon know her feeling and never once invited him to her house. This turned out to be a most expensive self-indulgence, since Herndon was the man who would do her in on the "Lincoln never loved her" theme after Lincoln's death, and he was the one who "found" the Ann Rutledge story—good lecture material for him for quite a while.

Less than five years after their marriage Lincoln was elected to Congress and took his family with him to Washington. There was a second son by this time, and they went to the capital city by way of Lexington, Kentucky, so that Lincoln could meet all the Todds. In Washington they lived in a boarding house on Capitol Hill.

The Lincolns would have four sons, and they adored their children. The first tragedy in their married life was the death and burial in Springfield of little Eddie before he was quite four. This was the child whom Lincoln mentioned as leaving behind when he said goodbye to Springfield twenty-one years later as he left for his inauguration. The year of Eddie's death, the third son, William Wallace (Willie), was born, and after him came Thomas (Tad), the pet of the family because he had a damaged palate and also because of his effervescence.

Robert, the oldest and always the most sedate member of the family, was sent East to school at Phillips Exeter and then on to Harvard. It is easy to imagine that Mary felt she had scored it over her sisters in being able to afford this expensive education for her son. She loved it when the railroads came to value Lincoln as a lawyer who won his cases—and she could travel on passes.

Carl Sandburg, Lincoln's most popular biographer, said

that the Lincolns always had good times
Mary kept up her interest in literature and
noted their many likenesses in temperament b
a basic difference between them likened Mary to
wildcat" and Lincoln to a "slow-moving wilder
Mary could blow her top in nothing flat, and life a
was never dull.

When Lincoln received the Republican nomination for
President in 1860, Springfield swarmed with reporters from
the East and Mrs. A. Lincoln was immensely proud that her
home could stand their scrutiny. "Whatever of awkwardness
may be ascribed to her husband," one of them wrote, "there
is none of it in her. She is quite a pattern of ladylike courtesy
and polish. She converses with freedom and grace . . . has
received a liberal and refined education and, should she ever
reach it, will adorn the White House."

On election night Mary was nursing a sick child, but Lincoln rushed home to exclaim: "Mary, Mary, we are elected."
As soon as possible, the First Lady-elect rushed to New York
to buy a breathtaking wardrobe, for she fully intended to be
a sparkling ornament. But little did Mary realize that every
stitch of her clothing would be in competition with attire
bought mostly in Paris and worn by sophisticated women who
never ironed a shirt in their lives.

The Civil War may have seemed far away in Springfield,
Illinois, but in Washington the old settlers already were locking up the silver and prominent Southerners were heading for
home. Along with the northern branch of the family, her
southern relatives had been invited to the inaugural. But most
of them would leave with bitter words. Emilie's husband, Dr.
Ben Helm, was offered a surgeon generalship by Lincoln but
refused it.

Her welcome was not at all what she expected, nor was her
ride into town what she had dreamed it would be. Instead of
being greeted by a wave of ovations, she reached the old
Willard Hotel several hours behind her husband, and was no
doubt irritated at finding that the wife of a President-elect
had so little power. She had not been permitted to leave
Springfield on the train with her husband, but had to dash
with their two little boys, Willie and Tad, to Indianapolis and
board the cars there. Rumors that attempts to assassinate
Lincoln would be made in Baltimore foiled her again and
her husband was rushed on ahead. Somewhere along the cir-
cuitous route she did manage to purchase a nice topcoat for
Lincoln so that he would look more imposing during the
inaugural ceremonies.

Instead of being welcomed with open arms, she was met
with rumors and snubs. The atmosphere was quite unlike

which any other First Lady has had to operate. Lincoln's prestige was exceedingly low, and extremists in his own party were openly antagonistic to him. What was said against him during his Presidency was every bit as harsh as what was said against Mary but by his leadership he eventually was able to neutralize much of it. Embattled Mary never had a chance and she took criticism much harder than he did. In small things as well as large Mary's wishes often were not considered—and almost never unless she made a scene.

For instance, Mary thought it odd that Secretary of State Seward had decided to give the reception following the inaugural. Mary thought that the first entertaining in the new administration should be at the White House (which is customary) and so she hastened to schedule the event. That meant she would need another dress, and here she was in luck. Among the oldtimers who had left town earlier were Senator and Mrs. Jefferson Davis, and this freed the best dressmaker in town. Elizabeth Keckley, a mulatto who was born a slave and who would become one of Mary's most loyal White House friends, was summoned to the Willard.

Gossip about Mary was so prevalent that Lizzie Keckley was embarrassed at the thought of sewing for Mrs. Lincoln. As she wrote later: "I had heard so much . . . of her low life, of her ignorance and vulgarity . . . Report was wrong . . . No queen accustomed to the uses of royalty . . . could have comported herself with more calmness and dignity." She made Mary a beautiful rose moire outfit for the reception and then helped her to dress for the occasion. It was an era of much color and voluminous skirts. Before the Civil War ended each woman was to require about six feet of space in which to maneuver her hoops. Mary wore fresh camellias in her hair for her first reception, and the flower wreath became her best remembered trademark.

It irked Mary to be told that the President should escort some other woman at his entrance to receptions and that she must come in on the arm of another man. She noted that women who paid no attention to her swarmed around her husband. Kate Chase, the beauteous daughter of Salmon P. Chase, Secretary of the Treasury, held a court of her own right under Mary's nose at White House events. Also, the wardrobes on display were magnificent.

As soon as Mary could manage it, apparently within a matter of weeks, she decreed that henceforth her husband's arm belonged to her and, under Lizzie Keckley's fine workmanship, her own wardrobe became ever more elaborate. Lincoln laughed at her jealous possessiveness, and formed the habit of jesting before parties: "Well, mother, just which women may I talk to tonight?"

In time the Lincolns took to giving two receptions weekly. The President called them "public opinion baths," and enjoyed them. He stood a little in front of Mary in the receiving line and tried to present guests to her in such a way as to save her hand in the handshaking crush. It was said his eyes often followed her during the mingling period which came later. One guest to whom he was talking noted his smile as he watched Mary and recorded that Lincoln said his wife was as handsome as when he fell in love with her years ago. "And I've never fallen out," he added.

Mary did not always get her way in matters of protocol and she clashed frequently with John Hay, the Presidential secretary who handled such things. Some of her ideas on White House entertaining seemed reminiscent of her belief that she could punish Herndon by not asking him to her home. For instance, she did not approve of all of Lincoln's Cabinet members. "Mr. Lincoln lets people take advantage of him," she said. So she had the idea that at the next Cabinet dinner she would ask only the "loyal" members. Hay went to Lincoln on this one and was told to do "what is expected" —and all the Cabinet was invited.

At first Mary's dinners were criticized as too extravagant during wartime. She talked Lincoln into skipping many of the set dinners and giving more receptions so that more people could be invited. Then she was criticized for stinginess and accused of saving food money to put on her back.

If Mary's troubles had been only social ones, however, her health might not have broken in the White House. But from the first she was accused of being in full sympathy with the Confederacy and in communication with the enemy. A presidential secretary was assigned to open all her mail to offset these charges, but they continued and were widely believed. The radical element within Lincoln's own party considered that the attack on his wife's loyalty was a choice instrument to use against him, and after a disastrous Federal battle the rumors about her flew swift as bullets.

Lincoln sympathized with Mary and knew what these attacks brought in headaches and jangled nerves. They also put a strain on her relationships with the White House staff. Mary, the record indicates, tried to spare her husband discussions about the charges against her and at times let her feelings go on the staff. John G. Nicolay, the young secretary whose job it was to open her mail, admired the First Lady but found it difficult to understand how a woman who was so kind, considerate and charming one day could be so unreasonable the next.

Mary was only forty-two years of age when she went to the White House. Her face had grown fuller (was sometimes described as too babyish) and perhaps she at times dressed too youthfully for her years, but her personality was as vivid as ever. Not everybody liked Mrs. Lincoln but none could be indifferent to her, although the rumors about her and her reputation for being impossible to deal with made many avoid her.

"Mrs. Lincoln? Well, she is Mrs. Lincoln," said Benjamin Brown French, the urbane Commissioner of Public Buildings, who liked her but found her difficult to describe. He worked with her on a job which she really enjoyed. Congress had allotted $20,000 to redecorate the old mansion, and Mary was in seventh heaven shopping and refurbishing. She took friends with her to New York when she selected such things as Victorian rosewood furniture, "patent spring mattresses," bedsteads, chairs, sofas, velvet wallpaper, hassocks, a footbath, wash stands, damasks, brocades, Haviland china, covered chamber pots, and magnificent carpets for two of the parlors.

She overran her budget by $6,700 and implored Lincoln to demand more funds, but he refused, saying he had liked the house as it was. French assured her that deficiency appropriations were usual, as was true, and Congress did appropriate the extra money to cover the outstanding bills.

The Lincoln children, Willie and Tad, had the run of the White House, which became increasingly crowded with wartime offices until it seemed more like an army barracks than a President's home. Little Willie died during the Lincolns' second year in the White House. This had a devastating effect on Mary who was even more morbid about death than Lincoln. According to the book which Lizzie Keckley later wrote, Mary continued so inconsolable that Lincoln took her to a window and, pointing to the asylum, told her that she must get hold of herself lest she wind up over there. Tad was loud in his grief about Willie until his father convinced him that "Willie is in heaven."

In the same year, 1863, Emilie, now the widow of a Confederate officer, showed up at the White House—against her will. She was trying to reach her mother's family in Virginia, but was not permitted through the Union lines. Lincoln was notified and he wired: "Send her to me." While she was with the Lincolns, Mary pleaded with her, "Oh, Emilie, love me . . . a little. I am blamed by both the North and the South." Lincoln urged Emilie to stay with them for the summer, saying, "Mary needs you,"

In her diary Emilie recorded the drain that the previous two years had made on Mary's health. She related how Lincoln and Mary were worried about each other's health, but tried not to let the other know it. Mary's nervous headaches grew worse under attacks which she could not fight. Robert Lin-

104

coln, not always generous about his mother's foibles, later related that he had never seen anyone endure more pain and with more elan as she tried to hide her suffering from his father "because she knew it would tear him to pieces." One of Mary's great virtues as a wife was that she sustained Lincoln during his own periods of dark gloom and put up a gay front about family affairs.

Emilie did not accept the President's invitation to stay. Later on she came again of her own volition to beg for medicines to take through the lines to suffering relatives and friends. These were denied her and she left with bitter words. Mary's Springfield relatives were no closer to her. Some of them called her "Princess Mary," and apparently none put herself or himself out to allay gossip that she was high-handed and hard to get along with. Lincoln asked Mrs. Edwards to come stay with Mary while she recovered from Willie's death, and the older sister was shocked enough by the state of Mary's nerves to write her daughter to be careful about joining in any gossip lest she make Mary's lot harder.

Mary was a prisoner of the White House and only Lincoln seemed to care. She entertained less after Willie's death, and apparently she also gave up any attempt to court public favor. She and Tad took many trips together, peppered constantly with telegrams from the President who knew Mary's need for personal assurance. She visited hospitals, but without fanfare, and her husband brought her more into his activities by discussing things with her. She gloried in his plans for the Emancipation Proclamation, and she was permitted to send advance copies to liberation societies in Boston. She did not need history's verdict to know that his Gettysburg speech was great. She liked it in manuscript.

But tales about Mary spying for the Confederacy did not lessen. In fact, Emilie's visits and other events fanned them. Congressmen discussed the possibility. Although there are no written records to prove it, and some historians doubt it, a story has persisted that Lincoln himself appeared in defense of Mary's loyalty to the Union before a joint congressional committee. This committee, under the leadership of radicals, was all set to go into the question of Mary's activities, when unannounced Lincoln came in the door, his face showing an "almost inhuman sadness" to say: "I, Abraham Lincoln, President of the United States, appear of my own volition . . . to say that I, of my own knowledge, know that it is untrue that any of my family hold treasonable communication with the enemy."

As the time for Lincoln's reelection or defeat for a second term drew nearer Mary had to face up to the fact that she was deeply in debt for clothes—and that her husband knew nothing about it. She owed between $25,000 and $70,000 for wardrobe materials for which she had said: "Charge it." (Lizzie Keckley in *Behind the Scenes,* the book she wrote after the "Old Clothes Scandal" broke in 1867, placed the sum owed at $70,000, but Mary denied it and the exact sum has never been known.) Mary worried about how she could tell her husband when his salary was $25,000 a year and she had heard him fret about not yet having a stone at his father's grave. But Lincoln was reelected and Mary consoled herself that somehow she could economize and get the debts paid without his ever knowing.

Mary's private worries apparently increased her touchiness. In the early spring of 1865, as the war drew to a close, Lincoln took Mary and Tad with him on some trips to the Virginia front. On one of them the First Lady made an unforgettable public spectacle of herself by berating the pretty wife of Major General Edward O. C. Ord for riding horseback beside the President. Lincoln had gone on ahead while Mary followed in a half-open buggy over corduroy roads with the wife of General U. S. Grant.

Upset because they were late, Mary was in a frenzy when her husband and Mrs. Ord rode up together, the latter to pay her respects. The scolding she gave the younger woman sent her into tears and embarrassed those nearby. As part of the tirade, Mary reportedly turned on Mrs. Grant with, "I suppose you think that your husband should be President, but it's mine who is." Lincoln, saying "Mother, mother," tried to quiet his wife by speaking gently. It was Mary's one public scene while First Lady, according to Ruth Painter Randall, the historian who probed most deeply into Mary's side of things. Mary was mortified later and, as Lincoln knew, really was a sick woman who needed medical care.

Times were going to be better during his second term, Lincoln assured Mary on a long afternoon carriage ride before they went to Ford's Theater on April 14, 1865. He was bone tired and near exhaustion but elated that the war was ending. He wanted Mary happy again.

Mary's collapse after his assassination that night was heart rending. President Johnson, Lincoln's successor, sent her word to stay in the White House as long as she wished. She mourned there five weeks, and only Tad could comfort her. "Don't cry, don't cry," the boy implored, "You are breaking my heart." Tad himself had cried until he asked a friend, "Do you think Pa is in heaven?" "I'm sure of it," the man assured the twelve-year-old youngster who then sought to soothe his mother.

Meantime the citizens of Springfield, without consulting

Mary, were collecting money and preparing to bury Lincoln at a downtown location. It was as if Mary did not exist and that when Lincoln died she had no friend left. She wired forbidding the burial place and said that Lincoln wanted to be beside his sons, Eddie and Willie. "The people are in a rage," ran a letter from Springfield at the time, "and all the hard stories ever told about her are told over again. . . . She has no friends here."

The packing boxes going out of the White House, between fifty and sixty, Lizzie Keckley wrote, were rumored to contain much of the nation's furniture. And when Mary moved from Washington to Chicago, rather than back home, the people of Springfield were irate all over again. Newspapers had said that Lincoln had left his wife well cared for and when she applied for a pension almost immediately, the reaction was swiftly vituperative.

Lincoln's estate when it was settled about two years later was shown to be a good one for a man who had started as a railsplitter—almost $80,000, plus the house in Springfield and one hundred and sixty acres in Iowa. Mary's income from it would amount to between $1,200 and $1,500 a year. She was granted the remainder of the President's salary for 1865, or almost $20,000. Most of this she used to buy a modest home for herself and sons in Chicago. Her obsession about poverty and debts, fed through the years, haunted her day and night.

Meanwhile William Herndon burst on her horizon with popular lectures about the love of Lincoln's life who, he said, was Ann Rutledge, a girl about whom Mary never before had heard. Ann was the young daughter of James Rutledge at whose tavern Lincoln lived in New Salem, Illinois. She was engaged to John McNamar, one of Lincoln's friends, and died in 1835 while McNamar was on a visit back East. Whether Lincoln ever courted Ann is conjecture. McNamar said he had never heard of it, and Lincoln, being dead, could not answer Herndon's stories. Furthermore, Herndon embellished the pretty legend with an account of Lincoln standing Mary up at the altar. He advanced the odd idea that Mary was so furious she later married Lincoln for revenge. "Where revenge entered the door, love flew out the window," was Herndon's theme.

Mary was mortified and humiliated, and she was suffering other worries—those secret debts for clothes. She concluded that it would be a good idea to start paying off those debts by selling her wardrobe, throwing in jewelry and all the bolts of lace and fabrics not yet made up. She thought she could do this without it becoming generally known. She wrote

Lizzie to meet her in New York, using assumed names for them both. They did find a dealer who assured them that he could "manage everything." Then he talked Mary into believing that the public would be only too eager to buy the things for larger sums if he could say they had belonged to Lincoln's widow. She agreed, and he ran advertisements. But the "Old Clothes Scandal" boomeranged so disastrously that it cost Mary $820 in cash, as well as travel and hotel expenses.

She talked to reporters about her living expenses and about how much the country owed her husband. She indicated that she knew of persons who had grown rich during the Lincoln administration. Thurlow Weed, New York political leader, retaliated by reviving all the smears against Mary, including accusations that she had padded White House bills and had carted off furniture.

Mary's son, Robert, engaged to a Senator's daughter, was so embarrassed by all this that he wished the earth would open up and swallow him. Then Lizzie Keckley wrote her book. Probably Lizzie thought she was doing Mary, whom she regarded as a friend, a favor, but Mary never forgave her. Somehow the clothes debts were paid with Robert's help, and possibly with aid from Republican friends of Lincoln.

After Robert's marriage in 1868, Mary took Tad abroad to school in Germany, and then in England. Obsessed by the idea of poverty, Mary lived in cheap lodgings and suffered continually from headaches. She still clung to the idea of getting a Congressional pension. Mrs. James H. Orne, abroad with her family, went to see Mary in Frankfort, Germany, and found her living in a back room on the fourth floor. She described it as "a small cheerless desolate looking room with but one window. I never knew what the word 'alone' meant before," she wrote Senator Charles Sumner who was trying to get a pension for Mary. In 1870 Congress finally voted Mary $3,000 annually, but by a narrow margin.

Next year Mary and Tad returned home because he was homesick and she wanted to see her first grandchild, Robert's daughter, who had been named for her. The New York *Herald Tribune* noted that Tad had grown into a tall fine-looking lad of eighteen. All speech defects caused by the palate were gone, but he spoke English with a slight German accent. Everyone said that he resembled his father.

But he had only been home two months when he died from a very severe cold. If Mary needed anything else to push her into insanity, this was it. She restlessly wandered the country with a companion, the latter at Robert's insistence, seeking seclusion and aid for a dropsical condition. But seclusion was rarely permitted her. Herndon expanded his lectures. She quarreled with him in print about Lincoln's religion.

Four years after Tad's death she was in Florida and had hallucinations that Robert was ill. She wired him: "Rouse yourself and live for your mother. You are all I have. From this hour all I have is yours. . . ." Then she rushed to Chicago carrying securities worth several thousand dollars in her purse. In desperation Robert asked the Cook County court to declare his mother legally insane.

Mary sat quietly while various physicians told of her hysterical behavior, and Robert wept as he told of his efforts to take care of her. The jury returned a verdict of insanity and Mary was ordered committed to the State Hospital for the Insane. That night in an effort to take her own life she asked at several drugstores for laudanum but was given harmless mixtures. The next day she was taken to a private sanitarium at Batavia, Illinois.

This harrowing news, of course, flashed over the country but Robert had done his duty as he saw it, and truly for the first time his mother was under the care of a doctor who specialized in nervous and mental illnesses. Mary never forgave her son. She immediately set about seeking her release, and four months later she was placed in the care of her sister, Mrs. Edwards. The next year the stigma of insanity was wiped out.

The efforts of the Edwardses in getting her released from the sanitarium erased the bitterness between them and Mary. Their grandson, sunny-natured and sympathetic Edward Lewis Baker, Jr., was delightful to her and he reminded her of Tad. But she did not want to live surrounded by people who knew her. "They will never cease to regard me as a lunatic," she said. . . . "I would be much less unhappy in the midst of strangers."

So Lewis escorted her to New York and she sailed for Europe, where she headquartered at Pau, France. She wrote frequently to Lewis but refused to communicate with Robert. She traveled to other parts of the continent, but illness was overtaking her. Three years after her arrival in Pau she fell from a stepladder while hanging a picture and was partially paralyzed from injury to her spine. In October of 1880 she wrote Lewis that she could not trust herself "any longer away from you all—I am too ill and feeble in health. . . . I entreat you, by all that is merciful, dear Lewis, to meet me on the steamer." Lewis met her.

Robert came to ask her forgiveness and love, bringing with him Mary's little granddaughter. She lived until July, 1882, when Chester A. Arthur was President, and died at the home of her sister at the age of sixty-three. Her funeral was most elaborate, with many costly floral offerings, including a very large one with "Mary Lincoln . . . the loving offering of the people" (of Springfield) spelled into it in forget-me-nots.

One could have assumed from the crowd that Mary had never had an enemy in her life.

ELIZA McCARDLE JOHNSON (April 15, 1865-69)

"Give Us Back Our Peace and Poverty"

ELIZA MCCARDLE JOHNSON, who succeeded Mary Todd Lincoln in the White House, was a woman of courage and integrity for whom life never was easy. She found it even more difficult during the Civil War when she, a staunch Union sympathizer, lived in a battleground state where Federals and Confederates fought almost daily and where neighbors were on opposite sides of the conflict.

Her home was the scenic and progressive little town of Greeneville, Tennessee, set in the mountainous and river-valleyed eastern section of the state. This area, thanks in considerable part to the work of her husband, Andrew Johnson, furnished forty thousand troops to the Federal army and many of its citizens remained loyal to the Union. It was a prize area needed for the movement of troops and it changed hands frequently. She was caught there when the war came, but without her husband.

She was forced to become a refugee and was often unwelcome wherever she turned. By sheer quiet strength of character she held her family together until the state fell into Federal hands. Then she was able to rejoin her husband in Nashville, the capital, when Lincoln named him military governor of the state.

The reason for the separation from her husband was the fact that she had returned home from Washington in 1860 because of her own poor health. Andrew Johnson was a United States Senator when the Civil War began and, not believing that the Union could be dissolved legally, he insisted upon retaining his Senate seat after his state left the Union. For two years his wife, Eliza, heard only recurring rumors that he had been captured and hanged.

Meanwhile her son-in-law, Colonel Daniel Stover, married to her daughter, Mary, led a group which became known as "The Bridge Burners." They subsisted in the high mountains of Tennessee and swept down on Confederate troop movements. Eliza and her daughters hid food for them at agreed places for as long as they could. Long before the Johnsons reached the White House, however, Colonel Stover would be dead from exposure and malnutrition. The oldest Johnson son, Charles, who rushed his medical education and joined the Union Army as a doctor, also would die during those tragic years.

Eliza Johnson was spared none of the horrors of war, and then none of the hates of the Reconstruction Era, nor any of the cruelty of politics. She caught it coming and going, and from all directions. Yet the nearest she ever came to complaining, it appears, was when as First Lady—during the impeachment trial of her husband—she murmured the desire that somebody somewhere would give the Johnson family back its "peace and poverty."

Aside from Mary and Charles, the other members of her family were: Robert, who went to the White House in 1865 as a bachelor of twenty-one; Andrew Johnson, Jr., who was only thirteen in 1865 when his mother became First Lady, and the oldest child, Martha. She was married to David T. Patterson, and was as charming a hostess as ever filled in for an invalid First Lady.

When Johnson was named military governor his first thought was to collect his scattered family around him in Nashville. Although usually the least demonstrative of men, he cried when they finally made it through the lines in a two-horse wagon sent by Confederate General Nathan Bedford Forrest under a flag of truce. The General had received orders from Confederate headquarters in Richmond to permit the journey of the Johnson family as part of an exchange of prisoners and refugees worked out with Federal headquarters in Washington.

The Johnson family would have had it much harder on its wanderings had it not been for Eliza. She never uttered a hasty word nor betrayed harrowed or irritated feelings in any way. It was reported that "wherever she passed, she won kind words and then often hearty prayers, and is remembered by friend and foe as a lady of benign countenance and sweet, winning manners."

Daughter Martha and her husband, David Patterson, with their two young children made it through the lines to Nashville some weeks later and found Eliza bedridden. Ever afterward she was almost totally an invalid, interested only in her family and a peaceful existence. She was not in Washington when her husband became Vice President nor when he succeeded to the Presidency after the assassination of Lincoln in April of 1865. She did not arrive until that June, and she soon learned that peace was not a commodity she could expect to find in the capital city.

Eliza Johnson's life was rich in independence, integrity, and innate dignity, but it was more lacking in worldly goods and opportunities for culture than that of any other First Lady. She was the daughter of a shoemaker and received a basic grammar school education. At the age of sixteen she married eighteen-year-old Andrew Johnson. Johnson, apprenticed to a tailor by his widowed mother, had run away from his master and finally—with his mother and brother— had crossed the mountains from North Carolina to the newer frontier to start his own tailor shop in Greeneville.

He knew his letters and could read a bit when he married Eliza McCardle. Then she taught him how to write and cipher and they studied at night. Came a day when he could afford to hire a man to read to him while he tailored, and the reading matter was often the Constitution of the United States, which he came to know almost by heart. He was a good tailor, ambitious, and much respected. He organized a workingmen's party and was elected town alderman at the age of twenty. Two years later he was Mayor of Greeneville, and rarely afterwards was he out of political office. By 1851 he was able to build the comfortable brick house with the cooling porches which still stands as a monument to him in Greeneville.

There was no deftness in Johnson's campaign approach, but it was a winning one. Once during a campaign he heard that he would be shot at, so—laying his pistol on the rostrum —he asked that the shooting begin at once so he could get on with his speech. He represented his district in the National House of Representatives for ten years before going on to the Senate.

Into the White House with the Johnsons moved their two daughters and two sons and their five grandchildren, the latter ranging in age from three to ten years, and their son-in-law, David T. Patterson. Patterson was newly a member of the U.S. Senate from Tennessee and would serve in that body during his father-in-law's impeachment trial.

At the White House the new First Lady selected one of the smallest bedrooms, on the northwest corner, to be her own and it became the busy center of family life throughout the ill-starred administration. In it she sewed and knitted and encouraged her family and from it at times she supervised White House doings. She made only one public appearance, however, and that was at a gala party for her grandchildren.

"She was seated in one of the Republican Court chairs, a dainty affair of satin and ebony," reported a *Chicago Republican* correspondent. "She did not rise when the children or old guests were presented to her; she simply said, 'My dears, I am an invalid', and her sad, pale face and sunken eyes fully approved the expression. Perhaps it is well to recall that it was this woman who taught the President to read, after she became his wife, and that in all their earlier years she was his counsellor, assistant, and guide. None but a wise and good mother could have reared such daughters as Mrs. Patterson and Mrs. Stover. . . ."

Martha, who became White House hostess for her mother, was thirty-six years of age and although old photographs picture her as a pretty brunette, she had blue eyes and fair hair. Her sister, Mary, was a statuesque blonde whom Washingtonians thought could have been a real beauty had she dressed more stylishly.

The Johnson girls, however, were not trying to outshine others in raiment and often wore dresses with sleeves and collars when bare shoulders were all the rage. Martha had gone to school in Washington at the Visitation Convent and during that time she often spent holidays in the White House with the Polks, but she had no pretensions. "We are plain people from the mountains of Tennessee, called here for a short time by a national calamity," she said soon after her father became President. "I trust too much will not be expected of us."

Martha's first job was to get the White House cleaned up. And it really needed it after the hard use of the war years and the vandalized untended months since Lincoln's death. She and her mother decreed lots of soap and water, insecticides, mending and patching. The floors were polished and the woodwork washed. Soon the old mansion began to sparkle with clean chandeliers and windowpanes. There were fresh bouquets in the rooms which resounded with the laughter of well scrubbed children.

By the time of the New Year's Day reception of 1866, the White House had a new air of homey friendliness and correctness which elicited wide approval. "To put aside all ceremony and work incessantly was the portion of Mrs. Patterson from the beginning. It was her practice to rise very early, don a calico dress and spotless apron, and then descend to skim the milk and attend the dairy before breakfast," it was recorded.

Congress in early 1866 appropriated $30,000 for more basic renovations. Martha supervised the expenditures so carefully, giving up all thought of a summer vacation, that the money stretched from garret to cellar although the first commerical estimates had indicated that the parlors alone would take all the appropriation. "When it (the White House) was opened for the winter season, the change was apparent and obvious, to even the dullest eyes, but very few knew that the fresh, bright face of the historic house was all due to the energy, industry, taste and tact of one woman, the President's daughter."

Martha, with true East Tennessee thrift, still stretched coverings over the new velvet carpets to prevent soil during big events, but the new wallpapers in the Red, Blue, and Green Parlors were so breathtaking that nobody minded and the opening reception of 1867 was splendid indeed. The President's daughter had excellent taste and shunned the ornate, preferring careful workmanship. Her extensive use of flowers in natural arrangements perfumed the rooms. White House events took on a look of perfection that was much admired and the state dinners were superbly served. Martha was popular with the White House staff and servants and her carefully planned details were dutifully executed.

White House affairs during the period were not so elegant as parties given by rich hostesses such as beauteous Kate Chase Sprague, whose father was Chief Justice and whose husband had unlimited wealth. Kate's house, run by forty servants, became the center of entertaining for the radical Republicans who disagreed with Johnson on Reconstruction. The president held that the Civil War was fought to preserve the Union and that Southern states automatically should be admitted or pressured back into it as soon as possible. The radicals' view was that the states were conquered territory and should be so treated.

The radicals in Congress found the President a dogged man with whom to deal. He was time consuming too, since he was prone to veto their legislation and they had the extra work of repassing it over his veto. The Executive branch was peppered with appointees not loyal to the President's views, and to show him who was boss, Congress passed the Tenure of Office Act prohibiting his removing them. This aroused Johnson's anger. While Congress was in recess, in 1867, he decided to test his hard-earned knowledge of the Constitution by removing his Secretary of War, Edwin M. Stanton. He appointed General Ulysses S. Grant to the post.

As soon as Congress returned, the Senate declared that the job belonged to Stanton, and Grant handed it over to him without even consulting the President. Johnson immediately fired Stanton again, but the Secretary refused to leave. He slept in his office, had meals sent in, and placed guards at the door.

The House of Representatives then voted unanimously that the President should be impeached and removed from office. The impeachment trial was a great show. It began in March of 1868 and lasted two months. There was never a vacant seat. Kate and her coterie and many other women adorned the galleries, but the Johnson daughters never attended. Asked what she thought the outcome might be, Martha replied that she had been too busy to follow the trial and had not the slightest idea.

The First Lady decreed that during the trial all scheduled White House events, including a diplomatic reception, must continue as usual, and she insisted on cheerfulness in family affairs. The diplomats were admiringly impressed when the President and his daughter, Martha, smilingly received them from eight until eleven o'clock on the appointed evening.

Some of the background charges made against the President were so extreme, including the insinuation that he might have been in on Lincoln's death, that public opinion against him began to change as the trial progressed. But the final vote was hair-raisingly close. Johnson was saved from impeachment by only one vote. A messenger speedily took the news to Eliza, who exclaimed, "I knew he would be . . . oh, thank you for coming to tell me."

The President began to get a good press during his last few months in office, and after Grant was elected to be the next President. At Johnson's last reception in the White House "every grade of citizens, representing every party and creed, vied with each other in their expression of admiration for the honest, upright conduct of the retiring Executive and his charming daughters."

Almost five thousand persons came through the Blue Room to shake his hand. "Mrs. Patterson, a handsome, though not tall lady, of very pleasing manners and appearance" stood nearby to receive the women guests. She wore a black velvet dress trimmed with bands of satin and black lace, and she had a shawl of white lace over her shoulders. One paper reported that "when some of the bare-armed, bare-necked, would-be-juvenile dowagers were presented to her, the contrast was entirely in favor of the President's daughter."

On the morning of Grant's inauguration the Johnson family left the White House and went to the home of friends rather than greet the incoming President. Johnson sought the personal vindication of one more political office, and in 1874 Tennessee sent him back to the Senate. When he took his seat the crowded galleries broke into thunderous applause. He served less than a year, and died six months before his invalid wife did.

Martha Patterson lived until 1901, and the Johnson home in Greeneville was occupied by his descendants until taken over by the National Park Service in recent years.

JULIA DENT GRANT (1869-1877)

She Enjoyed Being First Lady

ALTHOUGH Ulysses S. Grant in his last address to Congress felt the need to say that during his Presidency "mistakes have been made," he never had need to apologize for his delightful family, all members of which enjoyed his eight years in the White House almost as much as the adoring public of that day enjoyed all the Grants.

Julia Dent Grant, the First Lady, at first tried to persuade her husband that they should continue to live in the home on Eye Street which they already occupied in Washington, and use the White House for entertaining and offices. She feared what the increased spotlight and attentions caused by living there might do to their four children: Frederick, then aged eighteen; Ulysses S., Jr. (called Buck for the Buckeye State), sixteen; Nellie, already beautiful at thirteen, and Jesse, a wit at eleven. But later she called her years in the Executive Mansion "the happiest of my life."

Julia was a small and compact woman, spry and pleasant faced, and the older she grew the more her photographs looked like Queen Victoria. Her quiet and retiring manner was deceptive in that it gave no hint of the great influence she exerted on the lives of her closely knit family. But the family joke was that while she was an unyielding tower of strength in all crises, a mouse could unnerve her. Her family loved to tease her, and she liked to be teased. Her son, Jesse, who would chronicle family events with great humor, said, "For Mother the world contained three divisions—her family, sincere friends of father's, and his detractors. The last were totally black and there was no hope for them."

As First Lady she dressed with an ornate elegance befitting the Grant era and wore elaborate bustled skirts behind which often trailed ruffled and bunched up trains. Necklines were usually cut low. At first the President put his foot down against wifely throat exposure, but Julia finally won her neckline battle.

She usually won with the General, but one time she did not. She had a crossed eye, caused by a boating accident in her youth. Shortly after she became First Lady, she heard of a surgeon who, her friends said, could fix that eye in a jiffy. In order to look more imposing at her White House receptions, she was all set to give the man a try, but when the President heard about it, he exploded. He loved her as she was, he stormed, and anyway it looked to him more like a tiny squint than a crossed eye. She gave up the idea, but nonetheless, when having pictures made, the First Lady always tried to get her best eye nearest the camera and today it is almost impossible to view her full in the face.

To help her with her weekly afternoon receptions, Julia asked Cabinet wives and other friends to be her honor guard and she always gave them lunch in the family dining room beforehand. At times the ladies dallied over their food so long that impatient guests set up a foot-stamping in the East Parlor where they were waiting. Then Julia would lead her guard to the Blue Parlor from which even a hint of daylight had been fashionably excluded. Headed by Julia, the guard would form a receiving line and other women streamed by to have their hands shaken before going on to the State dining room for refreshments and chatter. Before the party ended, the President and a friend or two were almost sure to show up to add to the welcome.

Julia was perhaps the most relaxed First Lady that the nation has had. Probably this was because during the Civil War she had adopted her husband's fatalistic attitude about the outcome of battles and had extended it to life in general. She took everything in stride except criticism of her husband.

But of Julia Dent Grant herself there was no criticism worth measuring. People who did not know her well were inclined to think her rather dull and prosaic, but her friends and family knew better. One writer said of her that she was "too plain to arouse envy, too devoted to her husband and family to incite gossip, and not sharp enough of tongue to stir up controversy." Her bad eye caused her to mix up recognitions and names a bit in a big crowd but her friendliness was so evident nobody seemed to mind.

She was First Lady during a time of great prosperity and the display of wealth, by today's standards, was often heavily ostentatious. The Grants lived richly in the White House, where the President had all the household operations moving like a successful army bountifully supplied with men and materiel. Opulence became a way of life in the Executive Mansion as well as elsewhere among the country's well-heeled citizens. The display was nowhere more evident than at the state dinners which the Grants served in the White House.

Food was so superabundant that at times it had to be served in twenty-nine courses with a break after the roast course for Roman punch to fortify the guests to continue. A dinner for thirty-six guests might cost the President up to $2,000, although the average cost was around $700. If fewer than six wine glasses were needed, the affair was not topnotch.

As a fit setting for the heavy dinners the state dining room was decorated until it became a fairyland jungle of garlanded ropes of roses and smilax that looped from the chandeliers, festooned the mantel, draped the walls, and hung in odd shapes from the ceiling. Potted plants filled every niche and much floor space. Ten-foot pink azaleas bloomed behind the First Lady's chair. Epergne after epergne of fruit adorned the candlelit and be-smilaxed table. On the table there was often a mirrored plateau and on this frequently was placed the President's favorite decoration—a solid silver ship with a sail and one figure, depicting Hiawatha as he floated "through the clear, transparent water." It had been presented by the Mohawk Indians.

President Grant, despite the look of age caused by the whiskers, was only forty-six years of age when elected, or the youngest President so far, and Julia was only forty-three, quite young as First Ladies go. They had been through hard times together after he resigned from the army and failed to make a living on sixty acres given them by Frederick Dent, Julia's father. Grant then failed in two ventures in business. None of it had dampened her faith in him, and nothing ever would.

Julia's people, the Dents, were a well-to-do Missouri family. At first they did not look too kindly on the match between their daughter and Lieutenant Grant of Ohio, when he came visiting from West Point with his classmate, Lieutenant Fred Dent, Julia's brother. But when Grant saved Fred's life in Mexico, the family's attitude changed and Colonel Dent, the father, gave the young couple a fine St. Louis wedding.

Then came the Civil War and Colonel Dent again had doubts about his son-in-law because Grant rejoined the army and on the Union side. The Colonel was an out-and-out Southerner, and all during the war he maintained that while there always would be a place at his table for Julia and her children, watch out if that Federal son-in-law of his came around!

After the war, Colonel Dent, still unreconstructed, lived with the Grants in the White House and gloried in telling newspaper men his own version of the War Between the States. Grant's father, Jesse, a taciturn and self-contained Union man, also visited often at the White House and, to the delight of the public, the two quarrelled with each other in the newspapers. Jesse, the President's son, later wrote that his grandfathers made a great show of not speaking to each other directly and of being deaf when the other spoke.

During the Civil War years Julia frequently joined her

husband at front line headquarters, and at times remained several weeks. She thought that it did the General good to have his wife and children near him, and everyone agreed that life in camp always was more pleasant after Julia arrived.

When Julia took their children to camp she always had their only daughter, Nellie, the apple of the General's eye, dressed with doll-like prettiness because that was the way her father liked to see her. To learn how much his sons had grown since the last meeting, the General loved to wrestle with them. Once in Virginia an adjutant entered his quarters unannounced to find the General of the Armies pinned to the floor by sons Fred and Buck. "Now you know my weaknesses—my children and my horses," said the General.

Little Jesse, the youngest, often rode about camp behind his father on a horse named Mankiller, and also had ponies of his own, Rebel and Jeff. When the Lincolns visited the battlefields, Jesse and Tad Lincoln rode the ponies, young Grant being by far the better horseman. No horse was too mean for the General and he taught all his children to ride fearlessly. While in the White House he enlarged the stables and kept spirited steeds, but he rarely rode horseback after he became President.

The Grants were very indulgent with their children, whom he always called the smartest and best in the world. Fred wrote of his parents: "Their loving acts covered every day of our association, and I remember no unkind nor unjust decision." Each child considered himself the favorite—Fred because he was the oldest, Jesse because he was the youngest, Buck because he was born in his father's home state, and Nellie because she was the only girl. Nellie was born on the Fourth of July and believed it when her father assured her that the fireworks were in her honor.

The schooling of the older sons was sporadic during the war years, but they quickly made up for the lag later. Fred went to West Point and Buck chose Harvard. Nellie was sent to a girls' school in Washington, under orders to study hard. One afternoon the Presidential carriage came for her, but she was not released because she was making up homework. Two other carriage trips were necessary that afternoon as her staying-in period grew longer and longer. Next morning, the First Lady showed up with her to thank the teacher. "Teach her that she is only plain, simple Nellie Grant, subject to all the rules that govern all the scholars," her mother said.

When it came time for Nellie to go away to finishing school —Miss Porter's in Connecticut—the President escorted her because, he said, "Julia would only cry and bring her back." But by the time the President reached New York on his way home, his daughter had three telegrams awaiting him at his hotel. "I'm about to die from homesickness," they all said. And within a short time he wired her to come on home.

About a year later, Jesse also was sent away to school at Cheltenham's near Philadelphia, but he did not at all like the idea of staying. He wrote his mother that he really was making no progress, but she advised him to stick with it. He appealed to his father and said he wanted to be with his family. "We want you, too," the President wired. "Come home at once." Jesse later at the age of 16 entered Cornell and did very well.

Pretty Nellie did not return to school after her brief experience in Connecticut. At times she received with her mother at White House parties, but mostly she danced away the night with the younger set at all-night germans or was seen dashing around town in her phaeton behind a span of black ponies. The First Lady would not let her attend parties without one of her brothers and often it was reluctant Jesse who had to go. "I was not much of an escort," he wrote as he related how Nellie loved to dance so much that once when he took her to a Navy dance at Annapolis she was on the floor whirling away happily, not realizing she had forgotten to take off her galoshes.

Her popularity was unlimited in Washington and when she was a scant seventeen she topped it off with a trip abroad with the Secretary of the Navy and Mrs. Adolph E. Borie, longtime family friends. She was a sensation in Europe, was presented to Queen Victoria, had a gay time socially, and then had a shipboard romance. On the boat coming home, she met a handsome Britisher, Algernon Charles Frederick Sartoris, nephew of Fanny Kemble, the actress, and immediately fell in love. Neither the President nor First Lady enjoyed the prospect of Nellie leaving them to live abroad, but cupid won, and on May 21, 1874, they gave her a spectacular White House wedding in the East Parlor.

Gifts poured in from around the world. Valued at between $60,000 and $75,000, they were displayed in the oval library upstairs. The most priceless gift was a poem by Walt Whitman, "A Kiss to the Bride", in which he called her "O sweet Missouri Rose! O bonny bride!"

It was the first wedding in the White House since Elizabeth Tyler's in 1842, and it was quite a sensation. The ceremony was performed under a mammoth wedding bell of white roses hung from the ceiling. Smilax intertwined with flowers was looped everywhere. The Brussels point lace on Nellie's gown cost $5,000. Her eight bridesmaids wore identical dresses of white corded silk under white illusion. Four carried blue flowers, and the other four, pink. The First Lady, in mourning for her father, was gowned in an elaborate black silk with a sweeping train and lots of ruffles. The huge wedding cake was decorated with roses, bells, and doves.

The couple, accompanied by most of the wedding party, went to New York, and the farewells as Mr. and Mrs. Sartoris sailed away to England were gala indeed. When Nellie returned to the White House two years later she brought her first baby. But the marriage that began so romantically was not successful, and after a few more years she returned with her three children to live in America.

Julia saw another of her children married the same year as Nellie. The Grants' oldest son, Fred, married Ida Honore in a ceremony that cost even more than Nellie's. Ida was the beautiful sister of Mrs. Potter Palmer, Chicago's society queen. As a wedding gift the Palmers gave Ida $10,000 worth of diamonds in addition to her luxurious wedding gown and huge reception.

After his marriage Fred became an aide at the White House, and the young couple lived there with the Grants. Fred was excited that their first baby would be born in the White House, and he proudly planned to name it Ulysses. But the baby was a girl and he called her Julia Dent for his mother, the First Lady. Baby Julia was christened in the East Parlor and grew up to marry a Russian nobleman, Count Cantacuzene.

The Grants supposedly traveled more than any First Family ever did up to that time, and always with the flourish of a General accustomed to leading armies. When they went to their seaside cottage at Long Branch, New Jersey, each summer, the amount of luggage was staggering. The family traveled by Pullman palace cars, and on one occasion before their arrival eight enormous loads of baggage had been delivered.

Despite what the First Lady said, Jesse thought that she was happier at that Long Branch cottage than in the White House. He said she always looked a little sad in the autumn when it was time to start the parties, receptions, and dinners again. By spring she began to weary of the ceaseless throngs. Just before Lent one year, a guest reported that the carpets looked exhausted and so did the First Lady.

The planned splendor of the festivities for Grant's second inaugural on March 4, 1873, was marred by the bitter cold. It was so windy that most of the street decorations blew away. The ball was in a huge temporary building that had no furnace. Brass bands could not perform because the musicians' breath condensed in the valves of their instruments. The First Lady shivered in a white silk dress trimmed in black chantilly lace and much of the food, prepared at great expense, froze solid. Wraps were worn for vigorous dancing, but everybody gave up before midnight.

Julia continued her entertaining undiminished throughout all the Grants' eight years, and ended by giving a fine dinner for the incoming President and Mrs. Rutherford B. Hayes. Then Julia, her husband, and their son, Jesse, set out on a fabulous trip around the world.

They sailed from New York amid great ceremonies in May, 1877, and did not return until September, 1879, when San Francisco welcomed them back with a magnificent reception. The highlight of the trip for Julia was a precedent-shaking dinner in her honor in Tientsin, given by the wife of the Viceroy of China. No men were present, although great crowds pushed up to look in the windows and the Viceroy himself was seen occasionally peeping in to see how the innovation was working.

What surprised the Chinese hostess the most was that her guests only sipped their wine, as she had been told that barbarian American women drank their glasses dry. She and her daughters were most intrigued by the foreign jewelry, which was passed up and down the table. Since the Viceroy's wife had never seen a piano, one was sent in from the foreign settlement for the evening. A guest played a merry waltz while two of the others demonstrated the dance. What surprised the guests most was the cultured and courteous attention shown by the hostess, who made them feel so welcome.

When Julia returned home she had "traveled more than any other lady who has graced the White House and received at the hands of foreigners more attention than has fallen to the lot of any other American lady."

Jesse said that when his father left office his savings from eight years' salary were less than $15,000. Knowing he had cancer and fearing that he would leave Julia with nothing to live on, the ex-President wrote his memoirs under great difficulties during his illness, although she often begged him to stop and rest. He died in 1885, seventeen years before she did.

LUCY WEBB HAYES (1877-1881)

Let Them Drink Lemonade

SINCE March 4, 1877 fell on Sunday, the public inaugural ceremony for President Rutherford B. Hayes was deferred until Monday. But with only his wife and a few others in on the secret, Hayes, being in no position to take chances, privately took a preliminary oath of office at the White House seconds past midnight on the Sabbath morning. This precaution was purely political and had nothing to do with the rule about never on a Sunday.

His was the most disputed of all elections and the times were too tense to risk a minute's delay in getting a legal document to show, if needed. President Grant was delighted to speed things along because Hayes not only shared his politics but was from his home state of Ohio.

The margin in vote and time was narrow indeed. It was only on Friday, March 2, that Hayes had won the Presidential count by one vote. Democratic Candidate Samuel J. Tilden had won a majority of the popular vote in the preceding November election and then a majority of the electoral votes but he was one vote short of the one hundred eighty-five needed for certification. Twenty electoral votes were in dispute, and both sides claimed the votes of three southern states still under Civil War carpetbag government. How much the election was "fixed," if at all, is still good for an argument. Because of the uncertain outcome, no inaugural ball was planned nor given, but the new President and Mrs. Hayes received the public at the White House Monday afternoon.

The new First Lady was instantly popular, particularly with women of the press, who hailed her as the type of "new woman" for which the country had been waiting. The writers went into lyrics when describing her looks and activities. She was an attractive and animated brunette in excellent health and spirits, and her White House portrait indicates that she was as handsome as the chroniclers said. The rhapsodies written about her give intimate glimpses of the times.

One writer, Laura Holloway, said that Mrs. Hayes was of medium height, squarely built, and had large features. "Her hair is a particularly noticeably feature, partly from the manner in which it is worn (always parted in the middle and combed plainly straight back), and mainly for its abundance and beauty of color and texture. Her brow is low and broad, and is unmarked by care. The mouth is large and adorned with beautiful teeth. Her eyes are large and expressive, and deepen in color from gray to black as the feelings are wrought upon. . . She is as splendid a specimen of physical womanhood as the country can boast, and her presence is a tonic to weaker women."

Mary Clemmer Ames studied her during the Hayes inaugural address and wrote: "A fair woman between two little children looks down. She has a singularly sweet and winning face. It looks out from bands of smooth dark hair with that tender light in the eyes which we have come to associate always with the Madonna. I have never seen such a face reign in the White House. I wonder what the world of Vanity Fair will do with it? Will it frizz that hair?—powder that face?—draw those sweet fine lines away with pride?"

What the women liked about Lucy most of all was that she was a college graduate, the first First Lady to be such, a temperance leader, an activist in group activities, and always had identified herself with the public life of her husband while he was in Congress and then when he served as Governor of Ohio. Talk of woman suffrage and women's rights was in the air, and Lucy by nature and education was a reformer and crusader. Her arrival signaled a possible breakthrough into a new era for women.

In addition to her plain coiffure, Lucy was acclaimed for dress reforms. She wore no jewelry to the dinner which the Grants gave for them and her cameo-tinted silk dress had both sleeves and higher necklines. Her inaugural dress at the Capitol was "merely rich black silk with real lace," and at her first White House reception, given on the fourth Saturday after her arrival, her toilette was considered "remarkable for simple elegance rather than brilliancy or cost."

Yet Lucy's First Lady dress preserved in the Smithsonian's collection is as fancy as they come. She wore it when she hostessed her first state dinner, given for the Grand Duke Alexis of Russia. It is of ivory taffeta and satin and elaborately trimmed with beads, lace, rosettes, fringe, pleats, and drapery. Its train and bodice are brocaded in a golden rose design and it has a slight bustle. Julia Grant scarcely could have been more ornate, although Lucy's dress does have three-quarter-length sleeves with a rosette at the elbow, and the V-neck is filled high with soft net.

Nor do her parlor and dining room decorations for the Grand Duke sound very much like a new high in simplicity. A large oval mirror centered the dining table to simulate a fresh-water lake surrounded by tropical ferns and trailing vines. A description of that day had it that the "banks of the lake were strewn with graceful hills formed by vases of tropical fruit, and here and there a pyramid or column of candied fruits and bon-bons." At each end of the lake were tall frosted cakes decorated with white azaleas, tea roses and smilax. Banked around the room were potted plants, azalea trees, and camellias. Strands of smilax, strung on gilt wire, outlined table, chandelier, and pictures. At the plates stood alternately pink vases with white rosebuds and white vases with pink buds. These were to replace the wine glasses of former years, but the Secretary of State intervened and declared that the Grand Duke would not enjoy a dinner without wines.

The President and Mrs. Hayes were temperance leaders and although they yielded on this occasion, it was at the same time announced that all citizens of the United States who were entertained at the White House thereafter need not look for wine on the menu. This decree won both praise and gibes and led to the nickname of "Lemonade Lucy" for the First Lady, who received both the credit and the blame even though the decision was made by the President.

After one diplomatic dinner rumors flew around town that the oranges served, unknown to the First Lady, had been spiked with rum. Not so, said the President. "The joke's on the drinking people. My orders were to flavor them rather strongly with the same flavor as Jamaica rum. This took! There was not a drop of spirits in them!"

On their first Sunday in Washington, the President and his family were expected to attend services at the fashionable Metropolitan Methodist Church, but they endeared themselves to many by quietly going to the Foundry Methodist Church, which had a less stylish minister but was nearer to the White House. It became their custom to walk to services there each Sunday.

Morning worship at the White House was standard procedure during the Hayes administration, the eight-thirty breakfast invariably being followed by prayers. The President and Mrs. Hayes instituted Sunday evening hymn-singing in which Congressmen and Cabinet members participated. The First Lady's rich voice could be heard leading "Rock of Ages" and other favorite selections, and Congressman William McKinley helped boom out "Lead Kindly Light," with which the song-fest regularly closed.

Lucy Hayes was forty-six years of age when she became First Lady, and had mothered eight children, of whom three died as infants. Fanny was only nine years of age when the Hayes term began, and Scott, the baby, was six. There were

126

three grown sons—Richard, Webb and Rutherford P. The President was an affectionate father and on most days he found time to spend with Scott and Fanny. Because of them, he moved to save one of Washington's oldest traditions: the Easter Monday egg-rolling for children.

The custom, often called the oddest in Washington, is thought to have been started by Dolley Madison back in Jefferson's day. Originally it was held on Capitol Hill, but Congress had grown so heartily tired of damaged grass, stray tots, and smashed eggs that its members voted to end it and threatened that guards would run all prospective egg-rollers of 1878 right back home. Hayes became a popular hero when he invited the youngsters to use the White House grounds. Fanny wore white muslin, set off by a gay pink sash and pink boots, for the first egg-roll in the new setting. Scott was arrayed in tight, below-the-knee pants and high topped boots.

On December 30 of their first year in the White House, the President and Mrs. Hayes celebrated their twenty-fifth wedding anniversary with a renewal of their wedding vows at a service in the Blue Room. Lucy wore her wedding gown of white satin, attended by the same bridesmaids. The preacher who had first married them officiated. Among numerous friends who had attended the original wedding were Mr. and Mrs. John W. Herron from Ohio. They had with them their seventeen-year-old daughter, Helen, who as Mrs. William Howard Taft would become First Lady almost thirty years later. As part of the anniversary celebration, Fanny and Scott were baptized as was Lucy Hayes Herron, the infant daughter of the Herrons and namesake of the First Lady. The next night, New Year's Eve, the silver wedding celebration continued with a public reception.

Rather than "frittering away" appropriations made for running the White House, Lucy concentrated all leftover funds in the purchase of a dinner service of almost a thousand pieces, illustrated with animals, flowers, and scenes native to the United States. The designs originally were in water colors and it was necessary to invent new methods to reproduce them perfectly on porcelain in hard mineral colors. The set became a unique legacy for future First Ladies.

Lucy enjoyed the White House thoroughly and when in town, and not giving a dinner, was at home to callers on week-day evenings from eight until ten. Asked if she did not find all the entertaining tiring, she replied, "Oh, no. I never get tired of having a good time." She introduced the White House crest, a golden eagle similar to those on coins, at the top of engraved White House invitations, and she had elaborate charts drawn up to show state dinner guests where they would be seated and what was on the menu. The food she served, although by no means equal to that of the Grant dinners in quantity, was rated first rate in quality and still super-abundant by today's standards.

It was believed at first that she might somehow take an active part in trying to influence legislation, but if she did, it was through her husband. At one time, in answer to a comment about her lack of weight on Capitol Hill, her husband said, "Mrs. Hayes may not have much influence with Congress, but she has great influence with me." She departed from her hands-off policy about appointments once, however, to get a Pennsylvania postmistress reinstated who supposedly had been removed from her job for strong temperance activities.

Lucy was born in Chillicothe, Ohio, and lived there until her widowed mother took her two sons to be educated at the Ohio Wesleyan University at Delaware, Ohio, and entered her eleven-year-old daughter Lucy in its preparatory school. She was the only girl in the institution, and she studied there for six years. Then she enrolled in the Ohio Wesleyan Female College in Cincinnati, from which she graduated at the age of nineteen.

Lucy followed her husband to camp during the Civil War and won the gratitude of many Union soldiers for her sewing and hospital work. Hayes was elected to Congress during the last year of the war, and Lucy spent the winters with him in Washington. She had five years in Ohio as the wife of the Governor. She devoted much time to charities.

Lucy became one of the best loved women to preside over the White House. She was a popular hostess, sparing no effort to make the Executive Mansion a friendly and interesting place for guests and to insure that the official entertaining was attractively done.

During the last days of her husband's four years in office she received testimonials of appreciation signed by thousands of women who valued her interest in worthy causes. The Women's Christian Temperance Union, then headed by Frances Willard, backed its applause by presenting to the White House for its collection a life-sized portrait of Lucy Hayes by Daniel Huntington. The canvas is seven feet four inches high by six feet wide and its enormous frame, since replaced by a simpler one, was said to be "the finest ever carved." In it she wears a ruby red dress, with sleeves and filled-in neck, of course, and stands holding a small cluster of roses. Her hair is raven black and she looks every inch the beautiful and amiable woman "who had done such worthy things as to secure to herself a following such as no other member of her sex ever had in this country"—up to that time.

Martha Custis Washington

Abigail Smith Adams

Dolley Madison

Elizabeth Kortright Monroe

Louisa Catherine Johnson Adams

Rachel Jackson

Anna Symmes Harrison

Letitia Tyler

Julia Gardiner Tyler

Sarah Childress Polk

Abigail Powers Fillmore

Jane Appleton Pierce

Mary Todd Lincoln

Eliza McCardle Johnson

Julia Dent Grant

Lucy Webb Hayes

Lucretia Rudolph Garfield

Frances Folsom Cleveland

Caroline Lavinia Harrison

Ida Saxton McKinley

Edith Carow Roosevelt

Helen Herron Taft

Ellen Axson Wilson

Edith Bolling Galt Wilson

Florence Kling Harding

Grace Goodhue Coolidge

Lou Henry Hoover

Eleanor Roosevelt

Bess Wallace Truman

Mamie Doud Eisenhower

Jacqueline Bouvier Kennedy

Please see page 256 for artists, photographers, and sources of the portraits of the First Ladies.

LUCRETIA RUDOLPH GARFIELD
(March 4-Sept. 19, 1881)

Quietly Efficient and Bookish

"CRETE grows up to every new emergency with fine tact and faultless taste," President James A. Garfield said admiringly when he saw how smoothly things were going at the first reception given in the White House by his gentle and pretty wife, Lucretia. He knew that she shrank from the thought of being First Lady and that on election night, with tears in her eyes, she had exclaimed, "What a terrible responsibility to come to him—and to me."

Lucretia's philosophy was that if one has a job to do it is only good sense to learn to like it. This philosophy never failed her. She had evolved it to help her through the unwelcome routine chore of baking bread for her large family. Since the task was inescapable she decided to take a special interest in it, and bake the best bread possible.

"The whole of life became brighter," she declared. "The very sunshine seemed flowing down through my spirit into the white loaves . . . and this truth, as old as creation, seems just then to have become fully mine—that I need not be the shrinking slave of toil, but could be its regal master."

This philosophy worked just as well in the White House as elsewhere, and the sunshine of her spirit added an enviable dimension to her days. She was naturally hospitable, and the few social events over which she presided during her short one hundred and ninety-nine days as First Lady were called delightful. She was a slender, brown-eyed little woman who preferred literary society meetings and afternoons at the Library of Congress to partying. Usually she dressed with neat simplicity. But for her husband's inaugural ball, she selected a stunningly colorful dress of heliotrope satin made with stylish bustle and a spreading train. Its fancy skirt was trimmed in deep flounces of Brussels lace and, as noted with approval by the dress reformers, it had a high little collar and the frill-edged sleeves came to the wrists. She wore a cluster of pansies at the waist, but no jewelry.

Lucretia was a "new woman," like Lucy Hayes, her predecessor, in that she was a college graduate and took a deep interest in her husband's career. But unlike Lucy, she was not a speaker-outer for causes. She did not labor in the temperance movement nor espouse the cause of woman suffrage. The suffragists, in fact, considered her husband to be antagonistic to their cause, but the way he put it was that although he believed in an expanding role for women, he could not be for votes for women until he felt that most of them really wanted to vote.

As it turned out, shy Lucretia did not have to worry too much about the spotlight which would be turned on her at inaugural time because its brightest beam would fall on her mother-in-law, Eliza Garfield, the eighty-year-old mother of the new President. The family's pet name for the elder Mrs. Garfield was "Lady Kensington," which reflected her stature in the family. She was the first mother ever to see her son inaugurated President. That she was able to do so was a tribute to the nation's progress in transportation facilities as well as to her own stamina and lively interest in her son's career. Other Presidents, including Washington, Madison, Polk, and Grant, had mothers living when they took office but for various reasons they were not present when their sons were sworn in.

Since one Ohio President was succeeding another, the whole scene of the change-over in administration was homey, folksy, and gay. The fourteen-year-old daughters of both Presidents, Molly Garfield and Fanny Hayes, held hands during the inaugural address. Both Molly and Fanny were only daughters and each had four brothers. The older Garfield boys were Harry, seventeen, and James, fifteen, who would be tutored for college in the White House, and the two younger ones were Irvin, aged ten, and Abram, only eight.

The Garfields were a loving family and had good times together. The new President was as hearty and outgoing as the new First Lady was reserved and retiring. She always said that her husband was a charmer who brought out the best in people, but she at times worried that he was not always too good a judge of character. His zest for friendships could be a bit overpowering to Lucretia, but evidently his mother, who lived with them much of the time, usually shared his spontaneous enthusiasms. Lucretia's influence with her husband was in her studied opinions and quiet summaries, and he valued them highly. Her mother-in-law also loved and appreciated Lucretia, and they got along well together.

Lucretia was the daughter of Zebulon Rudolph, a leading citizen and devout member of the Disciples Church in Hiram, Ohio. He was determined to give his very bright daughter the best education possible. She and Garfield became engaged when they were students at Western Reserve Eclectic Institute (later Hiram College), which her father helped found.

They delayed their marriage until after he had gone east to Williams College at Williamstown, Massachusetts, for advance study and then had returned to be president of their alma mater at Hiram. Meantime Lucretia taught in the public schools of Cincinnati. She was an excellent teacher, and after her marriage she was very popular with Hiram students who needed tutoring.

She was twenty-six years of age when she and Garfield married in late 1858. Three years later he went off to the Civil War as a lieutenant colonel with the Ohio Volunteer Infantry. While he still was in uniform his fellow Ohioans elected him to the United States House of Representatives, and he resigned from the army as a brigadier general in December, 1863, to take his Congressional seat.

Lucretia economized during his absences and saved enough from his salary to buy their first home for $800. But she had not liked being left alone and thought that his election to Congress might mean more years of separation. When he returned from his first Congressional session he found she had prepared for him a written accounting of their wedded life to show that they actually had been together less than a year in all. Their first baby died while he was in the army, and their second was born during another absence. "I do not want to live in a state of practical divorce," she wrote in her memo. "I then and there resolved," Garfield said, "that I never would again go to Washington to a session of Congress without taking her with me." He kept his promise.

During his Presidential campaign, there was a rumor that she was thinking of divorce, but had dropped the idea when he was nominated. Some people always believed that except for intercessions by members of their church they might at one time have been divorced. But not even in her complaint about the separations had Lucretia even hinted she wanted a divorce.

Two of the five Garfield children were born in Washington. The family lived in rented homes until 1869 when Congressman Garfield bought a lot and built a house which cost him $10,000. Usually the family spent the summers at the Ohio farm of the elder Mrs. Garfield at Mentor. The family was there for the election returns which turned the Congressman into a President. For a time in late 1880 the popular Garfield could claim three political titles. Ohioans had elected him to the United States Senate, but he had not yet resigned from the House of Representatives, and he was the President-elect.

On election night the family wrote a round robin letter to Harry and James who were away at St. Paul's School in New Hampshire, and the Garfields also served a midnight supper to twenty-five guests. Pretty Molly Garfield helped wait on the table. Molly had been attending school at Madame Burr's in Washington and reentered after the election. Harry and James had a tutor in the White House to ready them for college, and the President himself took a hand in their training. Almost any mealtime could become schooltime when he started popping questions. The tutor also taught the younger boys, Irvin and Abram, but they were so noisily inattentive and eager to get back to their velocipides that he complained to their father. Garfield began grading their daily work, and its quality promptly improved.

Garfield, a born educator, always thought that learning should be an enjoyable process. He took it hard when as little boys, Harry and James did not immediately show his and Lucretia's love for books. This prompted him to send them to St. Paul's to study under Mark Hopkins, whom he venerated. "I cannot doubt that something is wrong with our system of education which has made both my (older) boys hate the sight of a school book," he said at the time.

The new President also believed in recreation, and he did not frown on a glass of champagne occasionally. He brought the White House billiard table out of storage and enjoyed games with his sons. He and Lucretia played bezique, and he and the children often played euchre and casino. He went to the theater and to baseball games. He and his wife planned to continue their membership in their literary society.

Throughout the campaign year and then on through the inaugural festivities, Lucretia carried a heavy work load. When the last inaugural guest left the White House it was April 7. That morning the Garfield family sat down to breakfast alone for the first time in seventeen months.

The White House was dingy and dreary. Even Molly, so cheery and bouyant, was depressed by what she called the ugly blue and the sickening green of the Blue and Green Parlors. Lucretia did not rush into a touch up job because she wished to consult historic sources and do a thoroughly authentic redecoration job on the entire main floor. She had the Library of Congress busy looking up books for her, but her aged mother-in-law became quite ill. By the time the older Mrs. Garfield was able to leave for Mentor for the summer, the First Lady was a victim of malaria and nervous exhaustion.

The President, knowing how heavy her schedule had been and that not even her bright philosophy could guarantee against physical strain, was worried when her temperature stayed at an unusually high level for days and days. When it subsided to little more than a hundred degrees his children heard him laugh for the first time since she was confined to her room. And joy was heightened when on June 12 her

132

oldest son and her husband "made a chair with their hands" and brought her down to the dining room again.

Washington's sweltering summer heat was in full swing, and a week later the President escorted the First Lady and their three youngest children to Elberon, New Jersey, for a temporary stay by the seaside. But they had plans for a summer that would provide deserved rest and a real change for Lucretia. The two younger boys were to spend the summer with Grandmother Garfield on the farm at Mentor. The President, on the occasion of the twenty-fifth anniversary of his graduation from Williams College, was to deliver the commencement address and make arrangements for the two older boys to enter in the fall. Then he and the boys would meet Lucretia and Molly in New York City to begin a tour of the New England mountains and afterwards embark on a recuperative voyage along the coast. It was such a welcome idea that the whole family eagerly anticipated it.

When the starting day, July 2, finally arrived the President was in such a gala mood that early in the morning he entered the room of his older sons, singing "I Mixed Those Babies Up," a popular tune of the day, and told the boys to prepare for a fine time. The Garfield Cabinet, its members all packed to go their separate ways for the summer, decided to give the President a happy sendoff, and many of them were at Washington's Union Station to cheer him onto his train.

The President no sooner had entered the station than two bullets whizzed in his direction from the gun of a disappointed office-seeker named Charles Guiteau. One bullet grazed his arm and the other entered his back near the spine. Bedlam broke out. Harry and James Garfield took charge of their wounded father, who was returned to the White House, borne high on a mattress, as gently as possible. "Whatever happens, I want you to promise to look after Crete," Garfield told Mrs. James G. Blaine, wife of the Secretary of State. She had her trunks packed for Maine, but the President implored: "Don't leave me until Crete comes."

A cautious wire, recounting the shooting and saying that the President needed her, was sent to the First Lady in Elberon. She and Molly left for Washington immediately on a special train which was routed around regular traffic and arrived early that evening. At first it was believed that Garfield could not live many hours, and then it was thought that he might recover completely. Fighting a gunshot infection in midsummer in Washington before the days of miracle drugs and air conditioning was not easy. An awkward and makeshift system of refrigeration was evolved for his room. Dr. Susan Edson, who had been an army nurse and knew the family well, came to the White House to be in charge.

Lucretia performed during his illness as capably and as patiently as though she also had trained for duty on the battle front. Her smiles in the sick room were confident. With unflustered calm she prepared special dishes for the invalid. She made an effort to radiate optimism always. She slept when she could find time. The President had been begging to go to the cool seashore of Elberon, and in early autumn it was decided that he had recovered sufficiently to be moved. He died at Elberon September 19. He had been President one day short of two hundred.

Lucretia was forty-nine years of age when she became a widow and, unlike what had happened to Mary Lincoln, the widow of the other assassinated President, Mrs. Garfield had the full sympathy of the public and of Congress. The latter granted her a pension of $5,000 annually in March following her husband's death and in July of the same year awarded her $50,000.

Lucretia Garfield kept her talented family together and its members were educated according to plans she and her husband had made. "Lady Kensington," the esteemed matriarch, died in 1887, and quiet Lucretia, lovingly called "Madame Garfield" by her offspring, took her place as the pivotal inspiration in the Garfield circle.

She lived to be almost eighty-six years of age and died in Pasadena, California, in 1918.

WIDOWER CHESTER A. ARTHUR
(September 20, 1881-85)

"Defeated by His Trousers"

FASTIDIOUS Chester Alan Arthur took a good long look at the White House in which the Garfields had lived and said, "I will not live in a house like this." If Congress would not appropriate funds for renovations, he would pay for them out of his own pocket, he declared as he huffed off to run the government from the granite mansion home of his personal friend, Senator John P. Jones of Nevada.

The elegant new President meantime placed his decorating orders with Louis Comfort Tiffany and went each night to the White House to make sure the workmen were fixing the place up to suit him. He earmarked wornout and unwanted items for the auction block, and Washingtonians joked about the contents of twenty wagonloads of White House accumulations that were to be sold. One wag said that the clearance sale included the trap that caught the rat that ate a suit of Lincoln's clothes. In fairness to Arthur, however, it was noted that the auctioned goods were mostly ancient belongings left behind by departing families who felt no further use for them.

After taking the oath of office on September 20, Arthur was able to move into the President's House in time for Christmas, and what a transformation had been wrought! The Blue Room was now a robin's egg tint, the East Parlor had a silver ceiling with designs on it in ivory, the Red Room had a frieze of flags and eagles and its ceiling was old gold, and the private dining room was papered in gold to compliment its luxuriant window draperies of heavy pomegranate plush. Two bathrooms and an elevator were installed. The old conservatories were enlarged and remodeled. Across the North Entrance Foyer—for privacy and to make for better heating—was stretched an opalescent glass screen which reached from floor to ceiling and featured a motif of flags and eagles "interlaced in the Arabian method."

Arthur's beautiful wife, Ellen Herndon, had died a few months before he became Vice President, leaving him a seventeen-year-old son, Alan, Jr., and a nine-year-old daughter, Nellie. Nellie came to live in the White House, for which

135

Arthur asked his youngest sister, Mrs. Mary Arthur McElroy of Albany, New York, to be the hostess. Alan often dashed down from Princeton University to drive the dark green Presidential landau which was drawn by two magnificent bays.

Mrs. McElroy brought her two young daughters, May and Jessie, with her and they shared a French governess with Nellie. The President laid down strict rules against photographers and news stories about his family. It was not until 1961 that the Library of Congress obtained a photograph of Ellen Herndon Arthur to put with its pictures of other wives whose husbands had become President.

It is now agreed that Arthur was a much better President than he was thought to be at the time. He worked long hours, instituted civil service reforms, and broke with his erstwhile political friends in New York over appointments. This left him without political backing, since he and Garfield's friends already had parted company. He was a lonely man in the White House and stories about him featured only his extravagant tastes.

His wardrobe was a rich one and he kept it up to date by ordering twenty-five suits at a time. He often spent as much as a thousand dollars on flowers for a dinner party. He was the first President to have a personal valet and when election time rolled around again the stories of his opulent living were so widespread that he did not have a chance. "Arthur was defeated by his pants just as Van Buren was defeated by the gold spoons," it was said.

Mrs. McElroy was a gracious hostess who at times asked up to sixty other women to receive with her at large parties. Among her co-hostesses frequently were two former White House occupants—Julia Gardiner Tyler, widow of the former President, and Harriet Lane Johnston, niece of President Buchanan. Both were then making their homes in Washington.

Mrs. McElroy was born in Greenwich, New York, the youngest in a family of nine. Their father was the Reverend William Arthur, a Baptist minister, who encouraged Mary to get a good education. She graduated from Miss Emma Willard's famous seminary for young ladies in Troy, New York, and at the age of nineteen married John E. McElroy, an Albany businessman. She was a woman of medium size, with a sweet and pleasant face, dark hair and eyes, and a delicate complexion.

After her brother's term ended, she and her husband continued to lead an active social life in Albany.

FRANCES FOLSOM CLEVELAND
(1885-89 and 1893-97)

The Youngest Ever and One of the Prettiest

AFTER twenty years of solid Republican family men in the White House, the voters in 1884 decided to try Grover Cleveland, a Democrat and a bachelor, and the first of either since pre-Civil War days. He became the twenty-second President and then, after a lapse of four years, he became the twenty-fourth President. Thus it is that Americans always have trouble remembering just how many Presidents they have had. Was Cleveland singular or plural, two Presidents or one?

He was quite singular when it came to upsetting precedents. He became President as a balding, mustached, heavyset bachelor of forty-seven years. Then he married in a White House Parlor, the only President to do so. One of his daughters was the first child of a President to be born in the White House, and his pretty wife was the youngest First Lady to date. Also, he bought one Washington home and rented another so that his family spent less sleeping time in the White House than any other First Family who had lived there for a total of eight years.

The preachers had sermonized against Cleveland's election and had called him an irreligious man. Some people had voted against him because of the charge that he had fathered an illegitimate child in his youth. "Maw, maw, where's my paw?" was part of the spicy campaign literature, and one version of the answer was, "Gone to the White House, didn'tcha knaw?"

Cleveland made campaign speeches to the men in saloons and some said that his election would mean "Rum, Romanism, and Rebellion." The Romanism part was aimed at Tammany Hall Democrats who were largely Catholics but who didn't like Cleveland much better than the Republicans did, because as Mayor of Buffalo he had been all-out for reform and as Governor of New York he had shown too much independence to suit them. The Rebellion part indicated that the South would vote for him, which it did.

Despite all these strikes against him, Cleveland won and a whopping big crowd of one hundred thousand people flocked to Washington to see their whopping big President inaugurated. He weighed almost three hundred pounds and his usual breakfast was oatmeal, beefsteak or a chop, eggs, breads, and coffee. He brought his cook with him from Albany so as to get his meals fixed as he wanted them. He asked his youngest sister, Rose Elizabeth Cleveland, to be his White House hostess.

Rose, as she preferred to be called although her brother called her Libbie, was an erudite headmistress type of woman in her early forties. She leaned toward women's rights and was a temperance advocate. She had taught in select schools for girls but in recent years had lived alone at the family homestead in Holland Patent, New York, writing learned essays and lecturing.

Many at her brother's inaugural ball admired the dashing double lighting, for which both electricity and gas were used, the fifteen hundred large flags waving, and the music from the Marine Band under the direction of John Philip Sousa himself, but Rose conjugated difficult Greek verbs in the back of her mind to get herself through what she considered a dull evening. She found the verb system so useful that she thereafter employed it frequently while shaking hands at White House receptions.

Rose tried to remove wines from official White House menus, but the President vetoed her plans and she received many protesting letters about him from her temperance friends. But when she gave her own luncheons and receptions she kept them dry—and she was successful in getting the President to church.

Cleveland's father had been a Presbyterian minister and one of his brothers still was, but he himself never quite pleased the church people. For one thing, he and his Cabinet traveled on Sunday, and on some Sundays the President fished around the clock. He was not a gregarious man nor one given to explanations. All the public had a right to expect from him, as he saw it, was that he do his work, and he kept longer work hours than any President since Polk. He broke his schedule with a ride each afternoon at three o'clock and he invariably rode into the outlying northwest part of the district which is now known as Cleveland Park. Then, after a large dinner, he returned to his office to work past midnight.

The President had a purpose in his lonely afternoon rides. Among the guests who had attended his inaugural and stayed at the White House were a pretty widow and her lovely twenty-year-old daughter. The mother had been married to Oscar Folsom of Buffalo, New York, Cleveland's law partner. After Folsom's death, there was speculation for a time that his widow and Cleveland might marry. The presence of the two women at the inaugural occasioned no new rumors whatever. It was well known that they always were on hand for high events in Cleveland's life.

"Uncle Cleve" had bought the baby buggy used for Frances Folsom, the daughter. He called her Frank and as her unofficial guardian took a hand in her upbringing. He let her copy legal documents in his law office before she was a teenager and urged her to go to college. All the time that she was at Wells College he wrote her regularly and kept her supplied with flowers. While he was Governor of New York she and her schoolmates attended public events as his guests. She and her mother were frequent visitors in the Governor's mansion. It was at "Uncle Cleve's" suggestion that Frank and her mother had left for a year's tour of Europe shortly after the inauguration. This was part of Frank's education.

What only the President, the Folsoms, and perhaps Sister Rose knew was that the new President was engaged to be married and the rides to the suburbs meant that he was looking for a house to buy so that his bride would not have to spend her honeymoon in the White House. And he was engaged not to the mother, but to Frank!

But Frank must have trusted one of her schoolmates with her secret engagement because when the President went to New York to meet the boat bringing the Folsoms home the bands were playing "He's Going to Marry Yum-Yum" and then went on into the wedding march. It must have surprised the heavy and solitary Cleveland that the public not only took kindly to but was excited at the prospect of a President marrying while in office. He took it with cautious grace as the headlines went wild with engagement news and as the bands continued to herald his public appearances with gay and romantic music. He was a most popular man during that spring of 1886.

The original plan had been that they would be married by one of Frank's relatives in New York State, but when that relative died, the President decided that the oval Blue Room in the White House would be a good marriage spot. Fewer than forty guests were invited to the greatest wedding of the year and the President himself wrote the invitations: "I am to be married on Wednesday evening, at seven o'clock, at the White House, to Miss Folsom. It will be a very quiet affair, and I will be extremely gratified at your attendance on the occasion."

Frank was a tall and beautiful young lady with pretty blue eyes, wavy chestnut hair, graceful ways, and an air of maturity. Her ivory satin dress was so full and corded that it could stand alone and her veil was described as being six yards long. The dress also had a train, but she managed the attire without an attendant or a mistake. Her jewelry was a diamond necklace, the gift of the bridegroom. He had worried a bit that perhaps it was too costly and had written his sister, "I want her to be happy and to possess all she can reasonably desire, but I should feel much afflicted if she gets many notions in her head. But I think she is pretty level-headed."

Plans for the honeymoon were a deep dark secret, or so the President thought, not knowing that reporters had kept their eyes on the railroad yards for weeks and had spotted the Presidential car, which was concealed far out on a Baltimore and Ohio track. The newlyweds waited until they assumed all right-minded people had gone home to bed and then they boarded the car for Deer Park in the Maryland mountains. The President was livid next morning when he learned that reporters had followed not far behind, taking rooms as close to the honeymoon lodge as possible, and bringing spyglasses with them.

Cleveland never became accustomed to reporters nor approved of their doings. The publication of rumors made him see red. One of them was that Frank's beautiful complexion was due to her eating occasional small doses of arsenic. One so-called doctor advertised that he knew the formula, and would make it available for a small sum. Photographs of Frank sold by the thousands. The President resented the scrutiny of his young wife on public occasions, especially after untrue rumors of her pregnancy. He interrupted one of his speeches at Harvard to call the oglers "ghouls of the press."

Although he thoughtfully had had a room redecorated and refurbished for Frank at the White House, he had carefully delayed other renovations of the mansion until after the wedding so that she could have her say. Meantime he had purchased for their use a rambling and roomy Victorian home out in the suburbs where he had taken his rides. Because of this transaction this area became known as Cleveland Park. He paid $21,500 for the place. It was a small farm, really, with several beautifully scenic acres. Except for the social season, when they moved into the White House, they lived at Red Top (a nickname evolved by the press from its red roof) for the remainder of his first administration.

Through the summer and autumn of the marriage year the White House underwent a thorough going over and redecorating. The Tiffany ceilings were left as they were, but all the first floor rooms were touched up and the outside of the house repainted a gleaming white. All the fence spikes were gilded.

Competent Frank planned the social season in advance and announced the schedule all at once and this plan would be adopted for several years to come. She also redesigned the invitations and place cards; on the invitations engraved for

Congressional families, the dates of all the special receptions were listed, since in those days "The Senators and Representatives in Congress and the ladies of their families" were automatically invited to all White House receptions.

The young First Lady's first public reception was on New Year's Day, 1887, and the crowd was enormous. Everyone wanted to see her and shake her hand, and they liked what they saw. She was lovely and gracious, friendly and poised, and looked quite mature for her age. She wore her long hair in a knot low on her neck at the back and it became the "a la Cleveland" style which was widely copied. Not liking bustles, she stopped wearing them and so did others.

She held her own afternoon receptions for women only and added one for Saturday so that shop girls and others employed the remainder of the week could come. All these affairs became increasingly popular, drawing crowds numbering from two to nine thousand persons. The most popular one was held on a Saturday and the line of ladies waiting to have their hands shaken stretched from the White House entrance all around the Treasury building. Young Frank had to have both arms massaged after this one, because her left one started aching in sympathy.

In the autumn of that year the President took his wife with him for a tour of the West and the South, where the handshakings were multiplied several times over at big receptions in numerous cities. Everyone, including the First Lady, expected that Cleveland would be reelected by a landslide, as his popularity tide seemed to be running so strong. But as the election of 1888 drew nearer, the whispering campaigns started and one of them, tailored for the pulpits, involved the First Lady herself. It was that the President woefully mistreated his young wife, beating her up when he got drunk and on occasions locking her out of the White House in the middle of the night!

Frank was so outraged at the unfairness that she authorized a unique statement in defense of her marital happiness. In it she said, "I can wish the women of our country no greater blessing than that their homes and lives may be as happy, and their husbands as kind, attentive, considerate and affectionate as mine." Some groups wanted to organize Frances Cleveland Influence Clubs and storm the country, but the President forbade it. Just before election day many factory workers received "Vote against Cleveland" notices along with their paychecks, or so it always was maintained, and Benjamin Harrison became the next President.

Frank cried when she told the White House staff goodbye, but she told them to take good care of everything because she would be back four years from that day—which she was, after a campaign in which the happiness of the Cleveland marriage was given an important role in the Democratic party literature. Frank's picture appeared on numerous posters, as well as with her husband's on lapel ribbons. Cleveland was not running alone this time, but as a husband, too. Frank became the first First Lady to run openly for reelection.

And when she returned to the White House she was the mother of a baby girl named Ruth. Ruth was more than a year old and the pride of papa's heart. "Frank, bring Ruthie in here," the President would call out when he had special guests. "Never mind the state of her apron. Bring her on in." Ruth was a sensation with the sightseers, too, and they flocked through the White House gates to see her when she and her nurses went for airings on the lawn. One morning Ruth's mother heard screams from the nurse maid and rushed out to find that Ruth was lost to view, having been taken from her carriage and passed from shoulder to shoulder, with kisses along the way. Frank frantically ordered the gates locked.

The public did not take kindly to the lockout and started ghastly untrue stories about Ruth, saying that she must be deformed in some way if the Clevelands wanted to hide her. The First Lady at the time was pregnant with her second baby. This one, another girl, whom the Clevelands called Esther, was born in the White House in September of 1893. Less than two years later Ruth and Esther were joined by a third sister, Marion, but Marion was born in July, 1895, while the President and First Lady were summering at Buzzards Bay, Massachusetts.

Cleveland had sold his Cleveland Park home for $140,000 when he was not reelected after the first term, thus becoming one of the few Presidents who left the White House (at least the first time) richer than when he went in. After Esther's birth, during the second term, he rented historic Woodley in the same suburban area so that his children could have more sunshine, pets, and privacy. The little girls received enough gifts from around the world to stock a children's store.

Ike Hoover, who came to the White House to manage the newfangled electric lights and stayed on to become its favorite usher, said in his reminiscences that the staff loved "the little Clevelands" more than other White House children because they were younger and so adorable. It was a pretty sight, he said, when their mother walked with them in the White House conservatories to show them the flowers, because they were like flowers themselves.

During the early days of the second term—in the summer of 1893—Frank shared in one of the greatest personal secrets

142

a President ever was able to keep from the public. The Cleve-lands had gone to Buzzards Bay, as usual. Ostensibly he would fish and rest most of the summer, but on June 26 he boarded a yacht in New York harbor and with three prominent doctors put out to sea.

Cleveland had developed cancer in the roof of his mouth. There was a financial panic in the land that year, and he be-lieved that for the good of the country, there should be no public knowledge of his condition nor of the operation in-tended. It was a frightening but successful operation and not revealed for medical history for a quarter century.

The whole upper part of his jaw was removed and the doc-tors had some fearful moments. The yacht landed him at Buzzards Bay on July 5 and he stalwartly walked from the wharf to Grey Gables, his home there. The First Lady cov-ered up his condition in notes saying that he had a bad case of rheumatism and the doctors had ordered complete rest for a while. Dental packing held his face in shape until a rubber replica of the part removed was installed in late summer.

The two Cleveland boys, Richard and Francis Grover, were born after their father was no longer President and when the Clevelands had moved to Princeton, New Jersey. The Ex-President lived to be seventy-one, not dying of cancer at all but of a stomach ailment.

After his death his widow remarried, the only former First Lady so far to do so, and she lived to be eighty-three. She married Thomas J. Preston, a professor of archeology at Princeton. In 1913 on the eve of her remarriage, the then First Lady, Helen Taft, invited her to a White House dinner for which the staff suggested the red-bordered china which Frank had selected for the Executive Mansion during her residency and her favorite flowers, pansies and jonquils. Grown-up Esther accompanied her mother to the White House and it was a nostalgic occasion for the bride and the child of the White House.

CAROLINE LAVINIA HARRISON
(1889-October, 1892)

She Helped Start the DAR

CAROLINE LAVINIA HARRISON, whose husband called her Carrie, was a handsome white-haired grandmother and fifty-six years of age when she became First Lady for the term sandwiched in between the two Cleveland terms. Caroline was a light-hearted and talented woman as well as a sincerely religious one and she lived in a swirl of people and activities. Nothing was too difficult for her to tackle. Her verve and good works already had made her beloved throughout Indiana and particularly in her adopted hometown of Indianapolis.

She had been active in civic affairs and been president of the Women's Club. A water color artist, she also did china painting and gave free lessons in her studio. She grew orchids. She played the organ at church and also taught a very large Sunday school class for small tots whose parents attended the First Presbyterian Church. Her class was not so famous as the Men's Bible Class taught by her husband, the grandson of a former President, but she was personally more popular than the diminutive and rotund man to whom she was married. Benjamin Harrison rarely laughed at all and Carrie had a smile for everyone.

The two had met sedately in Oxford, Ohio, where her father, Dr. John Witherspoon Scott, headed the Oxford Female Seminary and where young Ben was an honor student with a reputation for oratory at nearby Miami University. Father Harry Joseph Sievers, the biographer of Harrison, wrote of the difference in their temperaments. Ben could charm a crowd with his melodious voice but on a face-to-face basis had no personality whatever. Carrie was charming and lovable on all counts, and was the good mixer of the pair.

She taught and helped out at her father's Seminary while Ben finished his legal training. But he became so worried that all the work she had got herself involved in would ruin her health that they married before he was admitted to the bar. They lived on love—and very little more. When he decided that Indianapolis offered better opportunities for advancement than Ohio did, they piled all their belongings into one big box and moved there.

144

The Harrison name had great publicity value for a rising young lawyer in Indiana, where William Henry Harrison, Benjamin's grandfather, had cleared out the Indians and had been territorial governor before becoming the nation's ninth President. Carrie, who identified herself with church and civic work right away, was an asset, too. The couple prospered and soon were the parents of two bright children, Russell and Mary.

Russell was six and Mary four years of age when their father became a second lieutenant and went off to the Civil War with the Indiana Volunteers after first making a trip back to Ohio to say goodby to his aged grandmother, Anna Symmes Harrison, who had been First Lady for a month in 1841.

Lieutenant Harrison's war letters to his wife reveal a warm and tender side to his nature which the public would never see, and he immediately began to fret that she was not writing him often enough nor telling him all that she wished to know. He picked rosebuds and southern jasmine to drop into letters to her.

"Your daily domestic life I feel to be part of my life," he wrote her, "and I love every little event of it to feed my love of home upon." Another time he wrote: "I know that you love me, Carrie, with more devotion than most women are capable of and I, in so far as my heart or person are worth your acceptance, have given them to you." He also promised her that once the war was over he would spend more time with her and no longer be a slave to his profession. Nevertheless, he did well as a soldier and came home a brevet brigadier general.

Like nearly all the Harrisons he had a yen for politics, but he was unsuccessful when he ran for Governor of Indiana. It was not until 1881 that he won a six-year term in the United States Senate from that state. Carrie loved living in Washington and she had great curiosity about the city. She helped in hospitals, was active at church, and informed herself about the processes of government. When she became First Lady in 1889 after helping run her husband's campaign from the front porch of their Indianapolis home she already knew a great deal about the Executive Mansion and national political personalities.

She ran a four-generation White House. Dr. Scott, her father, lived with them as did their own two children, Russell and Mary, and three grandchildren. Mary had married James Robert McKee and had two small children, a namesake daughter and a toddler son, Benjamin, who became known throughout the country as "Baby McKee." Russell and his wife had a young daughter, Marthena. In addition, the

First Lady made room for her niece, widowed Mary Scott Dimmick, who would be her secretary, and she always needed spare beds for visitors and other relatives.

Carrie had quite a problem fitting her family into the nation's most famous home. The President's office staff in those days had its working quarters in the White House, and as the staff grew during succeeding administrations, First Families were forced into smaller and smaller space. Carrie determined to do something about it. She called in architects, who were soon at work on three separate plans for a new White House.

Her plans created a sensation. One plan was for a separate home for the President and his family to be located on Sixteenth Street, leaving the original structure for entertaining and offices. Another was for the addition of office wings to the main structure. (This idea was adopted in much modified form some years later.) The third plan called for going the whole way and building for all time by adding tall wings on both sides of the White House and then extending them on around the White House acreage. There would be an inner court with decorative fountains. Carrie expressed no personal preference. She told the press she was thinking only of the comfort of those who would come later.

It seemed for a while that Congress would authorize some part of her building program but in the end it was suggested that the First Lady accept $35,000 and give the old structure a thorough going over. And this was what she did.

Bess Furman in *White House Profile* entertainingly tells what happened as Caroline, unwilling to settle for less than a good job, found as many as five layers of old floors under parts of the structure and learned that one of her toughest chores would be to clean out the insects and rodents. It all made interesting, if grubby, news.

During her renovation the First Lady found some old china closets boarded over and, having already stumbled onto scattered china pieces from previous administrations, she thought it would be a fine idea to have representative pieces from all administrations. So she started the White House china collection which would be completed eighty years later by Mamie Eisenhower. She herself designed the china bought by the Harrison administration and thus added another unique flavor to the collection.

Not a woman to be content with collecting just one thing, she also started an orchid collection and spent part of her appropriated funds adding an orchid house to the White House conservatories, which were then in their heyday. She was wild about flowers of all kinds, but it was the orchid that she loved best and painted most frequently.

She had had her inaugural dress designed to feature the Indiana bur oak-leaf in its brocade, and her daughter Mary's dress featured a goldenrod design. To decorate the White House at party time, Carrie regularly used about five thousand plants including up to two thousand azaleas and eight hundred carnations. Hothouse plants were high style, and the more the merrier.

A new group, Daughters of the American Revolution, was forming in Washington. Through it the womenfolk hoped to participate in something as elegant and exclusive as the men seemed to have in their much envied Sons of the American Revolution. The First Lady, asked to join, dutifully worked up her credentials, sent them over by her niece, Mary Dimmick, and was certified for membership. Then she was asked, as a boost to women in their new found place in the sun, if she would be the first President-General of the organization. Her White House schedule was heavy but she consented when she was assured that her duties would be nominal.

Caroline was one of the busiest persons ever to live in the White House as she entertained for relatives, friends, and dignitaries and carried on her own projects, but her three grandchildren received more headlines than she did. They were cute as buttons and provided a field day for photography, which was beginning to be very much in vogue. Marthena, the toddler daughter of Russell, got the White House quarantined when she had scarlet fever. Mary's little daughter looked ever so angelic in the pictures, but it was "Baby McKee," her mischievous son, who stole the scene. "Baby McKee" was rarely out of the papers.

During the summer of 1892, when Harrison sought reelection, although Secretary Blaine openly wanted the spot, the First Lady became seriously ill of fast-spreading cancer and in October she died in the White House—the second First Lady to die there. Her funeral was held in the East Parlor and before the year ended another funeral would be held for her father, who also died in the White House. In November the President lost the election to Cleveland.

No White House reception was held on the next New Year's Day, but Mary McKee in late January resumed official entertaining in the place of her mother and continued as hostess until inaugural time, which was then held in March following the November election. When moving time came, the Harrisons were as happy to be leaving the White House as the Clevelands were to be moving back in.

A few years later the Ex-President married his wife's niece, Mary Dimmick, who had been her aunt's secretary, and fathered another daughter. The DAR, meantime, presented a large portrait of their first President-General to the White House collection, and its members have never relinquished the wearing of orchids, a custom started by Carrie.

IDA SAXTON McKINLEY (1897-September, 1901)

A Burden to Her Husband?

In her diary for September 6, 1901, First Lady Ida Saxton McKinley scribbled that she "Went to Niagara Falls this morning. My Dearest was receiving in a public hall on our return, when he was shot by a . . ." She failed to finish the sentence. Whether she was puzzled by what to call the assassin who had shot her husband or whether her strength gave out is not clear. She had been an incurable invalid for twenty-eight years and so it could have been the latter. When the President was mortally wounded that afternoon he had whispered to his secretary, Bruce Cortelyou: "My wife . . . Be careful, Cortelyou, how you tell her. . . . Oh, be careful."

William McKinley was a saint among husbands in that he lavished constant attention on his wife. If he had not been so attentive to her but had spent more time at exercise and recreation in the open air, doctors and others thought, he might have survived the wound. Because of his wife's condition, he slept in stuffy rooms, rode in closed carriages, was on twenty-four-hour nursing alert, and engaged in no pasttime more strenuous than a game of euchre with her and her friends.

On the morning of the day the President was shot, the McKinleys had made a side trip to Niagara Falls. The sun became too hot for Mrs. McKinley and the President personally saw her settled in hotel rooms put at the disposal of the Presidential party. Returning to Buffalo, Mrs. McKinley was to have gone to the Pan-American Exposition to receive with the President, but her doctor advised against it. At the station the President put her in a carriage that would take her to the home of friends where they were staying. He handed in her smelling salts and banteringly said: "Good afternoon, Mrs. McKinley. I hope you enjoy your ride. Goodbye."

Mrs. McKinley had been well for fewer than three years of their married life. An illness diagnosed as phlebitis left her a cripple who could not stand nor walk for long without difficulty, and after the deaths of her mother and her two children in rapid succession she became subject to seizures of epilepsy. Her epilepsy was of the petit mal type and her seizures, marked by sudden rigidity and loss of memory, usually came without warning and were over within a few minutes. At first her attacks were accompanied by violent hysteria but through the years the violence subsided.

If McKinley ever for a moment resented the years which he gave to Ida's illness there was no indication of it. Others resented it for him at times, but the general public loved his devotion to his wife and he felt lost when she was not nearby. She was visiting in New York the night he signed documents that took the country into the Spanish-American War, and he was so lonely that he asked Webb Hayes, son of the former President, to sleep in her twin brass bed.

Because of his wife's illness, President McKinley gave more stag dinners than usual. Also there was always the chance that the First Lady could not come at the last minute to official events at which both were to be present. Usually someone was handy to fill in, and Jennie Hobart, wife of the Vice President, often was a godsend in this respect. Ida McKinley, who never wanted to be left out, did go to more state dinners than she skipped, however.

The only change made in protocol in her behalf was that she sat beside the President rather than across the table. At the first dinner she was separated from him and he was miserable, fearing that she might have a seizure. "Could it possibly offend anyone," he asked his protocol officer, "for me to have my wife sit beside me?" This was arranged.

The First Lady's maid and often the doctor, too, were nearby during State dinners in case she needed to be removed from the table, but usually she could make it through the whole evening. At receptions she was usually taken to her room at the end of an hour. She entered the receptions on the arm of her husband, who knew just how to support her steps, and sat in a blue velvet chair as the line of guests passed by. The chair was cushioned to prevent her falling, should a seizure come. She held a bouquet in her hands to ward off handshakes. Occasionally a guest would extend a hand unknowingly and Jennie Hobart would say, "Won't you shake hands with me instead?" Mrs. Hobart gave unstinted hours of companionship and aid to Mrs. McKinley.

Ida McKinley's photographs during her White House years show that she retained much of the piquant beauty that had made her a belle during her girlhood in Canton, Ohio. Several of the photographs were made in the upstairs rooms of the White House and are period pieces showing turn-of-the-century decorating touches such as fringed covers for the heavily loaded mantels, ribbon-entwined horseshoes on the wall, conch shells on center tables, and wildly gaudy wallpaper and lamps. Her favorite spot to be pictured, however, was amid the plants and flowers of the conservatories. Her special bloom was the rose and the President's was the pink carnation which he always wore in his lapel.

Ida McKinley never lacked for company. Her sister, Pina Barber, stayed with her frequently, and her niece, Mary Barber, was nearly always there. McKinley nieces came often. She was particularly fond of children. Mothers often brought their youngsters calling and even to grown-up receptions to please the First Lady.

Her principal hobby—or timekiller—was crocheting bedroom slippers. Through the years she gave away thousands of pairs, many of them to orphanages. She also puttered with the cleaning of jewelry and liked to keep the Cabinet members' watch chains shining. Her husband usually gave her diamonds for birthdays and Christmases and she kept the settings spotless. For the White House Christmas which was to be their last she said she wanted nothing expensive, and the President was at a loss as to what to give her. He finally decided on a frame for a picture of Katie, their daughter who died before she was four. It had been a quarter of a century ago but Katie remained fresh in their thoughts and an oil painting of her was always on the bedroom wall. The other baby, Ida, had lived only a few months but she was remembered, too.

Despite her invalidism the First Lady dearly loved to travel, and her husband rarely made a trip without her. By preference they stayed in the homes of friends and acquaintances rather than in hotels. This was understandable because after her illness most of their private life was spent in hotels and a home was a treat. Thus they became the nation's greatest house guests, visiting not only Mark Hanna, who supported the Presidency of McKinley, but many others. McKinley died in the home of John G. Milburn, where they were staying while in Buffalo. Earlier, in May of that year, the First Lady was near death in the home of H. T. Scott in San Francisco.

The California trip, on which they took along forty-three officials and friends, was to have been part of a gala swing around the country after his reelection. To the Northwest and then on around to Buffalo by special train was the idea. But Ida developed a blood infection from a felon on her finger and as the train made its way up the coast toward San Francisco, doctors operated but despaired of her life. The President broke his lifelong rule of not traveling on Sunday and had the train rushed on to San Francisco so that she might get additional medical treatment. They went to the Scott home, and crowds assembled outside expecting momentary news of her death. But she rallied and the whole party hurried back to Washington.

Then, for the lengthy recuperation, her husband that summer took her to Canton, Ohio, on a trip of nostalgia—to live for almost three months in the home which Ida's father, James Saxton, had given them when they first married. They had sold it, possibly to help pay Ida's medical bills, when McKinley first came to Congress in 1877, but while he was President he bought it back for $14,500.

When in 1867, shortly after his Civil War service as a major, McKinley went to Canton to establish himself in law, Ida Saxton and her sister were traveling in Europe with a group of school girls under the chaperonage of a hometown teacher. Their father was the town's leading banker and Ida was an acknowledged leader of the younger social set. She had languorous blue eyes and frequently won prizes in amateur theatricals which included acting, singing and dancing for charity and cultural events.

When Ida came home from Europe her father put her to work in his bank, on the ground that young women should know how to support themselves. Major William McKinley was a handsome new banking customer and the new cashier could hardly wait to meet him personally. He taught a Sunday School class in the Methodist Church and Ida taught one in the Presbyterian Church. After services each Sunday they met halfway and chatted in full view of the townfolk. She thought that he never would propose and he was fearful that she would turn him down. Everyone else in town, however, knew that the banker's pretty daughter had set her heart on the Major. Finally he rented a rig, took her out riding, and popped the question.

They were married in the Presbyterian Church in January, 1871. Ida was ravishingly beautiful in her white attire with bridesmaids in blue and "corn," a light yellow fashionable in those days. Katie was born on the next Christmas Day and the McKinleys were supremely happy. The second baby girl was born fifteen months later, shortly after Ida's mother had died and Ida had become a victim of phlebitis. Little Ida lived only five months. Katie, a beautiful and apparently sturdy child, died when she was three and a half years old, and there was no doubt that twenty-eight-year-old Ida McKinley had become an epileptic as well as a cripple who needed a wheelchair. Epilepsy, an embarrassing disease in those days, was neither admitted by the family nor mentioned. Some of her sister's seven children grew up not knowing that Aunt Ida suffered from it.

McKinley took Ida to Washington with him when he became a Congressman in 1877, and they lived at Ebbitt House.

He set up his office across the hall from their living suite and spent as much time there as he could, ready to answer her calls at any time. President and Mrs. Hayes were attentive to the Ohio couple and Ida attended several White House parties and luncheons. Young Fanny Hayes thought it quite a lark to visit Mrs. McKinley in the Ebbitt.

During the year in which they rented and lived in their former Canton home for the Presidential campaign, the McKinleys celebrated their twenty-fifth wedding anniversary with as much aplomb as though Ida had not been an invalid for all but two of those years. She wore her bridal gown, and with "the Major" stood in a bay window, her arm in his, to receive their guests. An eight-piece orchestra played. They gave several other large parties that year, too. All thought of a stand-in hostess for the White House, should he be elected, was dismissed—or more likely never considered.

Her gown for the inaugural ball supposedly was one of the nation's best kept secrets. She bought it at Marshall Field's in Chicago. The husband of a cousin was an executive there, and the store's head designer worked with Ida on her White House wardrobe at the home of this cousin. A New York newspaper reported that the ball gown would be of grayish blue satin, but it was of heavy white satin elaborately embroidered in pearls from waist to hem. It was made with long sleeves, a net vestee with a high tight collar edged in a frill of lace, and the skirt had a ruffled train. With it the First Lady wore beaded satin boots and carried a gauze fan with pearls on the ribs. At her waistline she had a bunch of violets. She attempted a promenade around the floor of the big old Pension Building, but the inaugural crowds were too much for her. She collapsed, and the dress today still shows the black spots received when she fell to the floor.

The White House ran itself during the McKinley administration, according to Ike Hoover, the chief usher. But aides were capable, and the President was generous with food and money. The McKinleys had excellent musicals—a favorite form of relaxation with both of them—and the President reinstituted the Sunday evening hymnfests which he had enjoyed so much when Lucy Hayes was First Lady. He sang "Lead Kindly Light" in his renowned voice.

Ida Saxton McKinley, the invalid, outlived her husband by almost six years.

EDITH CAROW ROOSEVELT
(September, 1901-09)

Calm Center for "the Wildest Scramble in History"

As the new First Lady, Edith Carow Roosevelt, surveyed the black-draped White House during the funeral services for slain President McKinley in September of 1901 she was unusually depressed. It was not only the gloom of her surroundings that depressed her, but also thoughts of what the constraint and confinement of living in such a place and occupying such a demanding office as the Presidency might do to her always active husband, Theodore Roosevelt.

Furthermore she could not shake her fear that he might be the next one marked for an assassin's bullet. Three Presidents had been killed in office within less than forty years and Edith Roosevelt, generally the most cheerful of women, could not help dreading her new assignment.

She was forty years of age at the time she attended the funeral—a willowy and most attractive woman, wearing a black dress for which she hurriedly had paid $135 as she came through New York City. She also bought a black hat and a heavy black veil for herself and a black armband for her fourteen-year-old son, Ted, who accompanied her. The new President, who at the age of forty-two was the youngest Chief Executive as of that date, had left them and the remainder of his family at a camping site in the Adirondacks when he had rushed to be sworn in as President after the death of McKinley.

Edie, as her husband and friends called this First Lady, and Ted journeyed to Washington alone and went to the home of the President's sister, Mrs. William Sheffield Cowles, the former Anna Roosevelt, who was known to her relatives as "Bamie" and "Auntie Bye" and who also would figure in the story of a later First Lady.

The charming Bamie accompanied Edie to call on Ida McKinley on the afternoon of the funeral and to view the upstairs rooms of the White House. Edie's gloom further deepened amid the heavy and old fashioned surroundings and she wondered how, after the ten bedrooms of Sagamore Hill, she could fit her six rambunctious children into the space available. As soon as her husband left with the funeral train for

154

Canton, Ohio, she thought of the one thing that could possibly lift her spirits: her children. She wired Sagamore Hill: "Send down as many of the children as possible." Then she quickly countermanded the order and boarded the train to go and fetch her family herself.

The latter action was more in line with her character, and traveling with children was one of her specialties. Edie always could make order out of chaos, and create an atmosphere of unruffled calm and rightness just by being present. And what a family she had to corral and bring back to Washington! Five of the six Roosevelt children were her own. They ranged in age from Ted's fourteen years down to Quentin's three. In between were: Kermit, almost twelve; Ethel, ten, and Archie, seven. And then there was a beautiful step-daughter, Alice, who was seventeen.

Each of the six was as robustly outgoing and as individual as his father. Teddy Roosevelt had led his Rough Riders dashing up San Juan Hill and he demanded his own sort of strenuous life from all of his offspring just as he would demand it also of the country. Soon after the new President was in office, he led some military stalwarts and his family on an arduous jaunt through Washington's Rock Creek park. Noting some shortness of breath among the military, he immediately ordered a steady diet of calisthenics for the Army, Navy, and Marines.

Edith Roosevelt was back in Washington with her assorted young Roosevelts and ready to move into the White House ten days after the McKinley funeral. Ike Hoover, the head usher, said that the advent of the Roosevelts marked "the wildest scramble in history."

Each child was permitted to bring as much of his personal menagerie as he could manage in cages and in pockets. Freight vans filled in the gaps with loads of tricycles, bicycles, roller skates, stilts, ponies, boxing gloves, guns, books, costumes, and whathaveyou. Not that the young army needed so many props. Ethel and Kermit saw right away that climbing the lampposts along Pennsylvania Avenue to undo the work of the lamplighter as soon as he had finished it could be every bit as much fun as they had enjoyed at Sagamore Hill, where they had forty acres in which to keep their muscles and brains in trim.

The energetic First Lady, who could ride horses, row a boat, or climb a bluff with the best of them, pulled and hauled and rearranged White House furniture, put up new curtains, cleaned dark mahogany recesses, relegated horsehair sofas and heavy draperies to the attic, and dispelled the gloom by letting in fresh air and sunshine. She was so exhausted from the hard job and so pleased at finding places to put enough beds for everybody that she fell into her own bed and slept for the better part of two days.

Counting pennies was another of this First Lady's specialties. She was orderly by nature and also believed in knowing the cost. Money was a rather vulgar topic in those days to families like the Roosevelts, who always had had money and assumed that they always would have. But Teddy Roosevelt, as only Edie seemed to realize, was not really rich. His father had left him $125,000 but a third of this had "gone glimmering" in Western land investments. Sagamore Hill was a costly operation to maintain—always filled, as it was, with family and guests—and Edie's husband would have been thoroughly ashamed of himself if he had looked at the salary of public service jobs before deciding to take them.

His first such job, as Civil Service Commissioner in 1889, paid a modest $3,500, and necessitated moving his family to Washington. Edie was the one who knew that milk in Washington cost them $35 a month, and that one year their doctor's bill was above $500. Her family's trek, with nursemaids and servants, back and forth to Sagamore Hill in the summers was costly. When Roosevelt became President of the New York Police Board in 1895, Edie wrote her sister that if they had had to stay longer in Washington, "Theodore and I will not have two pennies to put together." Her sister would understand. Their father, Charles Carow, had suffered financial reverses which forced their widowed mother to take the two girls to live in Europe so that their small inheritances would stretch farther. Going abroad to live was a fashionable thing to do in those days, but Edie knew that the basis of their move was financial difficulty, and she was delighted when Theodore came to London to marry her in December of 1886.

Thus not only did Edie welcome the Presidential salary of $50,000, but she also appreciated it that the government shared the costs of White House entertaining and provided part of the household staff. She and the President were a hundred percent agreed that they wanted the entertaining of his years in office to be topnotch, and for the first time a social secretary, Belle Hagner, was added to the White House staff to make social events move more smoothly. A complete record of all protocol problems and decisions was kept as a possible guide for other First Families who might be interested in doing everything correctly.

It went without saying in those days that the socialite who married a chorus girl could say goodbye to his White House invitations, but the Teddy Roosevelts demanded the same sort of impeccable behavior from everybody, including the diplomats. One diplomat, or so it always was said, was embarked on an extramarital venture and received a White House note saying that the affair must be stopped or his invitations would be. Without hesitancy, the legend is, he ended the affair. A Roosevelt invitation meant this much. There was a conspicuous Russian Grand Duke who came visiting one summer when the Roosevelts were at Sagamore Hill. The Russian Ambassador wanted to bring him to lunch. Edie went off to spend the day with an aunt and let the President entertain the Russians alone rather than be hostess to a roué, however noble.

By the end of her first season in the White House, the First Lady knew that she would be the recipient of a windfall for which other First Ladies had longed for more than a quarter century. She would get a completely modernized and expanded White House. The best part of the expansion would be the office building added for the President's staff. She would get staff offices and Cabinet meetings off the bedroom floor and be the first wife of a President to have the so-called living quarters just for her family.

Congress rushed the appropriation of almost a half million dollars for the long-deferred project after an incident which Washingtonians found most amusing. Prince Henry of Prussia was in town and President Teddy invited him to go horseback riding. The Prince arrived with a valet who was carrying his riding togs. But not a single unoccupied spot could be found in which the Prince could change his trousers. The President asked the Prince to return to the German Embassy to make the change and come back.

In making the architectural changes in the White House it was decided to follow the plans of Thomas Jefferson and put low colonnaded wings at either end of the mansion, adding the office building at the end of the West Wing and using the East Wing for a new entranceway for tourists and for guests at large receptions. The wings meant that the sprawling greenhouses must go. These were dismantled and moved, along with their plants, to other parts of town.

The biggest change on the main floor was a doubling of the seating capacity in the dining room. This was accomplished by moving the family stairs down which the Roosevelt children had sailed on large cookie tins filched from the busy kitchen. Then the dining room was extended north and Edie could have up to a hundred guests without putting some of them in the corridor. The President ordered a special mantel for this room. The heads of American bison were to be carved into the design, but when the mantel arrived it was carved with more stylish lion heads. One of Roosevelt's last acts before leaving office was to have those lion heads recarved into bison.

The big East Parlor was restored to its more chaste look of

earlier days. When the Roosevelts moved into the White House they had described the decor of this room as "late General Grant and early Pullman." Others called it "early steamboat." President Grant in his re-do had added heavy beams and columns and President Arthur then had fancied it all up with painted ceilings. Brickwork of the four large mantels extended more than two feet into the room. This brickwork was cut back flush with the walls and the simplicity of an early day was returned in the removal of beams and columns.

The big trouble with this whole building project was that it was rushed too rapidly, as President Harry S. Truman would learn a half century later when bedroom floors began to give way. President Teddy Roosevelt had ordered, "Begin in June and finish by mid-November." During much of this time the First Family was at Sagamore Hill and the White House staff operated temporarily in a rented house on Lafayette Square.

Edith Roosevelt's quiet good taste had a great deal to do with the elegance as well as the convenience of the finished product. She was in constant touch with the architects about locations of bathrooms, storage space, wallpaper and paint colors. And she stretched her refurnishing budget with her usual economy. She salvaged good parts of fine old materials for the reupholstery of chairs and small sofas.

Edith Roosevelt was much quieter and more reserved than other members of her family. When they grew too much for her she retired briefly to her own sitting room with a book or needlework, just as at Sagamore Hill she had a habit of disappearing to a favorite bower with mending, while trying to get her smiling composure back. Despite the muddy boots and constant comings and goings, the White House during her tenure always retained a well-regulated order and when she spoke everybody from the President on down obeyed instantly, with the possible exception of Stepdaughter Alice.

This beautiful hoyden lived in two worlds: the youthful one of her adored stepbrothers and the grownup one in which a girl as sophisticated as Alice did not mind a cigarette now and then. Alice would stash her green snake named Emily Spinach and her blue macaw, Eli Yale, under the family stairs leading to the conservatory and slide down the stairs with the younger children. She and a girl friend would turn heads by motoring along the streets at the dashingly dangerous speed of twenty-five miles an hour. Alice was a sensation. The public loved her and so did the First Lady. No child of a President ever received more headlines, nor more approving ones. She amused and delighted the nation, but she was hard to handle. She truly loved Edie, the only mother she ever knew, and she resented it when Edie was tagged as her step-mother. But the First Lady had learned that to convince Alice against her will was to leave her with the same opinion still.

Edie and Teddy Roosevelt wanted Alice to go away to school, but Alice did not like the idea and threatened some-how to get herself put in jail so as to make the family sorry. Edie never for a moment doubted Alice would do just that if forced to do as her parents wished. Just as McKinley was an understanding saint among Presidential husbands, Edie was the saint among First Lady stepmothers, of whom there have not been many. The President also had his problems with Alice. When a good friend of his, Owen Wister, the writer, apparently shocked by some of the Alice headlines, once asked Roosevelt why he did not "do something" about Alice, the President replied that he could be President *or* manage Alice but that nobody could handle two such jobs at one and the same time.

Alice made her debut in the White House during the first season the Roosevelts were there, and crowds of youth flocked in from all over the Eastern seaboard. Everybody except Alice thought that it was the greatest party ever given. But Alice in her book, *The Crowded Hours,* said that she was mortified at the crush in the East Parlor, wanted a cotillion rather than a dance, and was chagrinned that her parents served punch rather than champagne. She was too hard on herself in her book. Her debut photographs show a breathtakingly lovely young girl who was trying her best to look bored.

But Alice did require almost constant attention, and there were five other children with whom the First Lady needed to share her energy. At times she must have worried lest she neglect them in the turmoil of Alice, who wrote that her chief characteristic at the time was "total irresponsibility." Ike Hoover, the White House usher, recorded that for two years after her debut and until her marriage, Alice was en-tertained at a party in her honor almost every night. She spent much time on trains commuting to New York and Boston. Her doting maternal grandparents lived in the latter city.

With her independent income from her own mother's side of the family—the Lees—Alice never in those years gave a thought to the idea that she was over-privileged. Her Grand-mother Lee of Boston, when her granddaughter became so attached to Teddy's second family, became a sort of stand-in grandmother for the other five Roosevelts. Edie's mother was living in Europe and Teddy's had died at almost the same minute as his first wife, Alice Hathaway Lee, following Alice's birth.

Shortly after the architectural restoration of the White

House, Roosevelt's genial Secretary of War, William Howard Taft, escorted a group of Congressmen, including Nicholas Longworth of Ohio, on a trip to the Orient and the Philippines. Alice went along, and before the party was at sea a week she was rumored engaged to the urbane Longworth, whose sister had married into the family of Lafayette, the French hero. Longworth was much older than Alice, but he played the violin beautifully and was in all respects as sophisticated as she. Alice had been rumored engaged to almost every eligible man in this country or abroad but even the easy-going Taft could not tell whether this time it was true.

When the glamorous group returned to Washington, the Ohio papers still pestered their capital correspondents to know whether Nick, one of their very favorite sons, was engaged to the President's daughter. One Cincinnati editor in desperation wired: "She was out driving with him today without a chaperone. If not engaged, she should be!" And almost immediately the White House confirmed it.

It was in keeping with Alice's individualistic viewpoint that she had no bridesmaids. Her father gave her away, and that was her side of the bridal party. Longworth, however, had six groomsmen. The gifts poured in from around the world. Not all were practical or feasible, Alice wrote, and not worth nearly so much as the newspapers said. Her favorite and most used among them was a fabulous pearl necklace sent by the Republic of Cuba to honor the daughter of the hero of San Juan Hill who had whooped it up for Cuba's independence and glory. When Alice donned her beige suit to start off on the honeymoon, as she later wrote, "Mother was dropping from fatigue and I knew what a relief it was to her to have the wedding over at last and me off."

Alice married on February 17, 1906, but she came back to the White House almost every afternoon for tea as long as her parents were there, and she frankly admitted that she never could visualize anyone except her father as President.

The First Lady, who had been sure of only the remainder of McKinley's term when she moved into the White House, thoroughly enjoyed the inaugural ball when her husband was elected for a full term in his own right. She bought a lovely blue dress with a silver feather design brocaded into it for this event and Alice, a year before her marriage, wore a stunning gown of gold gauze made with a white satin top and a train sprinkled with red roses. Alice, naturally, sat in the front of the box and waved to everybody in sight just as, she wrote, she had done four years earlier at the McKinley inauguration, not knowing that she should not sit in front of Mrs. McKinley. She assumed that her father was the be-all of all existence, and that of course everybody else thought so too.

And many did, of course, including Edie and the other five Roosevelt children, who assuredly were not behaving like little mice while Alice was having her escapades. When Archie had the measles his brothers smuggled his calico pony up to his bedroom on the elevator. Quentin ran the tongue of his red wagon through the large portrait of former First Lady Lucy Webb Hayes, and the scars are still there. One night the President yanked Quentin out of bed to remove spitballs one by one from the portrait of Andrew Jackson. Pillow fights, the President as often as not starting them, were commonplace in this lively household. Frequently the First Lady had trouble getting her husband downstairs to dinner without a mussed shirt front because he liked to stop and roughhouse with his sons on his way to receive guests.

In due course the children, except for Baby Quentin, went away to school. The youngest upset his mother by insisting he wanted to go, too, until he found that he would have her undivided attention at home. Then he was blissfully happy playing with his White House gang which included Charlie Taft, son of the next President.

The other girl, Ethel, as a youngster was truly the tomboy daughter of her Rough Rider dad. She just would not put up with the little girls who came a-visiting, bedecked with sashes and hair ribbons. Once she sent a little friend home in tears to change into "decent clothes" before she would deign to show her the greatest treat of all: the White House stables. But Ethel wanted to stay near her mother and she was sent to boarding school in Washington. She made her debut in the White House, too, and it was a very elaborate affair, but it didn't draw so many headlines as Alice's did.

Edith Carow and the future President grew up in the same New York neighborhood. The Carow family lived very near Teddy's family on Union Square and it soon was assumed that if "Thee," as he was called, took anyone to a youthful affair, it would be Edie. She was the girl he took rowing in the roughest waters, and the one to whom he could talk about animals, his travels, and books. All the Carows read voraciously. Edie's father owned a share in the old New York Society Library, and by actual count the family at one time drew out a total of six hundred and forty-eight books in a space of twenty-eight weeks.

Edie always was a most reserved young lady, however, and at Miss Comstock's fashionable private school on West Fortieth Street her classmates never could make her out. "She was pretty," they admitted, "and wore expensive clothes well," but she usually was not interested in school-girl chatter.

161

One of her schoolmates remarked one day: "Girls, I believe you could live in the same house with Edith for fifty years and never really know her."

She and "Thee" had a misunderstanding before he went away to college. In his third year at Harvard he fell madly in love with a charming and outgoing Boston girl, Alice Hathaway Lee, and on his twenty-second birthday they were married. Edie—the close-mouthed old love—was in the audience, indicating in no way that this meant anything to her. Three years later Alice died giving birth to her namesake daughter. And on the same day and in the same New York brownstone house the future President's mother also died. Teddy left his infant daughter with his sister, Bamie, and rushed out to his ranch in the Dakotas to ease his double sorrow. When he came home the one person he never wanted to see was his childhood friend, Edith Carow. One day the signals went wrong, and they ran into each other in Bamie's house. They never lost touch again, although Edie's mother took her and her sister, Emily, abroad to live.

But before she left she met her three-year-old future stepdaughter, Alice, who came down the stairs at Bamie's house carrying an armful of pink roses for the girl she was later to describe as "Mother—the only one I ever knew or wanted." Theodore Roosevelt went to London in 1886 to marry Edith, and it would be difficult to imagine a marriage more filled with love or meaning.

She was not his first wife but insofar as the record indicates, she loved him always. And she was Edie, who made life happy for all around her. As Ex-President, Roosevelt wrote his son, Kermit, years later: "Home, wife, children—they are what really count in life. I have heartily enjoyed many things: the Presidency, my success as a soldier, a writer, a big game hunter and explorer; but all of them put together are not for one moment to be weighed in the balance when compared with the joy I have known with your mother and all of you. . . ."

Lovely and devoted Edie survived her husband almost thirty years. By the time of her death in 1948 three of her four sons had died in two World Wars and her husband's timid little niece, Eleanor Roosevelt, had been a great First Lady—as had Edith Carow Roosevelt.

HELEN HERRON TAFT (1909-1913)

The Politician in Her Family?

THE William Howard Tafts began their tenure of the White House on the evening before their inauguration rather than after the formal oath of office ceremony the next day as did previous First Families.

It was the idea of outgoing President Theodore Roosevelt, who was so elated over the victory of his personally picked successor in the November elections of 1908 that he immediately extended an invitation to the Tafts to dine with him and spend the night of March 3, 1909, under the White House roof. In the four months between the election and the inaugural both families probably regretted the quick offer of hospitality, for the atmosphere of the famous night showed definite strain.

Helen Herron Taft, the incoming First Lady, felt that neither she nor the incumbent First Lady, Edith Roosevelt— if consulted about it—would have planned to be together on a night with so much personal meaning in it for both of them.

"Now there is always bound to be a sadness about the end of an administration, no matter how voluntarily the retiring President may leave office, no matter how welcome the new President and his family may be," Mrs. Taft wrote in her *Recollections of Full Years*. She said that Edith Roosevelt was depressed and that the table conversation never got off the ground. "The President and Mr. Taft, seconded by other guests, did their best with stories and conversation, made as light as possible, to lighten the occasion, but their efforts were not entirely successful."

Some of the strain no doubt was due to the fact that the long and warm friendship between Teddy and his jovial Secretary of War already seemed headed for the ash heap. Teddy was going off on a long hunting trip to Africa doubting that Taft, after all, would be the type of President he wanted him to be.

Soon after dinner the President-elect went off to attend a smoker being given him at the Willard Hotel by his former classmates at Yale. Helen Taft, thinking of her heavy schedule for the next day, excused herself to get what she hoped would be a long night of sleep. The First Lady held her hand and wished her a sweet repose but, as it turned out, the about-to-be First Lady slept scarcely a wink. She later admitted that when she went to bed her mind never was more wide awake and she began to think of every detail which possibly could or just might go sour on the morrow.

Would her dress for the inaugural ball really arrive by special messenger from New York as promised? The heavy white satin for the ball gown had been sent all the way to Tokyo to be embroidered in a goldenrod pattern, outlined in silver thread and besparkled with crystal beads. The material was back in this country, but the dressmakers surely had taken their time making it up into a revival of the Empire style which she wanted. Another worry was whether the cold and stormy weather would lift and the sun shine as the weatherman promised.

When she recalled that Captain Archibald Butt, who had been a perfectionist Master of Ceremonies for the Roosevelts, was staying on with the Tafts and would be in complete charge of her inaugural day, she became more like herself: level-headed and businesslike. Butt already had come up with one precedent-breaker for her and she was much pleased with it.

It was the custom at the time for the outgoing and incoming Presidents to ride together from the White House to Capitol Hill for the inaugural ceremony and then return together to the White House before they took leave of each other. President Roosevelt had announced long before the event that he would not return to the White House but would go directly to the train.

Archie Butt suggested that the seat thus vacated belonged rightly to the First Lady. It had been a struggle because nearly everyone on the inaugural committee felt that he was the one who should have it. But Archie won, and Mrs. Taft would be the first First Lady to ride back down Pennsylvania Avenue seated beside her husband! It was a small point in the affairs of men, perhaps, but it was a "right finally won for the wives and children." And Mrs. Taft, interested in all such nuances of political activity, saw it as a good omen for the new administration.

And on this happy thought, Helen Taft fell asleep in the early morning only to be awakened shortly by what she at first thought must be guns firing outside her windows. What she saw when she ventured to look belied all weather predictions. The noise was coming from ice-laden twigs and branches of trees being whirled against the White House in a storm that, far from abating, had increased in violence.

Weatherwise the Tafts would have the worst inaugural day

in history. Other First Ladies have had snowdrifts and torrents of rain, but Helen Taft had a freezing blizzard which tied up transportation all along the Atlantic coast, left thousands of inaugural visitors stranded on trains and roads leading into Washington, and temporarily halted the sending of telegrams.

After breakfast on inaugural morning President Roosevelt said that the storm was aimed at him and would abate when he got out of town, but Taft replied, "You're wrong; it's my storm. I always said it would be a cold day when I got to be President of the United States." Instead of being held in front of the Capitol as usual, the inaugural ceremonies were moved inside to the Senate Chamber. Helen found her three children snugly encased in the Senate gallery when she arrived under Butt's auspices, and she noted that Charlie, her eleven-year-old son, had brought along a copy of *Treasure Island* to read in case his father's speech bored him. The other two, the shy and demure daughter, Helen, seventeen, and the serious college student, Robert A., nineteen, would not have considered such heresy, but Charlie was a funlover and already knew, through his close friendship with Quentin Roosevelt, Teddy's youngest son, all about running the White House elevator. But Charlie did not read *Treasure Island*. Instead he listened to his father's speech, and President Taft always considered that a mighty compliment.

The new First Lady had her ride down Pennsylvania Avenue beside the President, and for the occasion she was wearing a lovely purple satin suit, so covered over with coats that it received scant mention in the newspapers. Her hat was trimmed with gold lace and a white aigrette. Reporters described the aigrette as a tall one but she knew that it had been taller on the day before when "it collided with a lighted gas-jet" at an afternoon reception. She feared it still smelled a bit from the burning.

When Helen Taft reentered the White House, preparations had been made for the usual inaugural luncheon, scheduled at one o'clock. But there was no need wondering where the guests were. They kept straggling in until long after dark, to apologize and grab a bite. They collided with guests invited to the inaugural tea that was to start when the parade was over. The President was late getting back, as the parade had to move very slowly over the slippery streets and there were long gaps. Charlie Taft and his friend, Quentin Roosevelt, shared the same chair at the parade. Quentin, left behind in school by his parents, had cut classes to see the icy pomp and ceremony.

It was a very mixed up day, and when the final guests had gone, the five Tafts, each worn to a frazzle, were at last alone in the State dining room under the steady gaze of the mooseheads on the wall. These mooseheads naturally had been added to the decor by Teddy Roosevelt. They were very fashionable at the time and there was no thought of changing them, but they were a little disconcerting on that evening.

Mrs. Taft recalled that she and her family gazed at each other, too, with slightly lost expressions, and then nature asserted itself in the new President. "Let's go upstairs, my dears, and sit down," he suggested with emphasis on the last two words.

His wife hated to remind him of the inaugural ball which they were to open that evening, but she was delighted to find that her dress had come and was spread out, beautifully pressed, on her bed. Hers was the first dress given to the Smithsonian Institution for its collection of gowns worn by First Ladies and White House hostesses, a project to which Helen Taft gave enthusiastic support.

The First Family participated in a nice private supper at the ball, held in the old Pension Building, but the other guests, for whom an elaborate repast had been planned, had tougher luck. It was quite difficult to dance in long coats and even the ice cream was too solidly cold for enjoyable eating.

Helen Taft, more fortunate than many First Ladies, moved into the White House after it recently had been done over to her liking. Edith Roosevelt had spent weeks getting everything into apple pie order, taking inventory and cleaning, but she thoughtfully left replacement purchases of such things as household linens up to her successor. Helen, or Nellie, as her husband called her, filled in the gaps and was so charmed with what she found that she made few changes. She had an over-sized bathtub installed for her three-hundred-pound-plus husband, and she moved the Lincoln bed, replacing it with two smaller mahogany beds. Into the family living room, she moved her own Oriental pieces—and that was about all.

Daughter Helen lived in the room occupied by Alice Roosevelt and then by the latter's sister, Ethel, without it being redecorated. Helen Taft decided to keep the Edith Roosevelt pattern of china. "Perhaps nothing in the house is so expressive of the various personalities of its mistresses," she wrote, "as the dinner services which each has contributed. For my own part I was entirely satisfied with the quiet taste displayed by Mrs. Roosevelt and contented myself with filling up the different broken sets in her service to the number necessary for one hundred covers."

She made an administrative change for which later First Ladies have been grateful, however. She replaced the male steward with an overall housekeeper to be in charge of cleaning as well as of food supplies. Also she hired a Swedish cook to replace the one who had gone with the Roosevelts. Her main energies she intended to put into original ideas for parties, civic improvements in the District of Columbia, and perhaps later into politics itself. She had lived a number of years in the Orient, her husband having been the first civilian Commissioner of the Philippines after the Spanish-American War, and she liked the Far Eastern idea of entertaining out of doors. Some of her garden parties were spectaculars with Japanese lanterns hung everywhere. She and President Taft often received under a big White House tree.

It was during the Taft administration and at Helen Taft's instigation that the first of the famous cherry trees were planted around the Tidal Basin along the banks of the Potomac. When she was in Manila, she loved the luneta, a parklike place where people at the end of the day could stroll or sit listening to music. She encouraged the landscaping of a luneta with Japanese cherry trees as a background on the Potomac Drive along the river. There were concerts by the Marine Band, and she and the President went to the first and to many others. They sat in a White House automobile listening to the band. Except for the automobile, which Americans were beginning to find more exciting than strolls in the dusk, lunetas might have continued beyond the Taft administration. However, there still are waterfront concerts, and the cherry trees have grown into one of the Capital's main tourist attractions.

But Helen Taft had trouble getting the cherry trees started. The Mayor of Tokyo, hearing of her love for the flowering Japanese cherry, sent her three thousand trees. But they developed blight and had to be destroyed. The Japanese grew others for her in sterilized soil, and meanwhile all that could be obtained from commercial nurseries in this country were planted at the luneta.

But the First Lady was working too hard on too many projects and after only a short time in the White House she collapsed. Archibald Butt thought that it was from sheer exhaustion. She recovered before the administration ended and was able to supervise many things, but she said in her memoirs: "I was permitted fully to enjoy only about the first two and a half months of my sojourn in the White House." In May of that first year she suffered a paralysis stroke while aboard the White House yacht giving an afternoon party on the Potomac River. She had been to the hospital that morning to see her son, Charlie, through a tonsillectomy. She lost consciousness on the yacht, and "was practically out of society for an entire season, having for a much longer time than that to take excellent care of myself." Among muscles affected were facial ones and she had to relearn to speak clearly.

Her four sisters came in turn from Cincinnati to fill in as

White House hostesses and young Helen, although not through school, helped out. Helen was formally presented at a tea for twelve hundred guests early in December, 1909, and just before Christmas a debut dance for her was held in the East Room of the White House. The guests numbered three hundred, and the Marine Band played from a special room constructed for the event just outside tall windows opening onto a terrace.

The New Year's Day receptions still drew between six and eight thousand people, and Mrs. Taft often gave up in sheer exhaustion and left the receiving line to her husband.

She recorded that to her personally the most enjoyable event of her four years in the White House was the Tafts' silver wedding anniversary. "I thanked the happy fate that had given me a summer wedding day because I needed all outdoors for the kind of party I wanted to give. That silver was showered upon us until we were almost buried in silver was incidental; we couldn't help it; it was our twenty-fifth anniversary and we had to celebrate it." Among the silver gifts worth a fortune was a solid silver service, costing $1,700, presented by the House of Representatives: an unusual gift from Congress to a President and a compliment to both Tafts.

Between four and five thousand guests were present at the garden party the Tafts gave that night in June of 1911. Archibald Butt called it the most brilliant function ever held anywhere, and the First Lady thought that a brighter assemblage of people never before had been brought together in America.

During his administration, the Tafts spent their summer vacations at Beverly, Massachusetts, where they rented a house. It was not considered proper for them to continue to use the Murray Bay, Canada, home in which they formerly had summered. The President once set his foot on foreign soil—stepping across into Mexico on a trip to Texas—and a great to-do was made about it. A President was supposed to stay inside the country!

When the Tafts left Beverly at the end of the 1912 summer, Helen Taft packed all their silver and household linens for moving, although her husband had won the renomination for a second term. Teddy Roosevelt was running against his old friend and heading the Bull Moose Party. This did not surprise Helen, nor did she believe that either Teddy or Taft could win in the three-cornered race. The Democrats had put up the Governor of New Jersey, that professor chap and former President of Princeton, Woodrow Wilson.

Helen Herron Taft was born in Cincinnati—just as her husband was. Both were from large and well established families with backgrounds of culture and wealth enough for foreign travel. They did not meet until he was nineteen and already a legal prodigy with an outstanding scholastic record at Yale University—where he also was the largest in his class, weighing two hundred and twenty-five pounds at graduation in comparison to the class average of around one hundred fifty pounds. Helen, who had a keen mind, also had a good education and could speak the stylish language, French. In her youth her big interest was music. It later turned to politics.

Helen and some of her Cincinnati friends established a political or public affairs "salon" modeled after those run by French women of an earlier day, and Will Taft became a member. During this time Helen was teaching in private schools, not because she needed the money, but because she felt that women should work and contribute their bit to the life in which they found themselves living.

She and Taft were married in 1886 when she was twenty-five, and the next year he was made a judge at the very early age of twenty-nine. By inclination he always was a jurist and not a politician, but his talents and charming geniality were such that he was always finding himself in jobs which he basically did not want—and that would include the Presidency.

His wife preferred politics, but how much she influenced his decisions along the way still is open to question. In some quarters she won the reputation for being a "driving" woman, and it is agreed that but for her he would not have accepted the Presidency—and he did accept it from the hands of Teddy Roosevelt, who, like the Presidents of former days such as Jefferson and Jackson, could name his successor. Neither liked the choice, as it turned out, and Mrs. Taft was too ill to enjoy it much.

When Taft went to the Philippines in 1900 as civilian President of the Philippines Commission, he already had been Solicitor General of the United States under President Benjamin Harrison. President McKinley insisted on his taking the Philippines assignment and while he was out there President Roosevelt practically ordered him home to become an Associate Justice of the Supreme Court. But he begged off from the job he really wanted because he did not consider that his work in the Philippines was finished. Apparently he got trapped by his kindness, geniality, and ability, rather than by his wife's insistence that he decide for the Presidency.

At any rate he seemed to dislike the Presidency even from the beginning. He wrote that "If I were presiding in the Supreme Court of the United States as Chief Justice, I should feel entirely at home, but with the troubles of selecting a Cabinet and the difficulties in respect to the revision of the tariff, I feel just a bit like a fish out of water. However, as my wife is the politician and she will be able to meet all these issues, perhaps we can keep a stiff upper lip and overcome obstacles which just at present seem formidable." That was before his wife was stricken by paralysis. The job must have grown even less attractive after her illness.

Mrs. Taft avoided a direct discussion of the question in her autobiography. It deals largely with her experiences in the Orient during her early married years, but it does give one of the clearest explanations of how the White House operates and what it looks like that has ever been written. Her mind was analytical and her sense of humor was not that of her family, who teased her for her matter-of-factness and thought that she took things, including White House housekeeping, too seriously.

She was forty-nine when she became First Lady. Previously she had taken her three children three times around the world. She enjoyed the customs of other peoples, and sought to evaluate the different cultures of the world without condemning them. But she did not go on the trip to the Orient when her husband, then Secretary of War, chaperoned a boatload of Congressmen—and Alice Roosevelt—to the Philippines. That summer instead she took the children to England.

When Woodrow Wilson was elected she did not invite him and his wife to spend the pre-inaugural night in the White House. But she and President Taft had them to tea, and she showed Ellen Wilson the workings of the establishment. Taft already had written to Wilson in Princeton telling him how to save a bit out of the Presidential salary. Taft considered the salary, $75,000 at the time, plentiful if managed properly. He had only praise for the regular White House staff employed by the government.

And Taft did become Chief Justice of the United States in 1921, after teaching at Yale. One of their sons, Robert A. Taft, inherited his mother's deep interest in politics. He became a United States Senator and she lived long enough to hear him called "Mr. Republican" and boosted for the Presidency. She outlived her husband by thirteen years. She died in 1943 at the age of eighty-two when another Roosevelt—Franklin D.— was President.

ELLEN AXSON WILSON (1913-August 6, 1914)

"An Angel in the White House"

WHEN the Governor of New Jersey won the Democratic nomination for the Presidency in 1912, a reporter noted that neither his radiant little wife, Ellen Axson Wilson, nor any of their three daughters ever wore any jewelry. "Do you have some sort of moral prejudice against jewelry, Mrs. Wilson?" the reporter asked and then did not want to accept a smiling "No" as an adequate answer. "But why, Mrs. Wilson?" insisted the reporter. Whereupon the prospective First Lady amplified with, "No, I have no prejudice against it. We just haven't any."

She must have remembered the question, however, for shortly after the election Ellen Wilson went into New York City on a mysterious errand and that night at dinner presented each daughter with an inaugural gift. For Margaret and Jessie, aged twenty-six and twenty-five, respectively, there were necklaces of seed pearls and for Eleanor, who was twenty-three, there was a bar pin, carved, and set with small diamonds. The girls were delighted with their gifts and eager to see what mother had bought for herself, an idea which really astonished mother since that thought had simply never occurred to her. So the President-elect, Woodrow Wilson, went out next day and bought his beloved wife a diamond pendant, which cost him $132.00 and which the family thereafter always referred to laughingly as the crown jewel.

The scholarly Wilsons were not given to thinking about jewelry one way or the other, with the possible exception of the youngest daughter, Eleanor, who became the family chronicler and often deplored their lack of worldly chic. The family money through the years had gone into such things as books, college educations for the daughters, household expenses (and there were always visiting relatives), a few thrifty investments, and—as their income went up—better vacations. After father became head of Princeton University, the girls had their trips to Europe.

Except for father, who learned that he liked politics, the transition from campus life was quite painful for this family. For Ellen Wilson even the move from their own home into the large edifice furnished for Princeton's presidents was a tearful occasion. She much preferred the smaller place which she personally had designed and where they lived while he was a Princeton professor. "I should not have brought you here, darling. We were so happy in our home," he said to soothe her.

"Oh, Woodrow, we felt like animals in the zoo," Ellen Wilson said on one occasion after his election to the nation's Presidency. She and her daughters had gone to their usual stores, but nobody treated them the same any more. Eleanor found the art lessons for which she had commuted to Philadelphia no longer enjoyable when her friends avoided her lest she think them currying favor. The hallowed treatment which she received as the President's daughter turned her into a cynic, she wrote in *The Woodrow Wilsons*. Brought up to discuss personal affairs with no one ever, the daughters found the prying questions of reporters almost unendurable. In trying to protect them, Eleanor felt, Wilson built up his press reputation for cold and pedantic aloofness—although his family knew him as a reciter of nonsense poetry, a dancer of jigs, and a relater of hilarious anecdotes.

Eleanor, who was the gayest daughter, wrote that her mother had excellent taste but no chic whatsoever and that until father became university president mother wore the same brown dress to all campus events. "Mrs. Wilson, that dress looks better every year," became one of their family jokes. Until then she had allowed herself only forty dollars a year for clothes. She bought a new blue dress for the ten faculty dinners she had to give in her new job and wore it for all ten. The clothes which they bought for the White House were, in Eleanor's opinion, all wrong, being artistic rather than smart. And the White House valet was so shocked at the state of the new President's wardrobe he insisted that some new and better suits should be purchased immediately.

But father liked politics and that was good enough for his wife and daughters, whatever it cost in lack of privacy. He often said that no man ever became a great success "without having been constantly surrounded by admiring females" and that he obviously "had no escape from extraordinary renown by that rule." At times, Eleanor said, they hovered around him like four mother hens. He was proud of his all-woman family and borrowed $5,000 for the move to Washington.

Ellen Wilson, a gentle but vital little woman, was fifty-two years of age when she became First Lady. She had been an exquisite copper-haired beauty when she married Wilson in Savannah, Georgia, twenty-seven years before, but by the time she moved into the White House, she was plumpish and her hair was darker. Eleanor deplored the rapidity at which

172

she had aged and suspected that her mother was really ill but trying to hide it.

There was no ball after the new President's inaugural, Wilson considering such frivolity not in keeping with the seriousness of the office. The First Lady on her first afternoon in the White House called her daughters to a south window and showed them where she would build two gardens, one formal and one informal, with nooks and a hidden telephone so that the President could escape there and still be in touch with his office. She was an accomplished gardener and an artist in all that she did, and all her touches in the White House were designed to make the place more comfortable and suited to the very personal life which she and her family preferred. The family dining room in the White House was dark, so she moved their table to the south end of the State dining room and put the President's chair where he could look down the Potomac without having to see Teddy Roosevelt's stuffed animal heads, which never failed to irritate him. She squeezed from the household money enough to build a skylighted studio in the attic for her painting. She located paintings which she knew belonged to the White House but which had been stored by former First Ladies because they had nudes in them. Some of these she had hung.

But first of all, she looked into the salaries and working conditions of the White House staff and began visiting the city's slums. "An angel has come to live here," the staff said when it became known that she hoped to do something about sanitation and housing for Washington's poor. She would be both ashamed and embarrassed, she once wrote in a letter, to leave the world no better than she found it, and she looked on her higher status only as a challenge to improve it.

The shacks and substandard lean-to's in alleys behind the Capital city's marble front and even within the shadow of the Capitol itself horrified her. She began doing what she could and soon asked Congress for remedial housing legislation. In a way she was the mother of slum clearance at the national level. When she was on her deathbed, Congress rushed through what she called "my bill" as a beginning.

Her year and a half as First Lady was crowded to the brim and, until she became really ill in the late spring of 1914—after fainting at a reception at which she shook three thousand hands—she was always busy. She was a placid and charming hostess with a warm Southern word for all who attended her semi-weekly receptions and the set state events. She was not a talker by nature and her husband said it took her longer to say anything than anyone he had ever known. He liked her drawl, however, and much admired her efficiency and business ability. He was not good at driving a hard bargain

173

cashwise but she was, and the great thing about it to him was that she remained softly Southern throughout the deals. Unlike him, she was not one for games and theatricals, and she often felt that she lacked a sense of humor. She argued with him but it was more to keep her mind active than for any other reason. He considered her perfection itself and she returned the compliment. When giving a party she always saw to it that he got to talk to "charming and conversant" women, since that was the type he liked. He detested what he called soulless society talk, so the women needed brains as well as nimble tongues.

Although less public entertaining was done at the White House during the Wilson's administrations than in any other eight-year period in the mansion's history, Ellen's more than a year was quite gala and socially most successful. The three unmarried daughters added a special social oomph, and Ellen became the only First Lady who ever managed two White House weddings for her daughters.

Margaret, who was serious about music and later would sing for the overseas troops during World War I, was the tiniest of the lot but she always photographed as the largest. Her face was almost a duplicate of her father's, although her body was her mother's. She almost always looked pugnacious in her pictures—which in a way she was. She was adventurous and definite, and was rumored to be engaged to almost every unattached man in the country, even though at times she had never met the man in question. Wilson, the first President to hold free-for-all press conferences, threatened to deal with the reporters man to man rather than as the President if these baseless rumors did not stop. She never married and, seeking philosophical peace in India, she died there alone at Pondicherry in 1944.

The other two were engaged but the public did not know it. Eleanor at times shook in her boots lest someone learn about her engagement, because she was falling in love with another man and he was the one she would marry. Jessie, a classic golden haired beauty and a Phi Beta Kappa, was engaged to Francis B. Sayre and would marry him at a magnificent big wedding in the East Parlor. When the presents began pouring in for her sister's marriage Eleanor decided that maybe there was something to being a President's daughter, after all! Jessie had wanted to be a foreign missionary and her parents never interfered with their daughters' deepest wishes, but there was "unholy glee" in the family when the missions board decided that Jessie's health was not robust enough for the job. She did YWCA work in Washington until her marriage. She came back to the White House to have her first baby, who later became dean of the Washington National Cathedral.

Eleanor was the gay one. She whizzed about town in the White House electric car and often would slip away from her mother's receptions to fox trot to victrola music with a younger group in the upstairs parlor. When on a trip to Mexico she had become engaged, but she found herself intrigued and then falling in love with William Gibbs McAdoo, a much older man who became her father's Secretary of Treasury. He was a widower with children, but this was no deterrent to Eleanor. They were married in the White House. Because she did not wish to inflict the strain of another large wedding on her already tired mother, there were few guests. But Eleanor gleefully noted that she received as many presents as her sister, Jessie, had.

The backgrounds of the First Lady and the President were almost identical. Both were the children and grandchildren of Presbyterian ministers. Both were Southerners and belonged to large families which included cousins many times removed, and both grew up in a gone-with-the-wind economy. One family joke involved his father, Dr. Joseph Wilson, when he lived in Staunton, Virginia, where the future President was born. "Good morning, Dr. Wilson," a parishioner said. "Your horse looks fine this morning—much better than you do, sir." "Yes," the preacher replied, "I take care of my horse and my parishioners take care of me."

Wilson, a struggling lawyer in Atlanta, was visiting relatives in Rome, Georgia, when he first saw his future wife. He was in church to hear his father's friend, Dr. Edward Axson, preach and into the church walked a stunning young lady in full mourning and leading a little boy by the hand. Although disturbed at the thought that one so young must be a widow, he knew that he had to meet her.

Wilson asked his cousin about her after services, and was told that she was Ellie-Lou Axson, that the mourning was for her mother and that the child was her little brother, Ed. Before he left town, Wilson swore he would be back and marry Miss Ellie-Lou, whose real name was Eleanor. She settled for Ellen when she went "No'th" and her husband at times called her "My Eileen."

Miss Ellie-Lou was intent on being an artist but at the time, she was keeping house for her father. She and Woodrow corresponded and became engaged but it would be some time before they would marry. Woodrow was having an unprofitable time practicing law; he gave it up to do graduate work in history and government at Johns Hopkins University. Ellie-Lou's father, unable to combat his heartbreak, moved his family to Savannah, Georgia, to live with his father, known in Presbyterian circles as "the Great Axson." This made it possible for Ellie-Lou to continue her art studies. She wrote Woodrow that perhaps they should forget their long engagement as she was heading for New York to study at the Art Students' League. He took the first train from Baltimore and ran all the way from the station to tell her that he would die if he could not look forward to marrying her.

She, on second thought, felt the same way about him and they became engaged again. But she did have more than a year of advanced study at the League before he became a professor of history at Bryn Mawr College in Pennsylvania at $1,500 a year, and they were married. Brother Ed and a sister lived with them some of the time and usually they had relatives visiting. Their home life was clannishly Southern. Ellen never relinquished her art entirely but three daughters took more time than three canvasses, she told those who complained about her small output. In the summer before her death she was doing landscapes, and as First Lady some of her paintings, given to worthy causes, brought good prices.

She was her husband's trusted and faithful proofreader, and he said that she "listened eloquently." Part of the time during their early years she tutored her daughters and always, until they were grown, made their dresses as well as her own. Eleanor said that the first time they all had storebought dresses was for her father's inaugural as Governor of New Jersey, but Eleanor judged a wardrobe by the standards of Mrs. Grover Cleveland, who lived near them at Princeton and always dressed with rich elegance.

About politics Mrs. Wilson would have said that she knew nothing, but Joseph P. Tumulty, the President's secretary and adviser, knew better. "I want to talk to Mrs. Wilson about this," he would say during the election campaign. "She knows more about politics than you do, Governor." When the Governor was off on trips grooming himself for the national office, he kept saying in his speeches that he was not thinking of the Presidency. Ellen wrote him, "Please, please don't say again that you are not thinking of the Presidency. All who know you well know that this is true fundamentally; but superficially it can't be true and it gives the cynics an opening they seize with glee."

He was away speaking when she learned that William Jennings Bryan, the Democrat who could not be elected, was coming to Princeton. She immediately invited him to dinner and wired her husband to make it home. "You have nominated your husband, Mrs. Wilson," Tumulty exclaimed excitedly after the simple family meal at which the two men sized up and charmed each other.

The 1912 campaign was no love feast and some of the

things said about her husband and the rumors circulated against him may have hurt Ellen, particularly those which played him up as quite the ladies' man. To a comely widow named Mary H. Peck, who had a home in Bermuda, it developed that the professor over a period of years had written around two hundred letters. In the gossip columns they were termed hotly romantic. Newspapers had copies and threatened to publish them, and it would have been better for Wilson in the long run had they done so, because all who read them called them harmless. But the gossip about them recurred for years.

Mrs. Peck at one time was a family friend. When she was Mary Hurlbert she had visited the Wilsons at Princeton and they had accepted her hospitality both in Bermuda and New York City. Ellen at times dropped into her New York apartment before concerts or for a cup of tea while shopping in the city. Eleanor wrote that Mrs. Peck was a charming woman and that after watching her smoke so attractively she thought that smoking could not be so bad after all.

There is no reason to believe that Ellen ever was—or had cause to be—personally jealous of anybody. Wilson's coterie of women friends was quite a large one and most of them remained campaign workers. Also Ellen knew she had received Wilson's real love letters. Her daughter, Eleanor, had these letters from her father to her mother published years later in *The Perfect Gift*. By today's standards they at times seem a bit saccharine and overly poetic, but they are filled with an ardor which was running just as strong the summer before Ellen's death as the first ones sent to Georgia.

Ellen's final illness, which apparently stemmed from exhaustion, lasted from May throughout most of the 1914 summer. She died in August and was buried in Rome, Georgia. Gloom settled over the White House. Wilson, concerned by the oncoming World War I, about which he was glad that Ellen did not know, was desolate. Margaret refused to discuss or think about plans for a resumption of White House entertaining, in which she had no interest. Belle Hagner, the social secretary, decided that it was a good time to leave and get married. Helen Bones, a cousin of the President and Ellen's devoted personal secretary, became ill and could not seem to get over it, although Admiral Cary T. Grayson, the White House physician, thought that all she needed was some exercise in the open air and a little laughter.

Without Ellen, it seemed, all cause for happiness was over. Her last words to Admiral Grayson had been, "Please take good care of my husband," but the doctor wondered what could be done about a man who now lagged about golf and never had an anecdote anymore.

EDITH BOLLING WILSON (December 18, 1915-21)

Indomitable and Lovely Helpmate

SKIES over the White House brightened perceptibly and the gloom of lonely President Wilson began to lift rapidly on a brisk March afternoon in 1915 when a stunning widow named Edith Bolling Galt walked into the old mansion for the first time. She was forty-two years of age and had lived in Washington for nearly twenty years. Perhaps because she had been around the capital city so long, she until that afternoon rather disdained politics and politicians. But, as she quoted, "You turn a corner and meet your fate."

She had been on one of her long walks with Helen Bones, the President's cousin, who had promised her definitely that Cousin Woodrow would not be at home. He and Admiral Cary T. Grayson were out playing golf and not due in until dark. She and Helen ran smack into them at the elevator, however, and the widow remembered to be glad that she had on a good, if old, Parisian suit even though her shoes were scuffed. The four had tea together in the family parlor and the courtship which would rock the city definitely was underway.

The President immediately was laughing again and enjoying the presence of a decidedly charming and well-informed woman. Any conversational tidbit which he threw her way she could bat back at him and at times she could top it. What had she thought of his inaugural festivities and the speech which he had made on that occasion, he wondered somewhere along the way. "Sorry, Mr. President," the widow had to explain. She had stayed home and cleaned out closets that day just as she did every four years. What she liked best about inaugurations was that they reminded her of that distasteful chore. He found the idea hilarious and the widow totally delightful.

The next time that Helen came by to take Edith Galt driving, there was the President himself in the car. An orchid a day began showing up at the widow's narrow red brick house on Twentieth Street and Wilson, grown a bit rusty in the poetry field, began to keep Ike Hoover, the head usher at the

White House, busy tracking down quotations to include in his notes to the widow.

"Who is Mrs. Galt?" and "How did she meet such an aloof President?" became the city's most consuming questions. The answer to the latter query was that Admiral Grayson himself had started it all by badgering the widow into including Helen Bones on some of her walks and rides. Mrs. Galt was the first woman in Washington to own and drive an electric car and the admiral knew quite well that she habitually drove it into Rock Creek Park and then set out on a long footpath trail. Please take Helen along at times, he pleaded, but the reply which he received was negative. Mrs. Galt had all the responsibilities she cared to undertake and was not thinking of taking on another. Let the White House take care of its own inhabitants!

The admiral telephoned one morning to ask whether she would be at home that afternoon. When he came by he had Helen and the President's daughter, Eleanor McAdoo, wife of the Secretary of the Treasury, in the car with him. The three women got along famously, just as he had expected and hoped would happen. And the walks with Helen became standard procedure. The reason that the admiral knew Mrs. Galt so well was that she was the unofficial guardian and the much loved older friend of the girl whom he expected to marry. The girl's name was Alice Gertrude (Altrude) Gordon, whose Scottish mining engineer father had known and admired Mrs. Galt's father, the late Judge William H. Bolling of Wytheville, Virginia. The Scotsman before he died asked the daughter of his old friend to keep an eye on his own young daughter.

Mrs..Galt, much more interested in traveling than in looking after orphans, had gone to call on the seventeen-year-old and, not knowing what else to do, impulsively exclaimed, "I'm going to Europe this summer. Don't you want to come along?" Altrude agreed that she did and off they had gone on the first of their several trips together. During the summer of 1914, the year before the widow met the President, they were on a canoeing trip which started in Maine and gave the admiral all kinds of trouble finding them when he set out to visit Altrude.

As to the "Who is she?" question, the overall answer was that she was an old-line Virginian, with all that it implied. Her family ran more to judges than to preachers, but she spoke a language which the President knew quite well. She was the seventh in a family of eleven children and their economic difficulties had been about the same as those of the Wilsons. Portraits of several of her ancestors hang in the halls down at old Williamsburg, but she went most of the Virginians one better. She was also descended from the Indian Princess Pocahontas, who married a Rolfe, one of whose decendants married a Bolling.

In addition to being part Indian, Mrs. Galt also was the owner of Washington's oldest and most respected jewelry store, named Galt's. Norman Galt, her first husband, left it to her and rather than sell it to live on the interest from her capital, as her friends expected, she consulted her lawyer and went over the books herself. Then she gambled on it meaning more to her family economically if she retained it. Three of her brothers worked there and her mother lived with one of the brothers. She never clerked in the store nor even managed it in the accepted sense of the word but, no doubt, she kept an eagle eye on it. She was never a half-hearted woman. (She sold the store to a group of the employees "at cost," incidentally, before she became First Lady.)

Mrs. Galt was a trifle big-bosomed, her photographs show, but she was a tall woman of five feet nine inches and held herself always erect. She had the fresh beauty of a full blown red rose. Her face was full, which at times made her appear heavier than she was in photographs, and her eyes were a deep violet. Her voice was husky but soft and, despite her height, there was always something playful about her—although never kittenish. She was a woman of strong likes and dislikes, which she formed immediately and rarely if ever changed. She had great dignity as well as a charming femininity, and could be most amusing. A woman of steel and roses, someone called her.

Soon after they met the President invited her, Altrude and others for a cruise on the yacht *Mayflower* and they ran into stormy waters. Everyone seemed to be seasick except Mrs. Galt, who went off to find some brandy for Helen Bones. As she was coming back with the bottle the yacht gave a fearful lurch and she fell sprawling. Turning on her back she held the unbroken bottle on her chest and closed her eyes while trying to get her breath back. "Are you ill, Mrs. Galt?" said a voice above her. "No, Mr. President," she replied. "I'll be all right in a minute." Then, realizing the absurdity of the situation, she sat bolt upright and they began to laugh. Nearly always there was something to laugh about when she was around.

She had the same sense of loyalty and warmth toward her own family as the Wilsons had about each other and although she could be forbiddingly aloof—like the President—she was lavish in endearments to those she loved. She kept a journal of her trips and wrote her mother or a sister or a brother almost daily when she was away from them. "My precious mother," her letters to her mother usually started. "It was the greatest pleasure in the world to care for her," the second

Mrs. Wilson wrote in her *My Memoir*. Wilson understood all this sort of thing without a blueprint, and they were most congenial as well as deeply in love.

The future Mrs. Wilson spent most of the summer of 1915 with Helen and Margaret in the rented summer White House at Cornish, New Hampshire. The President came up frequently and they courted in the moonlight with, as she said, "a Secret Service man behind every tree."

The summer in New Hampshire was a bit risky for the widow's reputation when the gossips took hold of it, but then she already had become "the scheming widow" among the gossips who felt that they did not know her, even though there was nothing to know about her that was not obvious. Of course, Mrs. Galt was not known to the big-rich Republican group which ruled Washington society at the time, since the Democratic Wilsons in the White House did not care to rule it and would have been no good at it anyway. They abhorred so-called "society." Mrs. Galt, one gathers, would not have accepted an invitation to one of Mrs. McLean's parties (and they were wonderful!) even if she had received one.

But then neither would she have been caught dead attending any of the White House receptions, often freely open to the public at that time, and especially that big free-for-all on New Year's Day. The life which she chose for herself, before she chose the President, was the purely "personal" one. She had all the friends whom she could handle on an intimate basis, and she cared for no other basis.

Her sister-in-law, Annie, was a very different type. She had worked hard and gladly for Wilson's election and had stood in the rain, with her dress shrinking, just to see her hero pass by. Thinking that perhaps dear reluctant Edith really wanted a special invitation, she wangled one for them to walk right in through the front gates and shake the President's hand, but dear Edith positively refused to go on grounds that she would not dream of taking up that much of a busy man's time. And if he were not busy running the country, he should be, in her opinion.

She drove Annie to this appointment, however, and the cop on the corner, who happened to be a special friend of hers, let her park and wait. She prided herself on knowing cops on the corner, doorkeepers at the Capitol, and assistants who could get her into the National Theater at the last minute. By the time she was First Lady, the cop on the corner at the White House wrote her that he had been moved. She had him put back, the President declaring an affinity for anybody who liked beautiful women.

The President proposed to Mrs. Galt near the end of April, having known her less than two months. She was reluctant, or conceivably just being Southern. She doubtless considered the fact that his wife had not yet been dead a year. Driving in the park one day in the autumn, he filled her in on his back-breaking worries about oncoming World War I and declared that he, naturally, could not subject her to such a strain. Whereupon, so she wrote, she—despite the ever present Secret Service man—threw her arms around the President's neck and said, "Well then I ask to be mustered into service and the sooner the better." And in September of 1915 they told their families of the engagement.

Edith wrote to her brother, Rolfe, and his wife, Annie: "I am writing to tell you that I am engaged to the President and we now think we will announce it early in October. Until we do don't even *think* hard about it lest the papers hear." She asked them to destroy the letter immediately after reading, but they, naturally, kept it.

But when the President told his advisers of his impending marriage some of them sternly advised against it, especially if he hoped to be reelected in 1916. "All that stuff about Mrs. Peck and the letters will be revived," they assured him, and the name of Mrs. Galt would be dragged in the mud. He never had discussed the letters with Mrs. Galt, apparently. He sent Admiral Grayson to tell her about them, with his offer to release her from their engagement. In *My Memoir* she wrote about sitting up all night to write her answer, but said that he did not read it until their honeymoon, when they read it together. He had sent Admiral Grayson to bring her to the White House and they personally resolved the answer—affirmatively.

She never forgave the advisers who would have separated them, but later on in California when Wilson was on his desperate League of Nations speaking tour she received Mrs. Peck just to show that the earlier rumors meant nothing. She found her a faded and sad woman who was intent on her own economic problems and who far overstayed the time allotted, although the President needed rest more than anything else. Eventually the Mrs. Peck letters were purchased by Bernard Baruch, who did many nice things for the second Mrs. Wilson, for more than $30,000—which Mrs. Peck badly needed—and they were placed in the library of Congress with a time release on their usage. They will first be available to Princeton University historians who now are editing *The Wilson Papers*.

Mrs. McLean in her book said that by 1916, the time of Wilson's re-election, almost every editor in the country had read copies of these letters. She passed copies of them around at her dinner parties and thought it about the silliest thing in the world that anyone would object to their being published.

She wrote: "There is not in a single letter one statement that is damaging, in any way compromising to the character of Mr. Wilson or Mrs. Peck. . . ." And the second Mrs. Wilson, being by no means the angelic type which the first Mrs. Wilson was, went to court after Wilson's death to obtain the ruling—always available—that letters to whomever written belong to the original writer or the heirs of same. She was not the daughter of a judge for nothing, but if Wilson did not want them published neither did she.

Wilson, the third President to marry while in office, was wed to Mrs. Galt in her home on December 18, 1915. For some reason which everybody forgot to check, the bride wore black, or what she termed to be a simple black velvet dress. The house was banked with orchids and American beauty roses and her mother gave her away with only family and very close friends present. The couple eluded reporters by boarding the train in Alexandria, Virginia, and set off for a Christmas honeymoon at the Homestead, also in Virginia. Colonel Starling, who was head of Secret Service, wrote that the President danced a jig on the train and sang "Oh You Beautiful Doll." Edith wrote her mother next day that on the train they had eaten a dainty supper of chicken salad and fruits at a table centered with orchids. "We both had a good night. Woodrow sends his love with mine and says we are as happy as children off on a holiday."

Contrary to what the advisers predicted, the public applauded the wedding. One editorial said that, "No man ever should be alone in the White House." The President was overwhelmingly busy, even on the honeymoon, and his wife studied how to make herself useful. With her, as with Ellen, he discussed his problems and asked her opinions.

Edith Benham Helm, who became her social secretary at the White House, wrote that Edith Wilson was "the best wife in the world" to a man who needed loving and constant attention more than most men ever do.

Into the White House with her the First Lady moved her three choice possessions: her piano, her sewing machine, and her mahogany rolltop desk. The President found the sewing machine most amusing, but she used it frequently and kept it going constantly for the Red Cross during World War I. In the summer before her death she still was making dresses on the same machine. She played the piano for the President, (having majored in music at school) and although in later years she stopped playing, she kept the piano in tune for the times when Wilson's namesake grandson would come by to serenade "Granny Edith," as he called her.

As a good example to wool growers she had sheep grazing on the White House lawn during World War I, and she

183

lived up to the rules about meatless and heatless days. She named ships galore and, to help her husband, she learned the wartime code and deciphered messages coming in from abroad. Then when the war ended she went to Europe twice with the President to attend the Peace Conferences and to visit the Allied countries. Thus she became the first First Lady to leave the country while in office, so to speak, and during the peace settlements in Paris she talked her husband into asking Clemenceau, the Tiger of France, whether she could see some of the signing of the papers.

Clemenceau agreed, with the strict understanding that she tell no one about it, particularly none of the other wives, and that she not let herself be seen. She sat behind heavy blue curtains in a balcony with Admiral Grayson and almost suffocated, but it was worth it, she felt, to see the Germans affix their signatures to peace plans. She was bursting with pride at the esteem in which her husband was held throughout the lengthy proceedings.

Too busy to keep an actual journal of those days, she wrote regularly to her mother and asked that the letters be kept. She started the letters as they steamed by the Statue of Liberty, telling of their emotional send-off from New York. She continued the letters sometimes hurriedly and in pencil, describing their rooms, schedules, and the clothes she wore on each occasion. She sent her mother pressed daisies picked by the Queen of Belgium and told how difficult it was to visualize cities and towns as they had been when looking at some of the shelled fields which she visited.

On December 15, 1918, she wrote that they had arrived in Paris at ten o'clock the morning before and that "There the *world* seemed to be waiting to welcome my wonderful husband . . ."

When the President "took the League of Nations to the people" on a cross-country speaking tour, hoping to influence opinion which in turn would influence Congress to ratify his peace treaty work without amendments, she was with him. One night he was stricken by partial paralysis, brought on by sheer exhaustion, as their special train sped from Denver toward Wichita, Kansas. She called the night "the longest and most heartbreaking in my life." The President fell asleep at dawn, but she knew that he was desperately ill and would not be able to continue the tour.

"The dear face opposite me was drawn and lined; and as I sat there watching the dawn break slowly I felt that life would never be the same; that something had broken inside me; and from that hour on I would have to wear a mask—not only to the public but to the one I loved best in the world; for he must never know how ill he was, and I must carry on," she wrote in *My Memoir*.

News of the President's illness shook the country. When his train returned to Washington on September 28, 1919, Margaret and the White House cars were at the station and so was a vast multitude of citizens. "My first impulse," his wife wrote, "was to escape them, to get away from what I regarded as prying, curious eyes, though now I realize that the gathering was a sympathetic one."

She was cruelly criticized for taking charge of his sick room and shutting out the world. Some called the last eighteen months of Wilson's eight years in office "Mrs. Wilson's Regency." She culled the papers which should come to his attention, spaced his visitors, relayed his messages, and stood like a granite wall between him and worry.

There is no doubt that Edith Wilson as her husband's chief close assistant and the only person with him around the clock became more nearly "Mrs. President" than any other First Lady ever. The length of his total incapacity to function as Chief Executive, some historians say, was only the two months during the gravest part of his illness and that this was the length of her regency, if such it could be called. The government continued to function. The courts convened, Congress legislated and the executive departments of the government went about their many businesses. His Cabinet had meetings, too, often taking up subjects and reaching decisions which irritated the ill President.

He still had his mind, if not his strength, although rumors that he was mentally deficient were widespread. He should resign or be ousted, it was said over and over. The Senate named a subcommittee to check on his mental condition. Senator Gilbert Hitchcock, always a loyal Wilson friend, accompanied Senator Albert B. Fall, a member of the subcommittee, in a call on the President. The First Lady wrote that Senator Fall entered the sickroom in an unctuous manner. "Well, Mr. President," he said, "we have all been praying for you." "Which way?" asked the President with a chuckle. The visit quieted serious talk that he could be ousted for mental reasons. But the Senate battle over the League of Nations went on and on.

The First Lady, seeing what the losing battle was doing to her ill husband, begged him to compromise. This was the only time that she tried to influence him during the illness, she said, and she soon felt ashamed that she had done so. She felt that the whole affair was becoming a purely personal struggle between him and Senator Henry Cabot Lodge, who was leading the opposition, and that a half loaf would be better than nothing at all. "For my sake," she pleaded, "won't you give in and get the whole deadly problem settled?"

"Now, little girl, don't you turn against me, too," he replied, "That I do not think that I could stand." Then he explained to her his view that neither amendments nor reservations could be accepted unless the documents went back to all the signatory countries, including Germany, and another agreement was worked out. He had done his best at the Peace Conferences and in cooperation with the other countries and the work either must be accepted in full or rejected in full.

But on his death bed in 1924, when his daughter Margaret had stopped reading to him, thinking that he was asleep, he murmured that probably it was a good thing that the League had failed to get America's sanction. Margaret gasped, it was recorded, no doubt believing her father to be out of his mind. But he, in a firmer voice, assured her that he was not dreaming and that it all would be done later and better, probably. "The country was not ready for it," he said.

Edith Wilson never apologized for what she called "my stewardship" during her husband's illness. The doctors told her that with rest and lack of worry he might get well, and that certainly he would live longer. She took the gamble, working around the clock, being always on duty. "He was first of all my beloved husband," she said, and then the President. She met Cabinet officers and relayed the President's wishes, but they did not get in to see him. She read the coded messages and told him their contents. She put papers before him to sign, but—she declared—she made no decisions on her own. Some of the letters of state began to come to her with the added note, "Bring it up if you think that the boss is up to it."

How she ever stood up to such pressures and all the hard work remained a mystery, and she had many astounded friends during the period as well as bitter castigators. Not all of her well wishers were Democrats, either. Dolly Gann, the sister of Charles Curtis, who would become Vice President under President Hoover, was among those who said, "Thank God that we had such a woman in the White House." Her stewardship did not go unappreciated, and it does remain unique.

This President never was well again, but his health did improve measurably. When the time came for the Wilsons to go out of office he bought a surprise gift house for her on S Street in Washington. It was one that she had looked at but felt that they really could not afford.

An elevator was installed to make it easier for him in his crippled condition and a terrace was added to the dining room entrance so that he need not tackle steps from the garden. Crowds often gathered across the street for bulletins on his health, and his wife continued to remain on constant duty.

He planned to practice law, an idea quickly abandoned, and to write other books. His main output was a marvelous little booklet called *The Road Away From Revolution*, which reads more like something done in the 1960's than in the twenties. His wife got up at any time of night to take it down sentence by sentence. He planned a "real book" dedicated to her but got only as far as the dedication "To E.B.W." On his typewriter, which is now in the White House as a choice possession, he wrote:

"I dedicate this book (to E.B.W.) because it is a book in which I have tried to interpret life, the life of a nation, and she has shown me the full meaning of life. Her heart not only is true but wise; her thoughts are not only true but touched with vision; she guides and teaches by being what she is; her unconscious interpretation of faith and duty make all the way clear; her power to comprehend makes work and thought alike easier and more near to what it seems." He never wrote the book, but what an accolade from a President, or even a husband, for that matter.

She lived almost forty years after his death, and in the same town house which he bought for her. She left the house, complete with endowment of $250,000, to the National Historic Trust and Council, to be kept as it was when he lived there—and there was scarcely a day in all her later life which failed to be dedicated to Woodrow Wilson. His aura followed her and she lived up to the standards of his memory.

Two of her brothers and a nephew died within a space of six months, but her oldest sister, Gertrude Galt (they had married cousins) moved in with her and continued to mend the finest linens well into her nineties. Mrs. Wilson became a legend in Washington, because personally and for sheer indestructibility there never was another ex-First Lady like her. She still was considered aloof by those who failed to know her. She never gave interviews, viewing them as beneath her dignity, but she deplored stories about her living as a recluse. When they appeared she usually permitted a rewrite to dispel the idea that she lived alone with her medals—because she really was always active, seeing her old friends and relatives with great regularity, playing bridge without her glasses, devoting much time to helping the authors of her husband's papers, and taking trips. One never thought of age in her presence and it was only after her death that her home, without her in it, showed that it obviously had been the abode of an old, old lady.

She continued to have a limousine with driver, even though the limousine in later years was bought second hand. She found the economics tough at times on her $5,000 a year pension as ex-First Lady, plus the interest from the endowment which she had settled on the house, but she kept up the elegant front. She always gave a lunch for the current First Lady and on public occasions she made the grand entrance. She still was lovely to look at and always dressed beautifully. She served her guests cocktails and very good food beautifully served, and there were always flowers in the house. But she was happy when the pension was doubled.

When she was quite ill once the doctor ordered her to eat a pound of steak and drink a split of champagne daily. "I call this really living," she said. Usually she was a late riser who had breakfast in bed and read far into the night. She kept up with all the latest books, preferring biographies and prize novels. She was reading *To Kill a Mockingbird* on her death bed.

She sparked the starting of the Woodrow Wilson Birthplace Foundation down in Staunton, Virginia, and continually helped to promote it. Just to watch her float in at the annual meetings, orchids in place and hat just so, was something to remember. She adored hats and as she grew thinner with the years was delighted that her face would "take the little flowered jobs which I never thought I could wear before."

She still relished her travels and visitors; family or close, trusted friends. Bernard Baruch remained a helpful friend and with his daughter, Belle, she had zestful visits to the shops and theaters of New York, even a visit to the Stork Club. She devoted her major energy to her husband's record, no request being too minute or demanding for a prompt answer in her deliberate, old-fashioned handwriting, now grown slightly quavery, to her distress. She mounted the stairs cheerfully to inspect the fourth floor walk-up office of the Princeton scholars working on her husband's papers.

Meticulous in all things, she had a fetish for punctuality and form. When she said she would be anywhere, she drew up in her limousine on the precise dot. At Washington's National Theater, where she enjoyed such musicals as *My Fair Lady* and *The Music Man*, she would look up at the box where she had so often sat with the wartime President. "You see so much better from down here," she would say in her fourth row orchestra seat. "We used to want to sit anywhere but in that box, where the noise of the drums was also a drawback, but the Secret Service wouldn't let us."

One of her final nights at the theater at the age of eighty-nine was in the open-air Carter Barron summer amphitheater where she reluctantly slipped on her hearing aid to chuckle at Danny Kaye's jokes and after the performance she was gracious enough to visit backstage to congratulate the company. Such efforts, she felt, were her duty as a former First Lady.

Born in 1872, she was almost ninety when she died on her husband's birthday, December 28, 1961, but she never seemed old nor did she even use glasses except for the finest work at her sewing machine. She played bridge with her close friends regularly on Tuesdays. Some of them fell by the wayside, but she did not.

On her last birthday celebration, an annual fete by Mrs. Charles Rollins in Alexandria, Virginia, she made a tiny speech but only because her arm was in a sling and she could not write. "I thank you all for your gifts vocally because I probably shall not be able to write to you for sometime," she said.

She was supposed, months ahead, to dedicate the Woodrow Wilson bridge over the Potomac on his birthday, December 28, 1961, but she was seriously ill by then. Her husband's son-in-law, Francis B. Sayre, Jessie's husband, did the honors in her stead, but she made herself live, barely conscious, until eleven that night. "How like her," some said. "She had accepted a duty for that day and she kept herself alive to see that her duty was done."

FLORENCE KLING HARDING
(1921-August 2, 1923)

The Stars Foretold Tragedy

AFTER she finished her labors as circulation manager for the
Marion (Ohio) *Daily Star* it was the pattern of Florence Kling
Harding's day that she bicycled hurriedly home thirty minutes
ahead of her handsome editor husband so as to have his
steak broiling when he arrived. "I have only one real hobby,"
she always said, "and it is my husband." She helped him make
a success of his newspaper and then promoted him politically,
being more ambitious for him than he was for himself, some
said. He called her "The Duchess."

She was more than five years older than Warren Harding,
and she had married him much against her father's wishes
when she was almost thirty-one. At nineteen she had married
Henry De Wolfe. That marriage was a short and unhappy one
which ended in divorce. She then returned home with her infant son, Marshall, to live again with her father. The first
husband died shortly before she married the editor who was to
become Ohio's Governor, then United States Senator, and then
President.

Her father, Amos H. Kling, was Marion's leading banker.
He felt so strongly against young Harding—doubting that he
would be successful at anything—that he did not speak to
his son-in-law for almost a decade and kept him out of some
of the town's best clubs. But Florence had a mind of her
own and loved a challenge. Harding built them a home and
they were married in it. Then she threw her energies, plus an
inherited business ability, into the newspaper and into pushing
Warren politically. She was an independent and enterprising
young lady for her day. Between her two marriages she taught
music. She had studied at the Cincinnati Conservatory and
her education in nearly all respects seems to have been better
than that of her husband.

Her handwriting was strikingly bold, and she herself was
beautiful at the time of her marriage. She had lovely corn-
flower-blue eyes, fairish hair, good features, and a command-
ingly erect carriage. She had a direct way of speaking, but
her voice was a bit loud and sometimes rasping.

By the time she became First Lady in 1921 she was sixty

years of age and looked older. She had been in wretched health from a serious kidney ailment for years, and under the constant medical care of Dr. Charles E. Sawyer, who had his own hospital on the outskirts of Marion. He kept her on a very strict diet. Harding made the little doctor a Brigadier General and attached him to the White House as the official physician. Dr. Sawyer has been credited with saving Florence Harding's life at least twice during her two years and one hundred fifty-one days as First Lady.

On one of these occasions he opposed specialists from the Mayo Clinic and the Johns Hopkins Hospital who said, "Operate." Evalyn Walsh McLean, the best friend Florence had in Washington, had rushed from Bar Harbor to be with her. Mrs. McLean wrote in *Father Struck It Rich* that she could have hugged General Sawyer when he stood his ground as the Harding family doctor, saying that he had operated on Florence twice before and knew that her body could take no more cutting.

In between her serious illnesses, Florence determinedly kept going and the White House was gay with entertaining. The public liked it when the gates again were thrown open after the dark Wilson months. Harding had won the Presidency by a sizable majority and his administration, which was to collapse in lurid scandals, came in on a blaze of virility and promises of a "return to normalcy."

The new President gave The Duchess a diamond sunburst pin for the inauguration. She put it on a black velvet band which she nearly always wore close about her neck, dog-collar style, and this became her First Lady trademark. Mrs. McLean supervised the First Lady's wardrobe, and it was an elegant one with plenty of changes.

Mrs. McLean's husband, Edward Beale (Ned) McLean, who controlled the Washington *Post* and the Cincinnati *Enquirer,* was inaugural chairman and had planned a magnificent ball for inauguration night, but members of the senate objected so loudly at the proposed display of wealth that it was cancelled. Instead, the McLeans staged a ball at their big estate, Friendship, personally spending about as much on it as the public one would have cost. Fabulous Friendship, with its golf course and swimming pool, became a sort of second White House for the Hardings, and each spring the McLeans took the Hardings yachting in Florida waters.

The First Lady loved garden parties and gave many huge ones. Quite a number of them were for veterans of World War I. The Limitation of Armaments Conference met in Washington the entire winter of 1921-22, and it brought many distinguished foreigners to town. All were entertained well and merrily.

191

It still is difficult to see the era as The Duchess must have seen it. As Bess Furman wrote in *White House Profile*, it was an "era of illusion" and to this she could have added "disillusion." The cut-short Harding administration, ending as it did in tragedy followed by revelations of the Teapot Dome oil scandal and other public lootings, only added to the disillusionment of a country upset by a costly foreign war "to end wars" and the collapse of peace efforts. Later it was said that everything in Washington during the Harding administration was for sale except the Capitol dome—and that it too could have been won in a good poker game.

But there were some who saw beyond the glitter. Alice Roosevelt Longworth, daughter of former President Theodore Roosevelt, called Harding a "slob" and stuck to it. She wrote in her memoirs that the country was so wild about making money and enjoying the postwar prosperity—so eager to get on with the Flaming Twenties—that few wanted to think about the government one way or the other. She had been egged on to tell the incoming President that many responsible Republicans did not want him to appoint Harry M. Daugherty, the Ohio political boss who spearheaded Harding's election, to be his Attorney General. But her efforts got nowhere. Daugherty was named.

Also Alice saw for herself that although the Eighteenth Amendment was part of the U.S. Constitution, liquor flowed freely at the White House. Wines disappeared from formal dinners downstairs, but good Scotch and Bourbon were available upstairs for the select. Nobody on the "in" needed to face a dry evening. For the daughter of crusading Teddy and correct Edie Roosevelt such disregard for the law and lack of good taste must have been galling. She openly wondered whether being an "out" did not have its advantages.

Before the Prohibition Amendment was finally ratified and while Harding was a Senator, The Duchess herself kept the glasses refilled at poker parties. "Duchess, you are lying down on the job," was the call for a refill. This indicates that she was wholeheartedly accepted by his political friends and card-playing cronies. "I owe it all to The Duchess" was one of his favorite expressions, and she loved to hear it.

Yet, without exception, the Hardings seem to have been the loneliest couple who ever occupied the White House. He insisted upon stag nights out. One night members of the White House staff were horrified to hear her scream down the marble stairs, "You're not going *anywhere* tonight!" It seemed like a scene out of the Maggie and Jiggs comic strip.

Yet the White House staff liked her. And her husband by all accounts rather expected and relished her nagging. "I'm bringing the Boss along to keep me in order," Harding wrote Ned

McLean about plans for their second yachting-golfing-poker playing vacation in Florida. Her "Now, Warren, you must be getting back to work" admonitions after golf and lunch at Friendship sometimes worked and sometimes did not. One time, Mrs. McLean recalled that after about her fourth such prod he exclaimed, "Five spades . . . and I'm going to play all afternoon!" But his recorded kindnesses to his wife and concern for her were numerous. He took her with him to most public events. She continued her concern with his career, but it is doubtful that she influenced much if anything about the administration.

Mrs. McLean was sincerely fond of both Hardings and did many things for them. In her book she said "The Duchess must have been a very beautiful woman at one time," but she also noted the discontented set of her mouth. She recorded that the First Lady after a big social affair would ask, "What did they say about me?" Mrs. McLean doubted that Florence Harding ever set her heart on being First Lady or ever pushed her husband for the Presidency until the nomination fell into their laps. Mrs. McLean thought the Hardings would have been happier had he remained in the Senate.

He was not an outstanding Senator but he was exceedingly popular with the other Senators. And he "looked like a President." The number of stories written about Harding's good looks now seems fantastic, but they may have been influenced by the charm of his kind personality. The Duchess was always saying, in effect, "You can catch more flies with syrup than vinegar. Now, Warren, watch what you say."

In the spring of 1923 it was decided that President Harding should go on a barnstorming tour throughout the West and go on to Alaska. At least two of the suicides for which the administration would become infamous had taken place by then, but there were as yet no open scandals. Harding had aged before the eyes of his Cabinet, but then it was the accepted belief that if any man lived through the Presidency, he would show the effects of his fearful responsibility.

The Duchess was going, of course, but the McLeans could not because Evalyn was ill. The President invited some, but not all, of his official family. Somewhat belatedly the Secretary of Commerce and Mrs. Herbert Hoover were invited, one reason being that the President apparently had a question he wished to put to Hoover, a man whose integrity never was questioned even though later his vision was.

"What would you do," the President asked his Secretary of Commerce, "if you learned that inside your own administration scandals were about to break?" "Expose them, of course, and the sooner the better," was the reply. But they were such different types of men. Harding did not act on his Cabinet officer's advice.

Harding developed ptomaine poisoning in Vancouver on the way home. He recovered, but became ill again in San Francisco. He died there in a hotel on the night of August 2, 1923, while the First Lady was reading to him an article favorable to him and which she thought he would appreciate. The White House physician, Dr. Sawyer, had left the hotel for a walk which was cut short. The nurses who had been attending the supposedly recuperating President were resting. The circumstances lent themselves to plays and books, and no doubt there will be more to come. But even at the time, or shortly thereafter, many believed that Warren Harding wished to die rather than to face the mess into which his trusted friends had dragged him. The funeral train rushed back across the country while newspapers tried to straighten out the details of the President's death. And a footnote on the period is that the Washington *Post*, with all its special lines to the White House, was scooped!

Evalyn Walsh McLean stayed in the White House with the First Lady during the night when the late President lay in state in the East Parlor. Mrs. McLean left a weird account:

"Right in the middle of the August night, at one-thirty, Mrs. Harding decided that she was lonesome for want of her husband's companionship. He was downstairs in the East Room of the White House, in his coffin. I held her arm, soft and dropsical, as we descended the curving white marble staircase. She was being game with all her might. Through all that time I never saw her shed a tear.

"George Christian, with a grief almost as deep as hers, alertly watched for any sign of weakness, of collapse; there was no such sign.

" 'Put back the casket lid,' she said to him, and he obeyed at once.

"In the night time the man who no longer was the President appeared quite alive from the rouge and lipstick touches that in daylight had seemed ghastly. But the softer illumination made him seem almost himself. Then I began to shiver, because I heard Mrs. Harding talking to her husband. The heavy scent of flowers cloyed my nostrils as we stayed on and on and Mrs. Harding talked. A chair was placed for her and she sat down.

" 'Warren,' she said, her face held close to him, 'the trip has not hurt you one bit.'

"That poor thing kept right on talking, as if she could not bear to hear the silence that would so poignantly remind her that he could not speak to her in turn."

" 'No one can hurt you now, Warren,' " she said another

time. "That one remark helped me to understand how she was weaving strands of comforting philosophy out of grief. I know how she had feared that some crank might do him harm. I too sometimes am conscious of a feeling of warmth when I think that my own dead are now beyond the reach of harm.

"Before we left she looked about at all the flowers, the costly sheaves of roses, the wreaths and the usual collection— oversize of course—of those stupid fabrications that the florists make, and then buy back, withered, from cemeteries for further use. Somewhere in those mounds she saw something that she wanted, and she stooped down as if she were in a growing garden to pick it up—a small bouquet of country flowers, of daisies and nasturtiums. These she placed directly on the coffin after she had told George Christian to close the lid. It was three o'clock in the morning when we started back upstairs."

It was ten days before Mrs. Harding left the White House and the Calvin Coolidges moved in. She went to rest a while at Friendship, and then returned to Marion, Ohio. But she had no real home there anymore and she spent the remainder of her life, less than two years, in Dr. Sawyer's sanitarium.

When the Coolidges' young son, Calvin, Jr., died, she sent the First Family a telling message: "No matter how many loving hands may be stretched out to help us, some paths we tread alone."

GRACE GOODHUE COOLIDGE
(August 3, 1923-29)

"I was Born with Peace of Mind"

AFTER Grace Coolidge became First Lady in the middle of a hot August night in the Plymouth, Vermont, farmhouse of her father-in-law, she went back to bed and slept easily. Not many women could have accomplished this feat, but then nobody else was married to Calvin Coolidge: the little red-headed President who always looked as if he smelled something burning and who never spoke to anybody if he could avoid the experience.

If Grace had not been an unusual woman she never would have married Coolidge in the first place and her mother, for one, could never see why she did. But Grace and her merry father, Captain Andrew I. Goodhue, a steamboat inspector for vessels plying Lake Champlain, always understood the Coolidge appeal. She was the completely happy wife, and that was the secret of her phenomenal success as First Lady.

Grace had found an extra kerosene lamp for the dramatic swearing-in rites so that anxious reporters, who rushed to Plymouth after news of the unexpected death of President Harding, could see what they were writing. She watched with interest while a telephone line was strung up by emergency crews. But at around two-thirty in the morning, after the hullabaloo connected with becoming President was over, it would never have occurred to her not to accompany her husband back to bed. Nor would he have permitted such deviation from the norm. And naturally she would go back to sleep if he ordered her to do so.

He appears to have been the tyrant among Presidential husbands, or would have been if Grace could have been tyrannized. But in his own way he was also a devoted and proud husband always. She knew him before she married him, and gave him every test imaginable, and decided that she loved him. She was a graduate of the University of Vermont, the first First Lady to have such an unimpeachable education from a real university, and was teaching in the Clarke Institute for the Deaf in Northampton, Massachusetts, when she met him. All her life she remained interested in education of the deaf and would do a great deal for Clarke Institute.

Yet when she married Calvin Coolidge, a Vermonter practicing law in Northampton, it had to be a complete surrender. He never even proposed to her properly but just announced: "I'm going to be married to you." But he dressed up and called on her father and showed himself off to her friends. She was very popular and wanted all her friends to like him, too. Some of them could not say that they did, but if Grace wanted him, it could be nothing but all right.

When he became Vice President in 1921 and they went to live in Washington at the Willard Hotel, he decided that on a salary of $12,000 a year they could not afford to rent a whole house. They had never had a whole house, for that matter, having rented half of a two-family home in Northampton from the first days of their marriage. When he was Mayor of Boston and then Governor of Massachusetts, someone was always advising him to move to more elegant quarters, but he held out against the pressures. When they first moved into their part of the house, the rent was $24 a month. This had climbed to a painful $40 by the time the Coolidges returned there for a while after his Presidency ended.

But when he was Governor of Massachusetts, he did make one concession. He took two rooms rather than one at Adams House, where he always stayed in Boston, so that Grace and the boys would have a place to stay. Heretofore he had kept her at home in Northampton as much as possible, going home weekends as often as he could. She was not part of his political life, but something apart.

It was said that Senator Henry Cabot Lodge of Massachusetts might have won for Coolidge the nomination for the Presidency in 1920, when darkhorse Harding won in the smoke-filled, deadlocked room, but that the aristocratic Senator could not fancy himself going all out for a man who by preference lived in a two-family house.

Coolidge's way of life offended the proper Bostonians. He might have been Mayor of their city, and then Governor of their State, but he was not one of them. He was a Plymouth, Vermonter, who in spirit never left the Green Mountains area. He was a hill man for whom Colonel Edward Starling, head of the Secret Service and a native of the Kentucky mountains, felt a liking and almost kinship.

Grace was not at all sure that he was going to take her to Washington when he became Vice President and she no doubt would have accepted the fate blithely if he had not. "He seems to need me," she wrote gaily to the group of friends with whom she exchanged round-robin letters for years.

As the Vice President's wife, Grace set a record by becoming the most popular official wife in Washington. Mrs. Harding could be stiffly acid and Mrs. Hoover, a future First Lady, was not warm with the masses, but Grace Coolidge always was a miracle of good nature, friendliness, tact, and charm. Wherever she was the people who were around her had a good time and felt welcome. Her philosophy about people was that short and tall, fat and lean, she loved them all! "That is the way I feel about people, and I have been fortunate in being placed where I had an opportunity to gratify my taste by meeting great numbers of them," she said of her days in Washington.

She was a pretty woman with masses of dark hair, large gray-green eyes, and a winning smile. She had sung contralto at school, and still sang whenever she felt like it.

She whistled, even yodeled, and was an ardent baseball fan. She grew enamored with the national sport when her two boys were small and she often played it with them. For as long as she lived, she was sent passes to the World Series games and, near the end of her life, she felt that President Eisenhower made an enormous mistake one year by not staying in Washington to open the baseball season.

The nearest she ever came to reprimanding her husband in public was at a game in Washington. She adopted the Senators as her hometown team, and they won the World Series in 1924—maybe because she cared so much. She and the President were at one of the vital and, to her, enchanting games when he, bored stiff, rose to leave before it was over. She caught his coat and exclaimed, "Do sit down. Where do you think you are going?" He sat, the horror in his wife's voice penetrating to him and her gesture being so unusual.

In the roaring twenties, the country found it amusing that the President went to bed at ten o'clock. And he thought six o'clock was plenty long enough for Grace to be out to tea. He rang her up if she overstayed. When he was Vice President and came home from the Senate, he wanted her there, too. Over the phone he would say, "Grace? I'm home. You get home, too." It was the same in Northampton in the days when she left him babysitting and went to visit or to attend a meeting. If he thought she was staying too long, he would call, "Grace? Hop home." And hop home she did—happily.

The things he would not permit her to do would fill a book. She was not permitted to drive a car, bob her hair, fly in a plane (not even with young Lindbergh himself as pilot), ride a horse, or ever to be unaccounted for. She yearned to ride horseback and when she became First Lady thought she had it all set to learn at nearby Fort Myer and then surprise him with her accomplishment. Her first lesson, unfortunately, made the newspapers and his verdict was that she did not need any new talents to be successful in her new job.

So about the only thing left for her to do was walk, which

she did with vim and vigor, often clipping off eight to ten miles a day without fatigue. In Washington she thought nothing of walking with her son John from the White House to the Union Station, when he was going back to college, and then walking back home again.

When the Coolidges were vacationing in the Black Hills of South Dakota one summer, the big political question in the country was whether he would run again. He announced his historic "I do not choose to run" decision without his wife's knowledge, and the newspapers made much of the fact she had to hear about it second hand rather than from him. She rallied to his defense to say that she was proud of a man who, after twenty-five years of marriage, felt no need to check with his wife before making up his own mind.

Nonetheless rumors circulated that she intended to divorce him. Mary Randolph, the White House social secretary, showed him some of the stories and made the suggestion that the couple be seen together more in public. He acquiesced, and crowds were treated to the spectacle of them walking happily together in downtown Washington during lunch hours and riding gaily in the park as workers came and went from their jobs.

Grace Coolidge never was surprised by anything which her surprising husband did and after his death she declared that she would miss terribly his habit of telling her what to do. She relished his sense of humor and apparently she had a freer hand in running her homelife than many of the stories indicated.

Coolidge adored his wife. He wrote his father from the White House, "I do not know what I would do without her." He pampered her in his own way. For one thing, he always wanted her to wear beautiful clothes, and this had held true in Northampton just as it did in the White House. The hats he bought her and took home to Northampton sometimes cost half as much as the month's rent. Once when they were leaving to vacation at the farm in Plymouth he ran back into the house to get the hatbox with the hats he wanted her to wear there.

Grace thought them quite fancy for the rural life, but she wore them with pleasure. She loved his attentions and his oddities.

Mary Randolph wrote that he would storm from the office side of the White House into the living quarters demanding to know, "Where's my wife?" She added that Grace Coolidge "was the sunshine and joy of his life—his rest when tired, his solace in time of trouble." He watched every dress she wore, often picking them out himself. Ideally he would have preferred her always to be in white satin and holding a single pink rose. Such a portrait was painted and hangs in Northampton. It probably shows her at her loveliest but it is not so dramatic as the one in the red dress which hangs in the White House and is often called the most charming First Lady portrait there. Her sorority and round-robin-letter friends had the latter painted and presented it as a gift to the Nation.

Grace Coolidge had the lovable qualities which turn aside antagonisms. The stories about her were uniformly favorable. "The triumph of his wife in Washington official society must have been one of the major satisfactions that he (Coolidge) found in office," William Allen White, the noted Kansas editor, wrote in *A Puritan in Babylon.*

None of this meant that he behaved like other husbands, however. He checked the White House menus right behind her, the housekeeper soon learning to send two copies for approval and to follow the changes which he made. He would go into the kitchen to lift the lids and peer into pots to see what was cooking. The story is that an angry cook once chased him out by brandishing a hot spoon at him.

When he was ex-President he was asked what he regarded as his greatest disappointment in the White House. His reply was that it was his inability ever to learn what happened to the leftovers. When ham was to be served Grace would write the chef a note to insure that the President received "the little round piece" near the bone. But he was in a dither at ham-time because, it seemed to him, only two pieces were ever taken out and then the big and expensive thing disappeared forever. He was in continuous argument with the housekeeper until she left and he found Ellen A. Riley who suited him to a "T". In addition to being a worry-bird about expenses, however, he always had indigestion, so perhaps he was not so meaninglessly finicky as he seemed.

Ishbel Ross wrote in her delightful book *Grace Coolidge and Her Era* that when he and Grace were first married, one of his ideas of fun was to drop a piece of her pastry on the floor, stamping his foot loudly at the same time to indicate how hard and heavy he considered it. Being married to him seems to have been as stiff a training course in poise as any royal princess ever underwent. Perhaps that was why she appeared so well schooled for her job as First Lady and why no one ever saw her flustered. She could carry on a bubbling dinner conversation while her husband cracked nuts for himself and ignored the talk. She had the ability to make whatever he did, even to leaving the table before their guests had finished dessert, seem natural and all right.

The Coolidges in the White House had a sensational

royal visitor who would be startling to a New Englander. She was Queen Marie of Rumania. One of Her Majesty's wishes was to be photographed with President Coolidge and he was dead set against it. Marie wore the very short dresses of the period and was an extremist in glamour.

At a White House reception for the Queen, the harassed social secretary warned the First Lady about leaving Her Majesty alone for a second. The First Lady sat beside the Queen on a sofa, but she sensed that the party was bogging down and felt that there were other guests to whom she should be talking. The minute Grace arose the Queen motioned Alice Roosevelt Longworth to join her on the sofa, and she never let her go, to the horror of Teddy's fearless daughter who felt herself to be under some queer Balkan spell. Another upshot, was that, thanks to photographers planted behind palms, the Queen also got her pictures.

Charles A. Lindbergh flew the Atlantic and was received with his mother at the White House amid great excitement and festivity. He later married Anne Morrow, daughter of the Dwight Morrows, old and close friends of the Coolidges. The country was laughing at Will Rogers' vaudeville take-off of Coolidge—and the Coolidges invited him to the White House, too, so that he could gather new material. The years were busy, and generally happy.

The Coolidges suffered a great personal tragedy in the White House, however, in the death of their youngest son, Calvin, Jr. The Coolidge boys, John and Calvin, Jr., were handsome lads of seventeen and barely fifteen years of age when their father unexpectedly became President one August. They had left for summer jobs before the event occurred, and they stayed on the jobs as if nothing unusual had happened. Young Calvin's job was on a tobacco farm. "I would not be stripping tobacco if my father were President," a working companion assured him. "If my father were your father you would," Calvin replied.

In 1924, however, the boys for one unusual summer were doing nothing but having a good time and enjoying life at the White House. Young Cal was so eager to get onto the tennis courts each day that one morning, not finding his socks immediately to hand, he put on his tennis shoes without them and rushed out to play in the July sun. He blistered a heel but thought nothing of it. A few days later he died at Walter Reed Hospital from blood poisoning. His father always thought that if he had not been President it would not have happened, and all her life John sent his mother flowers on the anniversary of Calvin's death, knowing how much this son had meant to her. Young Cal had her sunny disposition and was happy-go-lucky by nature. His grades in school were not as good as John's because he did not apply himself so sturdily, but he was exceedingly popular. John said that even at home he could get by with more mischief around his father than he himself ever would have dared. John was the quiet one and especially enjoyed riding horseback.

Mrs. Coolidge refused many invitations to return to Washington after her husband's administration ended. She did return once, unannounced. She and a neighbor from her early married days, Mrs. Florence B. Adams, with whom she spent many summers in the North Carolina mountains after her husband died, were motoring north and stopped to see the new National Gallery of Art and do a bit of sightseeing. The only place at which Grace Coolidge was recognized, wrote Ishbel Ross, was at the art gallery, where she met one of the guards who once had served on the Presidential yacht and also at the White House.

After the White House the Coolidges found it difficult to live again in a small two-family house, so the ex-President bought a big tree-encircled place for them. It was called "The Beeches" and after his death, in 1933, she sold it and had an especially designed smaller home built for herself. It was an advanced sort of house, the living room being on the second floor where she could be up among the treetops and birds. When World War II came along and the Navy headquartered the training camp for its women WAVES in Northampton, she happily let them use her home. She did much work during this war, but never as the chairman of anything. She also continued the fine needlework for which she was well remembered in Washington. She did petit point chair covers for son John's family and perhaps thought back occasionally to the years in the White House, when she had crocheted a wool spread for the Lincoln bed. She died in Northampton in 1957 at the age of seventy-eight years.

LOU HENRY HOOVER (1929-1933)

Adventure, Geology, and Girl Scouts

INTO California's Stanford University in 1894 walked a female freshman who was determined to become a geologist no matter what anybody thought. A senior who was working his way through college as a geology laboratory assistant, as well as handling numerous other remunerative chores, thought that the least he could do was be attentive to the attractive nineteen-year-old maiden with the whimsical mind and laughing blue eyes. After a field trip during which he was pondering how to get her gracefully over a fence and she just took a running start and jumped it, Herbert Hoover knew that Lou Henry would be the girl for him. He graduated with forty dollars, but no debts, and set off job-hunting while she completed her three additional years.

They were both born in Iowa. Lou's father, Charles D. Henry, was a Waterloo, Iowa, banker who developed a bronchial disorder and went West for his health. He settled in Monterey, California, and, having no sons, often took his daughter on camping and hunting trips into the hills. She rode like an Indian, learned about fishing and taxidermy, and fell in love with the thought of knowing more about minerals and mining.

Hoover was born into the West Branch, Iowa, Quaker family of Jesse Clark Hoover, who died before his son reached the age of six. When the son was ten years old he went to live with relatives in Oregon and then made his way to Stanford, where he soon became a "big man" on the campus.

In 1899, by which time he had held engineering jobs in Australia and other places, he came home to marry Lou Henry. She was determined to become a Quaker like him, but in Monterey they could find no Quaker to perform the ceremony, so they sought a dispensation and were married as Quakers but by a Catholic priest. The next day they sailed away to China, where the adventurous but scholarly Lou plunged into the serious study of Chinese. Hoover was so busy that he never had much more than a working knowledge, but when Lou was First Lady and was talking

203

sotto voce to her husband, she more than likely was speaking Chinese.

In the Orient she also developed an expert knowledge of antique Chinese porcelains. After a while she narrowed her interest to blue and white pieces of the Ming and K'ang Hse periods, and over a period of forty years she assembled one of the world's best collections of them.

The Hoovers were caught in the Boxer Rebellion and were under siege in Tientsin. She immediately became a nurse in their embattled compound and learned to ride her bicycle close to walls of buildings to avoid stray bullets. She also found a native who drove in a small herd of cows so that the sick could have milk. Once food ran so low that one of the cows had to be killed for soup. One day she was resting in her home and playing solitaire when a shell went right through the house. But she did not interrupt her game. Joaquin Miller, the California writer, showed up as a war correspondent and wanted to go on to Peking while it was still under attack. Lou bribed his rickshaw boys to desert him and he had to stay on with the Hoovers, where it was a bit safer.

During much of his career before he went into government, Hoover was with a British mining and engineering company. Globe-circling to the home office in London became a way of life for the Hoovers. Both Herbert, Jr., and Alan were born in London. When Herbert, Jr., was five weeks old, the family was off again to Australia. By the time the tot was three, he had rounded the globe three times.

Traveling with children was no problem to the Hoovers ever, but as the boys grew to school age the nomadic life had its drawbacks. The Hoovers had had homes everywhere, rented several and bought at least two in England. They tried a cottage in Monterey, California, then a six-room one on the Stanford campus and later a house in the town of Stanford. In order to be with his children more, Hoover began a free-lance engineering career, based in Stanford, California, and Lou began building her dream house—a large white one in a style borrowed from the Hopi Indians, not from the Spaniards, she always insisted. But before the house was finished, the Hoovers were off again, this time caught up in World War I. The house is now the home of Stanford's presidents.

In 1914, the Hoovers with their sons, now aged eleven and seven, were in London on a summer vacation when the war conflagration began. Into the city from all over Europe flocked well over a hundred thousand Americans, eager to get home on the first boat. Some, including the cast of a Wild West Show, had lost everything. Many had fled ahead of the guns on the Continent with only what they had on their backs.

Hoover was asked by President Wilson to chairman the American Relief Committee in London, and Mrs. Hoover formed her own committee of Americans to care for unattached women and children. She often had to find lodging and sometimes clothing for them. While they awaited homeward passage, Lou Hoover would send them on trips to Shakespeare and Lorna Doone country and to see England's cathedrals.

In October Lou Hoover took her children home to school and then returned to England to continue her relief activities, which soon included Belgian relief, too. Among other things her women's group talked the main committee into underwriting the lace industry of Belgium to save the art of lacemaking, as well as to provide work for women who knew it. The women's group also built a hospital in England for the Yanks who served "over there". Hoover's writings are filled with admiration for the way in which the American women's group always made good on its end of the bargain. But he did admit that he had had some doubts about filling warehouses with Belgian lace, which was not exactly a weapon of war. But every yard of it was sold when the war was over, and the skill was preserved.

When summer came, Lou Hoover returned home to take the boys camping, as promised. Then in 1916 she took them back with her to London so that the Hoovers could all be together, at least occasionally. The youngsters were sent to a small private school near a home the Hoovers had bought. One night when the air raid warnings sounded, she rushed to take the boys to the cellar and found their beds empty. Herbert Jr., and Alan had gone to the roof to watch the action. Their parents joined them and they saw a German zeppelin brought down in flames over the northern part of the city. Next day they all drove to the scene to gather souvenirs. When the threat of bombs and the submarine menace grew graver, Mrs. Hoover and the boys went home to California.

It was in England that the Hoovers spent what seems to have been the happiest part of their lives. There in 1907, Herbert and Lou began their scholarly translation of Agricola's *De re Metallica,* the first great treatise on mining, written in Latin in 1556 and never before successfully translated into a modern language, because linguists expert enough to tackle the languages invariably knew nothing of the subject matter. The Hoovers knew both. Mrs. Hoover was a good Latin student, and in addition to Chinese, she could speak four modern languages and had a reading knowledge of two more. And Hoover had available laboratories in which the experiments about which Agricola wrote could be checked. They worked over the treatise sentence by sentence. Over a period of five years, the manuscript traveled with them to many countries. The translation was finished in 1912. Not many husband-wife teams would call this project fun, perhaps—but the Hoovers did.

Hoover, revisiting London in 1938, after he had been President, made a pilgrimage of what he termed "unalloyed sentiment" to the Red House in which he and Lou had lived for so many years. In his memoirs, he apologized to his readers for including a letter to his wife about this visit. It shows more about their life together than these reticent Quarkers ordinarily would let others see.

Hoover stole out of his hotel, found a taxi, and traveled back into memory. In part he wrote:

"On the way my mind traveled over the thousands of times we had driven along Pall Mall, Knightsbridge, and High Street to take the second turning to the left beyond the church. And the church was the same as when the boys used to attend all weddings as doorstep observers—returning to tell us if the red carpet and awning were up—that service being five shillings extra—and how many bridesmaids or how many peals of the bells there were—those being two shillings sixpence each. I came to the door of the Red House, flooded with memories of the months we lived there, alternately with our New York and California homes, for nearly twenty years. How we had first come, as a couple, from stays in Australia or China or Russia or Burma, or New York, or the Continent: then when we had brought the babies; then when I would return from long journeys to meet you all again. . . ."

At the Red House he automatically fumbled in his pocket for the key, but was let in by a butler who had not the remotest idea who he was. After looking the place over nostalgically, he continued with: "I imagined again sitting on the opposite side of the desk from you, with the manuscripts and reference books of Agricola piled between us as we worked over the translation of *De re Metallica*. Again I saw 'Pete' at the little table in the corner making marks and announcing that he was writing a book, too; and 'Bub' clambering into his mother's lap and demanding to know what the book said. . . ."

It sounds un-Hoover, as Americans later grew to think about him, but perhaps it was more realistic than impressions of him during his years as President. The Hoover family relationships always were close knit and warm. Lou learned to live anywhere, under all conditions, and always happily;

and to be a homemaker wherever she might be. Even in hotel rooms for a two or three days stay, she invariably moved the furniture, put the telephone nearer to where her husband would be using it, and changed the lights for better illumination. "Whatever it was that she did," a secretary said years later, "the rooms were better and easier to work in after she finished." Usually she had along in her baggage gems and stones, precious and semi-precious, not because of their value as jewelry, but because she liked their beauty and wanted to study them as geology specimens. As a Quaker she wore little jewelry—many times none at all.

When President Wilson asked Hoover to be War Food Administrator in 1917, the Hoovers moved again, this time to Washington, where they eventually stayed thirteen years. When he became Secretary of Commerce under Harding, they purchased a big house with an acre-sized garden on S Street and entertained around the clock—not in the capital "S" for Society way but more in the open-house manner. After his war relief chores and the "meatless, heatless" days of World War I, his was a household name at home and widely known abroad. The Hoovers rarely sat down to a meal alone—even breakfast.

In 1922 Lou Hoover accepted the national presidency of the Girl Scouts. She built that organization from a membership of a hundred thousand to close to a million girls and raised about 2 million dollars for its treasury.

She was also attracting attention as a hostess and for the interior decoration of her home. Her flair for decorating in which she borrowed freely from the Orient was considered novel and daring. Edith Helm, who had been social secretary at the White House in the Wilson administration, wrote in her memoirs that Mrs. Hoover in furnishing her large living room had achieved a striking effect by the use of black and gold. Mrs. Helm described how sofas done in black satin enlivened by a gold flower motif were set out from the walls so as to form centers for conversational groups and how large bouquets of yellow chrysanthemums or other yellow flowers stood on end tables to heighten the dramatic effect. In a day when furniture went solemnly around the four walls and there were still high center tables in the middle of the room, such an arrangement was most unusual.

Lou Hoover was fifty-four years of age, with prematurely white hair but with a happy youthful face, when Herbert Hoover became President in 1929. She was never considered a height-of-fashion woman. She wore clothing of beautiful materials but conservatively styled. She liked tailored suits and in evening clothes never yielded to the short dresses then in vogue. She wore the cloche hat of the time or a sailor, but shunned floppy brims. "She seemed almost unaware of clothes," one of her husband's former secretaries said years later.

As First Lady, Lou Hoover continued her Girl Scout activities, supervised the building of the Hoovers' Rapidan Lodge in the Virginia mountains so that she and her husband could continue the outdoor and camping vacations they loved, and interested herself in a program of authentic redecorating and restoration in the White House.

She studied old paintings and engravings like that of Lincoln signing the Emancipation Proclamation to see how the furniture was arranged. She had copies made of many pieces of the original Monroe furniture. With the cooperation of the Frick Art Reference Library, she started a systematic cataloguing of the art work in the White House and compiled a reference book in which all portraits of the former First Ladies were included.

She bought a hundred gilt chairs for White House musicales, and, it was said, put three secretaries to work to make the White House parties conform to engineering principles. And she was credited with setting the best table the White House had known in many a year.

Lou Hoover made two White House social innovations for which her successors can be thankful. One was the discontinuance of the custom that required Cabinet wives to return endless calls and to be "at home" to the public on set weekly days. She had detested the system when she herself had been a Cabinet wife. So with White House blessing, the wives of members of her husband's Cabinet were released from the ordeal. Although vestiges of these customs lingered on until World War II, being revived a bit when the Democrats came back to power, there was never again the same hard peonage.

The other custom, the public handshaking on New Year's Day, the Hoovers obliterated forever. It was started by Abigail Adams who, by best accounts, had on her big day in 1801 a total of one hundred thirty-five callers, that being all who cared to go the White House—or could get there. It was a different story by the time Lou Hoover became First Lady.

At about 7 o'clock the morning of New Year's Day in 1930, she looked out a window and was shaken considerably to see thousands of people circling the White House grounds. Some had been there since midnight for a reception that was to begin at 10 o'clock. The event had become something like a one-cent sale and no price in human discomfort was too high to pay to get in and shake the hands of the President and First Lady on New Year's Day.

Mrs. Hoover quickly dressed, called her husband, and told the guards to throw open the gates and doors. During the hours which followed, the President begged her to take more rest but she refused, so eager was she to finish the spectacle and end it forever. Next New Year's Day the Hoovers left the White House after many announcements that they would not be at home. No other First Lady has wished to revitalize the custom which had become both impossible and meaningless.

The President would have been willing for his wife to cancel other big receptions which had become traditional, but her sense of duty would not permit her to do so. A quarter century later these had dwindled in size and number, but Lou Hoover gave them while she was in the White House as a matter of principle.

Herbert, Jr., by then married and the father of three small children, developed tuberculosis during the early days of his father's administration and was hospitalized in Asheville, North Carolina. His wife and the youngsters moved into the White House. Peggy Ann, the oldest child, in looks was—or so Alice Longworth wrote—a tiny feminine counterpart of her grandfather. Young Peter was too innocent to care about clothes. He stood in his birthday suit at a window fronting on Pennsylvania Avenue one morning, but only the staff was shocked.

Alan, only twenty-two and unmarried when his father became President, was very popular with the young crowd in Washington, but is credited with saying about the White House: "If I can't get out of this place soon, I am coming down with the willies."

It would be a surprise if Lou or her husband really liked their White House days. The First Lady, an urbane and sensitive woman, and perhaps the greatest scholar among all First Ladies, resented criticism of her husband. He tried to tease her out of it by saying that one of the good things about religions like theirs was that there was a hell to take care of non-believers—so why bother? But she never appreciated that bit of whimsy.

And Hoover perhaps had more than his share of criticism. He went out of office, a one-term President, with a public image that bore no resemblance to the one Lou had of him—or even the one the voters had when they elected him—that of the Quaker who helped feed Europe's war victims and who, a Republican, had answered a Democratic President's call to be this country's Food Administrator in World War I. The great depression changed many concepts.

Lou Hoover died unexpectedly in early 1944 in New York City where they were then living. She had come home from an afternoon concert, and he went into her room to tell her goodby before going to a dinner. He found her dead. He had never wanted to know what she did with the money which he deposited to her account, and it was only after her death that he realized how many people and organizations she had helped through the years. She had given away most of her possessions and had never cashed the repayments for loans she had made to people in need.

Attached to her simple will was "the sweetest compliment ever given to men", in her husband's opinion, although he was most reluctant at first to have it published. In a letter addressed to her sons she wrote: "You have been lucky boys to have had such a father and I am a lucky woman to have had my life's trail alongside the paths of three such men and boys."

ELEANOR ROOSEVELT (1933-April 12, 1945)

Woman of the Century

FOR sheer length of occupancy of the White House alone incredible Eleanor Roosevelt set a record which no other First Lady can hope to equal. After her they changed the law! Which was just as well, perhaps, since so few women would want to face her term of twelve years and thirty-nine days at 1600 Pennsylvania Avenue in the job which she welcomed and in which she continued to pick up momentum.

Some of her fellow citizens burned incense to her always, just as Jefferson irritably said that many did to Martha Washington. Others criticized her bitterly throughout her First Lady days and even beyond. Emotions ran high, wide and not always handsome during her husband's New Deal era. She was the sparkplug, as well as a continuing publicity outlet, for several of the era's most controversial aspects. She was more active in politics and government affairs than were all of the other First Ladies combined, and she was a social revolution herself. Her impact on her times would be hard to exaggerate.

She lived to hear herself unchallenged for more than a decade as "the woman Americans most admire." The American Indians, and she no doubt visited each of their reservations, called her "The Princess of Many Trails." Later on "First Lady of the World" was added to her many unofficial titles. She became the best known woman on the globe. She traveled more miles, came to know more people, and talked to more world leaders than any other woman in history.

When her husband was elected President she said, "I will take to Washington with me the same interests I have." This sounded so ordinary that it took the country a few days after March 4, 1933 to realize that it had attached itself to something resembling perpetual motion. She certainly was the biggest surprise package as a First Lady that the American public ever opened on any inaugural morning.

Editors took on more reporters to handle the upswing which she caused in the news. So one of her first imprints was to create new jobs—which was what the country needed. Ten million jobs for the unemployed must be found or created, her husband said, to put the country back into orbit. They were created, mostly at government expense, so rapidly that the alphabet had to be called back into special service. Americans lived on new "alphabet soup" around the clock. It contained NIRA, NRA, TVA, REA, NYA, WPA, PWA, etc., etc. And nobody was as active around-the-clock as the new First Lady.

She set up a system of regular press conferences for herself. No other First Lady had ever done this. She welcomed the idea and opened the doors, and she talked about the New Deal rather than about teas, although she gave them, too. Some who attended her weekly news sessions felt that they picked up college educations just by attending her "seminars" and trying to absorb the array of national and world affairs which she spread before them. One reporter asked her how she dared to speak so assuredly about government policy and wouldn't the President mind. The answer was that he and she saw alike on basic issues. She decided to check with him, however. He reminded her that she lived in a free country and told her to go ahead. If she put him on a limb, he continued, he could get himself off.

The first controversy which she ran into as First Lady was about the White House trees. She had swings strung on them for her two grandchildren, "Sistie" and "Buzzie" Dall. "That will ruin them," someone howled immediately—but she went ahead. Within a week she had fitted her large and noisy family into the old white mansion and done over the family living room in chintzes so that it would look more like rooms at Hyde Park, the Roosevelt estate up on the Hudson River. She had found wall space for her husband's collection of ship prints and places for his ship models.

Then before some of the Cabinet ladies had their inaugural gowns rehung, she was off over the country to see at first hand what the great depression was doing to families everywhere. She square danced with the farmers and the miners and came home with numerous notes. These notes were typed and, after she added her comments, she dropped them into a basket beside the President's bed for reading at his leisure. Thus as First Lady she was continuing to be "eyes and ears" for her crippled husband. It was a job she had assumed after he was stricken with infantile paralysis twelve years before.

When he was Governor of New York he had sent her on inspection trips of state institutions, and she learned to be a keen observer. As President he continued assigning jobs to her on a national and then an international basis. During

World War II he sent her to both the European and Pacific war areas. Her code name was "Rover," and she always believed that he was the one who suggested it.

Her trips became legendary and they were great cartoon material. The classic one showed two grubby miners in a coal cut looking up to exclaim, "For gosh sakes! Here comes Mrs Roosevelt." She did not know whether to be pleased or embarrassed when her plane put down on a Pacific island and she heard a soldier say, "I do declare I believe it's Eleanor." The President called her secretary once to ask, "Where's Eleanor?" and was told, "She's in prison this morning, Mr. President." "I'm not surprised," he quipped, "but what has she done now?"

Her voice at first was a drawback. Each sentence seemed to end in a nervous little laugh. It was good for vaudeville acts, though, and the imitators were popular. Mrs. R., one of the world's great examples in self-improvement, took on a speech teacher and set out to make her voice pleasing. The teacher went along on her trips so that no shining moment would be lost. The First Lady drove her own car and refused Secret Service attendance as not needed, but a teacher along fitted in with her ideas about continuous learning.

Some complained that "She's never in the White House," but this was untrue. It only seemed that way because she was also in so many other places. She skipped none of the so-called First Lady duties and gave all the expected receptions and dinners. But she added, added, added. The New Deal parties were fabulous not only for their numbers and the size of the crowds invited but for their informal elegance. They glittered with famous names and entertainment, and everybody—no matter how un-famous—basked in the glow of the Roosevelts. The tall First Lady looked regal in evening attire and often was decked out in family heirloom jewelry. She said that a First Lady often feels that she is dressing not herself but a national monument, but she did it with great effectiveness. The President at times came in a little late in his wheel chair, but his exciting presence was felt immediately. A man could not be elected President four times, even back when it was legal, without having unusual appeal.

These Roosevelts gave so many parties and such phenomenal ones that they almost wore out the White House which the First Lady's uncle had gone to such trouble to renovate. Uncle Teddy would have been proud of his niece's physical stamina, though. She often topped the evening off by leading the Virginia Reel in the East Parlor. And if anyone going through the receiving line told her some news

—such as that an old acquaintance of hers was in the hospital—the next day flowers would show up at the correct hospital. How she did it without a notebook at hand one wondered. She was more than a seven-day wonder.

Clothes per se meant little or nothing to Eleanor Roosevelt, or so it often seemed. She would wear a bargain basement dress costing no more than ten dollars with as much pride as she did an ermine stole and not many women would go on a trip with so few belongings as she learned to take along. But she was well groomed always, her nails manicured in a clear polish and her hair usually in good order. Anyway, it was the remarkable woman herself who was remembered and not what she wore.

One of the more amusing incidents connected with her wardrobe concerned the visit of King George and his wife Queen Elizabeth of Great Britain in a torrid June before World War II began. Someone had the bright idea that both the Queen and the First Lady should wear wool dresses, to encourage the production of wool which would be needed in the war ahead. Full descriptions of the dresses were released ahead of time but when the royal party appeared at the Union Station the Queen obviously was not in blue wool. The weather had forced her to change into a light satin of pale gray, but there Mrs. R. was at the station in the sweltering wool which was "expected."

She felt about food much as she did about clothes. It was just something to sustain one through the day. Her husband happened to have gourmet tastebuds, however, and occasionally wrote her saucy notes on the subject of meals. In one he claimed that he "bit two foreign powers this morning," and all because he had been living on sweetbreads—a plight in which he found himself after complaining about having chicken for two solid weeks. Housekeeping was not one of her many talents and she was so immune to her physical surroundings that the household help may at times have let her down. "I ruined my white gloves on dust at the White House," one irate guest complained to the press.

Mrs. R's specialties were people and how to make democracy serve their needs. "She loves humanity so much," Bernard Baruch once said, "she is not afraid to meet it face to face". She long since had turned her back on her aristocratic mother-in-law's idea that people should be judged "almost solely by their social position." She liked people just as well, and at times it seemed, better, if they had been down and out or were up against economic and social difficulties. Before her "emancipation" she had not been permitted to do charity work in the slums lest she "bring

214

diseases home to the children." But she stopped believing such, if she ever had, and began trying to do something about the diseases. She was an activist and just to talk about the government and democracy was not her way at all.

She took on so many projects that some in the country were just as much shocked by her activities as her mother-in-law had been when she began them.

When FDR ran for his first reelection, criticism against the First Lady had snowballed. She was told that she could go along on the campaign train but must stay in the background and make no speeches. To the surprise of the advisers who feared her presence, she was called for all along the way. A Gallup poll made the next year, in 1937, showed that sixty-seven percent of her countrymen approved of her multiple activities. A taxi driver, that much quoted Washington observer, declared that her criticism came mostly from "lazy wives who are jealous."

She began a daily column for United Features while she was First Lady and kept it up for twenty-five years. Only in the last years of her life was it cut to three times weekly. It was filed from every place imaginable and her fun-loving secretary, Malvina Thompson, once complained that she— not Mrs. Roosevelt—kept the longest hours of anybody. After the First Lady finished dictating, Tommy had to do the typing and get the column off. On her Pacific war trip, however, Mrs. R. did her own typing and filing. Typing was another thing she had "made" herself learn to expedite her programs.

She added a monthly question-and-answer column in the *Ladies Home Journal* in 1941, but soon switched to *McCall's* magazine where she remained for more than thirteen years. In a final article for *McCall's* she expressed belief that the strict disciplines which she underwent as a child enabled her to get through some very bad periods in her later life, and were responsible for her accomplishments. ". . . Because of all this early discipline I had, I inevitably grew into a really tough person," she wrote. And she deplored again that her own children had not been subjected to more rigorous discipline.

All five of her children married, two of them while she was First Lady, and four of them later remarried. The divorce rate among the First Family was shocking to many. The only daughter, Anna, was separated from Curtis Dall, the father of "Sistie" and "Buzzie", when her father became President, and would marry twice more. Oldest son, James, had three wives in his mother's lifetime; Elliot had four, and Franklin, Jr., had two. Only the youngest, John—at times referred to by Mrs. R. as "my Republican son"—remained with the one and only. For his fourth inaugural the President wanted all of his grandchildren present. Mrs. R. demurred but he insisted. There were thirteen of them, and they were collected from numerous households. "Sistie" was a grown young lady and the President held one tot on his knee for a sensational family photograph.

The most dramatic and amazing political speech Mrs. Roosevelt ever made was at the Chicago convention which nominated her husband for his precedent-shattering third term. Not all the delegates liked the third term idea, although a majority did—but there was bedlam when the convention learned that FDR wanted Henry A. Wallace for his Vice President. Nearly everybody wanted to be Vice President that year and the delegates would have preferred almost anyone to Wallace. Convention officials, including National Democratic Chairman James A. Farley, were fearful of the consequences if balloting began before the angry and unruly atmosphere cleared. Farley himself was resigning, supposedly over the third term, but was trying to do one more job for his commander-in-chief.

But who could quiet the undisciplined mob? The name which inevitably came to mind was that of Eleanor Roosevelt, at times known as "the conscience of the New Deal." If she indicated that the choice was all right maybe Wallace could make it. The President, reached by telephone in Washington, agreed that it was worth a try if she could be persuaded to come. She was in Hyde Park when the call from Chicago came through, and she refused to agree until she talked to Jim Farley, one of her most loved political mentors from her early days in the public arena. When she called to ask if he thought that she should come he told her, "We really need you." So she went to face the angry crowd of thirty thousand people.

She sat on the packed platform under klieg lights and waited while the nominations for Vice President went forward. Loud boos and foot-stamping greeted every name put forward and once the First Lady had to settle an argument between two of her sons: Franklin, Jr., who knew what his father wanted, and Elliot, who was a delegate from Texas and had been out on the floor promoting the choice of Jesse Jones, a fellow Texan.

All the nominations ended eventually and now was the time for the First Lady to speak—before the balloting began. Senator Alben Barkley of Kentucky banged the gavel and presented her. "I will not speak of her many virtues. . . ." he said, "not the least of which is that she has not felt it necessary to retard her efforts to advance the

216

good of humanity because she happens to be the wife of the President. . . ."

The crowd rose to clap and roar its approval. Not a boo was heard. One could almost feel the spirits of the Democrats rising again. She spoke without notes and her words were exactly correct for the occasion although not great oratorically. As always in her speeches, the woman herself and the hopes which she could engender were the sensation. She brought no message from her husband, she said, as "he will give you his own message, but as I stand here I want you to know that no one could not be conscious of the confidence which you have expressed in him . . .

"You cannot treat it as you would an ordinary nomination in an ordinary time . . . No man who is a candidate for President or who is President can carry this situation alone. This can be carried only by a united people who love their country and who will live for it to the fullest of their responsibility, to the fullest of their ability, with the highest determination that their party shall be absolutely devoted to the good of the nation as a whole. . . ."

Oldtimers called it the most effective political speech they ever heard, because it did exactly what it was intended to do and left the audience exalted. Everybody was ready to sing "Happy Days Are Here Again."

Eleanor Roosevelt was forty-eight years of age when she went to live in the White House. "I am getting old," she said when her husband died soon after his fourth term began, but she was a mere sixty at the time. By seventy-four she was saying, "My sons tell me to take it easy, but I notice they tire before I do."

The momentum which she picked up as First Lady carried her into the international arena at a time when the world seemed to need her most. Against the pleas of such political stalwarts as Senator Arthur Vandenberg of Michigan, who later proclaimed his great respect, President Truman named her to the United Nations. She was the only woman on the United States delegation which went to London in 1946 for organization of the UN General Assembly. If she had known that her appointment had to be approved by the Senate, she wrote in her autobiography, she might not have accepted it. She believed that "certain Senators would disapprove of me because of my attitude toward social problems and more especially youth problems." To her great surprise, "and I still marvel at it," she wrote, only one vote was cast against her. It was by Senator Theodore Bilbo of Mississippi who refused to specify and declared that his oppositions to Mrs. Roosevelt would "fill a book."

She remained with the UN for seven years, during four of which she was the first chairman of its important Human Rights Commission. Her countrymen loved and the world admired the tireless manner in which she worked and struggled with the Russians during those formative UN years. She called 1947 "my year with the Russians." She fought them on such issues as freedom of the press, and she was selected by the State Department to answer in the General Assembly the Soviet denunciation of democracy as a philosophy of government. She was a dogged and effective spokesman for the human rights longings of everybody everywhere. That was when she began to be called "First Lady of the World."

Her opposition to Soviet principles and tactics also did her a world of good at home because it began to lessen the criticism that she was "soft on Communism." Her patronage of the American Youth Congress, which admittedly had Communists on its roles, had done more to feed this idea than all her other actions while First Lady. This Congress was not a New Deal agency and had no connection with the government other than through the First Lady's interest. It should not be confused with the National Youth Administration, which was government-run and met with wide general approval. Mrs. R. had mothered the NYA idea as a means of helping needy youngsters get an education. What the A.Y.C. stood for never was clear. "Whether they were Communist-inspired from the beginning I have never known," she said in her autobiography.

She turned her back on A.Y.C. when she learned that she could not trust its members "to be honest with me," but that was after the group had shocked the Nation by booing the President on the White House grounds. Its 1940 convention was held in Washington and the First Lady went all out to find free lodging for many of its five thousand ill-mannered delegates. The White House was filled to the rafters with them and some were quartered in barracks at nearby Fort Myer. This was a use of government property which Congress questioned most heartily.

Her flood of critical mail, adverse editorials, and denunciation on Capitol Hill reached an all-time high during this period. "I never have felt the slightest bitterness toward any of them," she wrote of A.Y.C. members years later. "I learned from them what Communist tactics are. . . . In fact, I think my work with the American Youth Congress was of infinite value to me in understanding some of the tactics I had to meet later in the United Nations!" Of the Russians she wrote, "You can't understand them. You just have to outlast them. We have the ability (to cope with them), but do we have the patience?"

After her terms with the UN ended she began her travels again in earnest. She went twice to the Soviet Union and after that to the Arab countries and to Israel, to Japan, Yugoslavia, India, Morocco, Hong Kong, and elsewhere. When she visited Sheik Suleiman near Beersheba, he already had thirty-nine wives, but he put up Mrs. Roosevelt's picture and assured her son, Congressman James Roosevelt of California, that she really should have been his fortieth. The only place she wanted to go and did not, it appears, was to Red China. She cancelled her visa for there in 1954 because "other reporters" were not admitted.

Whatever Mrs. R. did as First Lady always seemed to be easy for her and she appeared to lack self-consciousness when things went wrong or when she was criticized—but probably it was only her rigid discipline taking over. As someone who once must have been her pupil at Todhunter School for Girls wrote in *The New Yorker,* "She was incapable of discouragement. . . . and watching her and listening to her, we began to see that she not only believed in but lived all the difficult, optimistic bluestocking virtues."

As a child and as a young wife she was ultra shy and self-conscious, and apparently devoid of rebellion. She did not rebel against her background and sheltered life until her husband was crippled in 1921. Then she "made" herself learn to swim and dive, drive a car, become adept with horses and go camping because the children would need her more, as would her husband. Her real rebellion was against her mother-in-law, who thought that Franklin should succumb to the wheelchair and forget about politics. Mrs. R. was determined to keep him in the career where he wanted to be and where his future had seemed so bright. So she "made" herself learn politics. She started at the doorbell-ringing level and with the help of her husband and men like Governor Alfred E. Smith and Jim Farley, she became an effective campaign worker.

Once started she kept going on to other areas, too. With some friends she established a furniture factory on part of the Hyde Park estate and built herself a cottage there. It was "my own place," the first she ever had. Her husband had spurred the furniture factory idea. When "the girls" kept talking about it he dared them to go ahead and gave them a ninety-nine-year lease to the land. One of the ideas behind the factory was to provide jobs for some of the country boys in the area. After that was done she and her friends bought Todhunter School for Girls in New York City. Mrs. R. became vice-principal and tried her hand at teaching civics and literature. When writing the Bill of Rights on the blackboard, she would become so excited about its contents that she often broke the chalk.

Her parents were Anna Rebecca Hall and Elliott Roosevelt, a brother to Theodore. She adored her father and it was mutual, but she always felt that her beautiful mother was ashamed of her looks and awkward ways. The mother called her "Granny," she was so serious, and laughed at her attempts to dance. Both parents died by the time she was nine. She and her little brother, Hall, lived with their maternal grandmother, Mrs. Valentine G. Hall, on part of the old Chancellor Robert R. Livingston estate, also on the Hudson. The home was palatial but gloomy for an overly sensitive little girl surrounded by adults. Grandmother Hall was the great granddaughter of Chancellor Livingston, so little Eleanor had an abundance of social status and good governesses. One of them was so strict that when the child had darned a hole, the governess would cut it out and tell her to try again, which she obediently did. Once she went to visit Uncle Teddy at Oyster Bay on Long Island and shook with fright when told to plunge into the bay and swim with her gay and vigorous cousins.

She was sent to Mlle. Souvestre's School in Europe and became a paragon of obedience and study. Mlle. Souvestre was a demanding headmistress who insisted on much quick memory work. Eleanor learned to concentrate so well that she could read a poem once and repeat it. The headmistress was fond of her serious American pupil and took her on vacations with her. When she was eighteen Grandmother Hall ordered her home to make her social debut in New York City. She would have loved to study more but to Grandmother and all old New York families of the day one "came out" at eighteen and there was no escape.

During Eleanor's debut season her beautiful aunts drummed up escorts for her. This was easy to do for a Roosevelt who was descended from a Livingston, but getting the same lad back twice apparently was difficult. Eleanor was not the type who came home with dates for tomorrow. One gay and handsome young man paid her more than usual attention. He was her fifth cousin once removed, Franklin Delano Roosevelt, the only child of James and Sarah Delano Roosevelt, whose family seat was rich and ancestral Hyde Park, also on the Hudson. His interest in the shy tall maiden who eventually would become his fearless wife was a lasting one.

They were married on Saint Patrick's Day of 1905, the President of the United States going up from Washington to give his niece away. Uncle Teddy walked away with the show, naturally. Everybody in New York wanted to see him and when the minister asked who was giving the bride away his "I do" sounded like a cannon going off. When Mrs. Roosevelt's own children married—and two of them did while she was First Lady—she tried to make her husband stay in the background.

The young couple went to live with Franklin's autocratic mother as a matter of course and there never was any doubt that they were "her" homes: the big place at Hyde Park, the New York houses, and the summer place at Campobello in New Brunswick, Canada. When the children came she claimed them for her own, too. During World War I when Franklin became assistant Secretary of the Navy under President Wilson, the younger Mrs. Roosevelt escaped temporarily by living in Washington. But eleven years and five children after her marriage, the basic mother-in-law situation was the same. The stroke that crippled the future President came at Campobello. Years later, when she had become a far different type of woman, Mrs. R. was resenting her mother-in-law in retrospect and apparently still worrying that she had not been in control of her children when they were growing up.

Mrs. R. was a great one for earning money and always preferred what she earned to any she inherited. This seems to have been connected in some way with one of her maxims that "You must be important to yourself." When she was First Lady it caused raised eyebrows and the recurring question, "Why in the world does she want it and what does she do with it?" The official answer was that she gave it to charities, needy individuals, and to worthy causes—and apparently this was the truth. In her lifetime, it was estimated, she gave away about a million dollars. Let her rich mother-in-law top that! Her earnings for a long while totalled in the area of $100,000 a year. Her income from her parental inheritance, she wrote, was about $8,000 a year and her husband's estate when settled was worth about a million dollars. Yet in *On My Own,* published in 1958, she wrote with apparent pride: "I live on what I earn by writing, appearing on radio and television and reading manuscripts at $100 a month for the Junior Literary Guild. . . . Actually these earnings total more than I spend in living expenses, and it is a good thing that they do, because all the income from my inheritance and more besides is required to pay my annual tax bills."

Edith Helm, her White House social secretary, and her other secretaries there learned to hesitate before telling her of charity appeals, she was so quick with the checkbook. Many thought her overly generous, not only with money but with herself. She charged $1,000 to $1,500 for many of her lectures, but would pitch in for free if the cause appealed enough. She kept three secretaries busy in her later years but always found time to get in on the causes of the sixties such as finding tractors with which to ransom prisoners held in Cuba by Fidel Castro.

President Kennedy returned her to the UN and when one of her secretaries was asked how this could be wedged into her overflowing schedule—and could she give, say, an eighth of her time to it—the answer was, "Why, where would Mrs. Roosevelt find an eighth of her time for anything? She's much too busy for that!"

She did her work under any and all conditions and never went anywhere without it. In her earlier days as First Lady she knitted through conferences, but she changed that to paper work. In railway stations, on airplanes and under the hair dryer she was always working. She learned to enter her beauty parlor with a smile big enough to include everybody (it would have hurt her terribly to leave anybody out) and then to get on with her massive correspondence.

Some said that she lacked a sense of humor and that she was not warm personally. Certainly she lacked the gay and swashbuckling type of laughter which her debonair husband so fortunately had in his makeup, but she enjoyed a chuckle. When a big campaign button one year proclaimed, "We Don't Want Eleanor, Either" she found it funny—but her speeches contained neither jokes nor anecdotes, nor would she have known how to relate them. She wrote matter of factly many things which amused Americans, however, and was so frank that it was refreshing. She wrote about Madame Chiang Kai-Shek and her silk sheets which had to be changed each time she got out of bed at the White House, about how uncomfortable the hard bolsters were when she visited Queen Juliana in the Netherlands, and eventually she revealed that her husband made a miserable martini even though he considered himself to be an expert in the field.

As for personal warmth, she spread it over such a wide area that it rarely seemed intimate except to her earlier friends and to those who needed her help. One of her grandchildren said with understanding, "Grandmother lives upstairs."

Her last assignment was to be chairman of the President's Commission on the Status of Women. After her death in late 1962, President Kennedy decided to leave the chairmanship vacant, declaring it to be his judgment "that there can be no adequate replacement for Mrs. Roosevelt."

About her forty years of marriage to Franklin Roosevelt she wrote: "He might have been happier with a wife who was completely uncritical. That I was never able to be, and he had to find it in other people. Nevertheless, I think I sometimes acted as a spur, even though the spurring was not always wanted or welcome. I was one of those who served his purposes."

BESS WALLACE TRUMAN (April 12, 1945-1953)

Gallant Lady from Independence

On a memorable April afternoon in 1945 Bess Truman was going her own quiet way about the modest Washington apartment in which she had lived for a decade, being company for her aged mother and enjoying her gay college daughter's preparations for a dance. Within the next hour she was en route to the White House to become First Lady.

The homey scene to which she would think back with longing for the next seven years was changed for her by the ring of a telephone. Daughter Margaret grabbed it, as usual, and as usual started right in joshing with her father, the Vice President. He asked her to call her mother, but she had more to tell him. "Margaret!" came a voice which Harry S. Truman rarely used with Margaret, "I want to speak to your mother!"

The next thing Margaret remembered was her mother, with tears streaming down her face, going in to tell her own mother, Mrs. David Wallace, "President Roosevelt is dead." In what seemed to be the twinkling of an eye the doorbell rang and Margaret went to answer it. "Don't open that door again unless you know who's outside," ordered a Secret Service man. The Trumans' lives and the type of life they liked to live changed in a few minutes.

To all who saw the photograph of the swearing in of the new President, it was obvious that Bess Truman's eyes were swollen from crying and that she stoically was trying to prevent the tears starting again. She was looking straight into the camera, her spring hat tilted toward the front and her hair nicely curled, but she presented as grief-stricken a picture as ever a woman could. Her tailored suit was light colored and she was holding a largish dark purse in a way which indicated that she might let it drop at any moment.

Many of her tears, no doubt, were for the late President, the news of whose death was then spreading over the country and beginning to circle the globe to American troops still in combat overseas. Some were for her husband, for the shocking swiftness with which he had to assume not only leadership of the country but the carrying on of a great war which was by no means over. Dry-eyed Mrs. Roosevelt had felt for him, too. When he asked what he could do to help her, the going-out-of-office First Lady said that the question should be: "What can we do to help you? You have the burden now."

Truman was entering a lonely job and at the same time he was taking his family into the glare of a spotlight which his wife never would have chosen for herself. She was a reserved and private sort of person who relished her life-long friends, preferred her home town of Independence, Missouri, to any other place in the world and had her own strong convictions about what made life worthwhile. She was not eager to share her thoughts with casual comers. She was the wittiest member of her family, but she did not spread her wit before strangers nor waste words in conversation. She was from show-me Missouri and apt to speak in mono-syllables. "Nope" was one of her best known words around Washington and she became known as "the independent lady from Independence."

Just as her husband was taking on a job which many thought would be impossible for him, so was she stepping into the shoes of Eleanor Roosevelt and that was about the toughest assignment which a First Lady ever had. Bess Truman did fill the job of First Lady with poise and charm, but she did it by remaining herself. It took her a few weeks to decide what her roll would be and there were some false starts.

In late May on her first official appearance she went out to the airport to christen two hospital planes. Margaret went along as maid of honor and the new First Lady had prepared a speech to give. It read: "We send these planes forth with our love and the sincere desire that the comfort and solace derived from them by our fighting men will let them know firmly that we are behind them."

The speech was lost in the shuffle when the First Lady, swinging with all her might and main, was unable to break the champagne bottle. Whoever was in charge of the arrange-ments had neglected to have it scored for easy breakage as customarily is done for any launching. Also the planes had new soft-type aluminum noses and the harder she swung the more they dented. After six failures Margaret said, "If mother can't break that bottle, nobody can!" "Be quiet," her mother hissed. It took her eleven swings and then the champagne spilled all over her dress. "Fine thing for a woman who won the shot-put championship at her school's track meet," Margaret teased later to make her mother feel better about her debut in what became known as "the battle with the bottles."

Mrs. Truman scheduled a formal press conference, but then cancelled it and never scheduled another. After two years in the White House she answered a list of written questions submitted by reporters. After the one which asked what qualities were most necessary for a First Lady she wrote, "Good health and a strong sense of humor."

Her daughter in *Margaret Truman's Own Story* wrote: "Mother is perhaps the least understood member of our family—a woman of tremendous character, a warm hearted, kind lady with a robust sense of humor, a merry twinkling wit and a tremendous capacity for enjoying life.

"From all I can gather, although not from her, as her modesty is so deep-seated nothing can be done about it, she was an Independence belle. Her pictures show her to have been as slim as a willow wand with large blue eyes and a cap of fair wavy hair that fitted her head like a helmet. . . . She was a crack tennis player and distinguished herself in boarding school by winning the shot-put in a track meet. Her own comment on this last is that it certainly has come in handy for shaking hands with a thousand people at a time. It's also reported that mother could whistle through her teeth, play baseball, and beat all comers at mumblety-peg . . ."

Margaret could have mentioned, too, that her mother nearly always was the best skater on the pond and that Harry Truman wrote his supposedly one and only musical composition around her whistle. It was the whistle which she used to call her girlhood friends to her home at 219 North Delaware Street in Independence. He kept hearing it as he practiced the piano and, ever conscious of Bess (nee Elizabeth Virginia Wallace), he set it to music.

The home in which Bess lived was the one from which the Trumans moved to Washington and to which they returned when the White House days were over. Margaret was born there and the house was a story in itself. It was built by George Porterfield Gates, the future First Lady's grandfather, not many years after he took his family out to Missouri from Vermont shortly after the Civil War ended. It was known as "The Gates Victorian Mansion" and it never seemed to matter to whom the deed belonged because it was the "family home" and its seventeen rooms welcomed three generations at any time.

Grandfather Gates made a comfortable fortune in Queen of the Pantry flour, which was advertised as making the best hot biscuits in the world, and it was said that the elegant young lady on the flour sack, so proudly wearing the bustle dress of the 1880's, was patterned after one of his three daughters: Myra, Maude, or Madge, who was Mrs.

Truman's mother. She, Madge, would die in the White House while her son-in-law was President, and was considered to be "about the queenliest lady" ever to live in Independence. She married David Wallace, whose father had been mayor, and after his death she gave up her home a few blocks away and moved back to live with her mother. Bess, her only daughter, had three younger brothers. The brothers married and built nearby. Bess, as was proper, remained with her mother and grandmother.

In later years, when tourists came seeking the Harry Truman house, it delighted his friends to say, "Why I don't believe that Mr. Truman, if you mean Harry S, owns a house here. He lives right down the street there, though in his wife's mother's mother's house." There never was any doubt, though, that when Harry Truman married Bess he would move into the Gates mansion nor that Mrs. Wallace would move to the capital city if the Trumans did; nor that they all would go back to Independence every summer. They were a "family" and family ties meant much to the Trumans.

Harry Truman first saw Bess Wallace and became smitten with her in the Presbyterian Sunday School kindergarten when he was six and she was five. He was a Baptist, incidentally, and the Wallaces later became Episcopalians—which caused their daughter Margaret in her White House years always to have two trips to make on Sunday: one to early services with the Episcopalians and then one at eleven o'clock to church with the Baptists. The legend went that Harry as a boy went to the Presbyterian church just to see Bess, but one of his friends said, "Heck, it was nearer to where he lived and he had to go to church somewhere."

During their grammar and high school years all that he asked of a day was the privilege of carrying her books home. His aunt coached them in Latin and knew that he had his heart set on the popular Bess.

When he came back to visit this aunt years later she sent him across the street to return a cake plate to the Wallaces. He stayed and stayed and came back walking on air and saying, "Well I saw her." They did not become engaged until he was going off to World War I. She and her engaged girl friends, for fun, called themselves the I.W.W.'s which stood in their code for Independence War Widows. She was the first I.W.W. to be married. That was in 1919, when she was thirty-four years of age. Margaret, the only child of the future First Family, was born shortly after her mother's thirty-ninth birthday.

When Bess Truman became First Lady she was sixty years of age and, like Martha Washington before her, she at times thought this to be unfortunate.

Asked a decade later whether she thought that Mrs. John F. Kennedy's youth would be an asset or a liability she quickly responded, "An asset. On that point I have no doubts whatsoever." She never looked her age as First Lady and a decade later she not only was looking much younger but much happier than when she lived in the White House.

Margaret wrote that under criticism, and no First Lady ever can escape it either about herself or about her husband, "Ma goes to bed with a sick headache but Dad and I bounce back." The husband and daughter were extroverts by nature, and the peppery President could blow his top to rid himself of irritations. These blow-offs often were enjoyable to the public, but not to the First Lady. One of the stories of the administration was that just as she finished calling the President to task for language he had used about a columnist his daughter telephoned. She wanted to take up the same subject. "Now, see here, Margaret, I've just had two hours of that from your mother, and I'm not going to take it from you," said the President.

One of the toughest flurries of criticism which Bess Truman had to face happened right after her husband was nominated for Vice President. She held a press conference at the political convention in Chicago and neglected to say that she had been on her Senator husband's payroll. When it came out that she had started as a clerk at $2,600 a year and was raised to $4,500, the headlines were rough. Congresswoman Clare Booth Luce called her "Payroll Bess," a barb for which Truman never forgave the phrase maker.

The truth was that Mrs. Truman worked for her money by handling the Senator's personal mail and later helped edit reports of the important Senate war investigating committee which he headed. When the committee work became so voluminous he had asked her to take on the personal-mail chores because he trusted her above all others and could work with her at home on them. "She is my chief adviser always," he declared. There was nothing illegal or even unusual about her job, but a Congressman's payroll is one of those recurring areas of doubt in the public's mind.

Another area in which the public is very much interested is that of gifts to the First Family. Some Presidents accept everything in sight and nobody minds, but others accept nothing at all. Thomas Jefferson belonged to the latter group and his poor daughter, Martha, in love with a shawl brought personally to her by a foreign potentate saw it sold at public auction before her own agent could get there to bid on it. Congressional committees love to investigate in this area and usually come up with some bit of wisdom such as that it's all right to accept a ham (especially if it's cooked!) but not a rug, say, nor a hotel bill. Bess Truman, as First Lady, ran into this one, too, by permitting someone to give her a deep freezer. By that time, however, her character was so well established that even her husband's most bitter enemies, such as Senator Joseph McCarthy, rose to her defense. "The nicest thing about Harry is Bess," the Senator said.

When she first became First Lady one of her friends who had been an I.W.W. called to congratulate her and to add that she assumed things would be different now. "Indeed they will not be," declared the First Lady.

The I.W.W.'s became the nucleus of Mrs. Truman's famous bridge club, the members of which were invited to the White House for a gala visit during which they swam in the President's pool, saw everything in town, and had a posh luncheon given for them by the First Lady. When Bess went home to Independence, as she did every summer, the bridge club once tried to play a trick on her. They rose in a body at her entrance and on cue, bowing formally, said in unison, "Welcome home, Madame President." She did not disappoint them but said in disgust, "Oh, sit down. Sit down! You all make me so mad!"

She was a member of Chapter S of PEO, a sorority, and it was rumored around Washington that she had been slated for its presidency. "Don't be silly," a member said, "Bess never would consider being president of anything." Mrs. Truman never craved top honors. She had attended the Senate Wives Club off and on for years but when her husband became Vice President and she was entitled to preside over it, she stopped going. The thank-you notes which she wrote in her own slanting hand are said to outnumber those of any other First Lady in modern times. She was so personal about all that she did that she could not imagine letting a secretary answer the letters she received after her mother's death, for instance.

Another friend, whose daughter was to give a musical recital, called the new First Lady shortly after the President was sworn in, to say that there was still time to re-do the program, which Mrs. Truman as wife of the Vice President had agreed to sponsor. The friend assumed that now Mrs. Truman might consider the idea presumptuous. "Leave my name on that list, and expect me," said the First Lady.

She took special dishes to the sick, and by hand. Going to leave a hot dish for a sick friend one day when she was en route to a gala First Lady event she was told "No visitors allowed." "Well, will you please eat it then?" she said as she put a ten dollar bill on the dish and fled before being recognized by the janitor.

One of the nicest and most revealing things about her was

written by Edith Helm, who stayed on at the White House as social secretary although she was of retirement age. Mrs. Helm was sitting with head bowed at the funeral services for President Roosevelt at the White House when she felt a hand slipped into hers. It was the new First Lady's, who sensed what the older woman, who had served also during the second Wilson term, must be going through. "I'm so grateful that I did not retire but had a chance to serve under the Trumans," said Mrs. Helm. Mrs. Helm waxed furious when anybody criticized this administration, and it was much criticized—with "belittling" being perhaps the better word—as many will remember. President Truman's job, many thought, was to finish out the incomplete fourth term of President Roosevelt and then get out of office as quickly as possible. Then, when President Truman won an election on his own, the election which was considered impossible, the tune changed; but the First Lady never did. Nor did she need to do so ever.

"Now you leave *her* alone," almost anybody who set out to criticize her husband in the presence of anyone who knew Mrs. Truman was apt to hear. "Say what you feel you have to about him, *but not her!*" It was a great relief to some of the country that she was *not* a Mrs. Roosevelt, for instance, and anyone who ever knew Bess Truman became fond of her for her own qualities. She was not a glamorous woman, at least not at the time, nor did she ever photograph well. And small wonder that she did not, for she refused ever to pose. One of the jokes about her was that when she came home to Independence and tarried at the train for the local photographer to take the pictures, her mind was always on something else. She pulled her hat smack down over her eyes, squared her already square shoulders, clothed in the square clothes of the time, and just waited for the ordeal to be over. She nearly always looked belligerent in her press photographs. The Independence view was that "Bess does not care how she looks . . . and Hoorah for her!" As for what President Truman thought, he made the classic remark that "She looks exactly like a woman who has been married for twenty-five years *should* look."

She wore nice clothes, as she always had, and she possessed innumerable hats. The dressmaker and shop owner who made her inaugural dress for the term which her husband won on his own said that she looked for the practical and always asked the price. Her "poodle hair cut", one of the first in the country, and her salt-free diet were featured in many a headline.

Bess Truman not only was an excellent housekeeper but she knew all about good food and would have been embarrassed to serve her guests anything else. Being the daughter of a hot biscuit king, as well as from Missouri, naturally she liked her breads hot and preferred them homemade if possible. The White House long since, it appeared, had shifted exclusively to bakery products and those in charge of the kitchen failed to see the difference between piping hot and lukewarm. Morning after morning the First Lady's rolls went back uneaten. So she sent for Vietta, their wonderful cook in Independence, so that the First Family could have biscuits and rolls so fresh and piping hot that they melted butter instantly. After all, what's a biscuit for?

The staff loved the warmth and informality of the Trumans and about the only advice which Bess Truman ever offered to future First Ladies was for them to have confidence in the staff provided to them and not to consider the personal part of the job too hazardous. Through the years, her experiences indicated, the government must have grown more efficient in assuming responsibility for seeing a job well done in the White House, on the housekeeping level. No more wandering around in the dark like President Franklin Pierce, for instance, and falling into an unmade bed on inaugural night!

One of Mrs. Truman's biggest worries about the White House was what it might do to her daughter, who was about to graduate from college. About this point she need not have worried. Margaret was so well adjusted that nothing fazed her. She rather liked to see her picture in the papers, she admitted, and as for riding to school in a White House car, "what could be nicer?" She was made much of, as she wrote, and became a belle almost by national law.

Margaret had her own piano at the age of eight and was bent on a singing career, something to which her parents had no objection as long as she finished college first. This she did and her father gave the commencement address. Then she went to New York to continue her music lessons, the First Lady sending along her own secretary to be chaperone. Margaret began to give concerts, as well as to appear on radio and television. Whether a President's daughter has a fair chance at a career, her experiences did not necessarily prove. Critics hit her harder just because she was a President's daughter, some more pro and some more con than they might have done otherwise. But her main problem, it appears from her book, was one of time. Margaret in her early twenties was always tired. She was leading about eight lives in one, it seemed. Being a White House daughter and a theatrical character all at once was far from simple. For instance she could not, if she had wanted, miss the visit of Princess Elizabeth and her husband, Philip. Events of this kind were happening regularly in the Executive Mansion. She wrote that she never had time to shop and that she rarely if ever faced a concert rested and in good shape. But the show must go on at the White House just as inexorably as it does on the stage.

Margaret was young and gay and lovely, with blonde hair and big blue eyes. Her school chums came to sleep in the Lincoln bed, for which the mattress was "exceedingly lumpy," she said. She was the life of the family and any time she stepped an iota out of line she heard from the President. Evidently thinking that on a few of her radio and TV shows she tended to show off, he wrote her in New York to remember that she was brought up to be a lady and must give every performance all she had.

The Trumans had the White House fall down around them —almost. They were giving a reception when the President kept hearing the big chandelier above their heads in the Blue Parlor go tinkle-tinkle. He asked the Commissioner of Public Buildings, W. E. Reynolds, who happened to be at the party, to have someone take a look at the old place. "You're going to have to get out of here," a survey committee said before long, but not before the leg of Margaret's piano started going through the upstairs floor. Patched and repatched, and so hastily renovated in 1902, the structure was wobbly all over. Its electric wiring was decidedly unsafe, too.

This time it was decided to strip the house down to the masonry and start over, so to speak, regardless of what it cost; which turned out to be around $6,250,000 plus the cost of some new furbishings. In the renovating the President was able to make a change which he had been wanting to do. The main stairway before this had come straight down, ending right outside the door of the East Parlor. He wanted it to be more graceful and to open into the large foyer where, with a little managing, it could be quite ceremonial. Although they were not credited with it at the time, the Trumans entertained with elaborate formality and color and their crowds were the largest yet seen. Mrs. Helm said that the Roosevelts topped them for sustained elegance, but that the Trumans returned to rituals not possible to the crippled Roosevelt, and the postwar growth greatly increased the number of their guests. They gave large parties.

President Truman's desire to change the White House stairway caused adverse headlines, but not so many as when he earlier had built his balcony so that today's First Families, so often trapped in their quarters upstairs while tourists take over below, at least can go out on the porch and see what the weather is like. He did it for architectural reasons, however, thinking that the tall columns at the south entrance needed the balcony. Also, having the balcony rather than the awnings which were formerly put up each summer let more light in. Architects later said that he did the structure a favor, but at the time it seemed to many that he was going to ruin the place before he got out of it! The Truman administration was marked by many such quibblings.

Nobody expected him to win an election on his own—except a healthy majority of Americans, as it turned out. But the family whistlestopped the country and picked up crowds everywhere. He introduced his wife as "my boss" and then Margaret as "her boss." The sophisticates called it kid stuff, but it did not turn out that way. There have been other elections just as exciting, perhaps, but not in modern times. Margaret said that getting on and off the campaign train and helping keep track of appointments at the various stops were at least slimming. After their victory they gave a tremendous inaugural reception at the National Gallery of Art, with ten thousand guests invited. That was the largest inaugural party in history up to that date, on an invited rather than a free-for-all basis.

Everybody assumed that Bess Truman was happy when the White House gave way and she could move across the street to smaller Blair House, where no more than twenty could come to dinner. The truth is, however, that living in Blair House complicated her life rather than simplified it. For every tea which she might have given in the White House she now had to give a series of them. She did it all with steady graciousness and added a featured set of parties for convalescent veterans from military hospitals in and around the city. The President, looking over the intended beverages of tea, coffee and soft drinks, added a light beer to this menu. Once, when him wife was ill, he ran a veterans' party on his own.

When the White House was gutted and then rebuilt, the fireplaces worked again and there were such up-to-date innovations as air conditioning, clothes closets, a basement complete with an air raid shelter, and lots of plug-ins for TV. The First Lady showed the women of the press over it from top to bottom, but she never once mentioned that her mother was dying in one of the family bedrooms. That was too personal for her to mention.

The President went down to the station to meet Margaret almost every time she came home and one of the most comforting sights of the hectic era in which all were living in those days was to see the President at the station sending his wife off on her brief trips to New York to see Margaret and maybe do a bit of shopping. He loved his "womenfolks" and the country came to love him for it.

He wrote that someone should evaluate the role of First Ladies and give the wives of Presidents due credit. When

Bess Truman went back to Independence many a Washingtonian realized that they missed her dreadfully. "Didn't you just love Mrs. Truman?" they asked each other. Not all First Ladies leave behind such a warm afterglow.

MAMIE DOUD EISENHOWER (1953-1961)

Smiles, Bangs, and Jewelry

WHEN breezy Mamie Eisenhower moved into the White House in 1953 it was her thirtieth move in thirty-seven years and, as always before for her, it was into a place not her own. Nonetheless, she was determined to continue being a perfect housekeeper and to leave the white edifice in as good shape as she found it. "Don't step on the rug," was rather startling when first enunciated by her secretary to the newswomen who went to view the table decorations before a state dinner. "What does she think we're doing—wearing cleats?" one upset reporter demanded. But the secretary was only reflecting the lengths to which the staff went in trying to meet the spit-and-polish standards set by this First Lady with a military background. It was said that even the Secret Service men ran around with dust pans during her eight years.

Mamie enjoyed being First Lady and did not mind who knew it, and she kept a top sergeant's hold on all the homemaking facilities. She was strict about the menus, saw to the flower arrangements, inspected the table, checked the place cards, tried on her dresses in trial runs, and wanted to find the dining room exactly as she left it. Unfluffed carpets irritated her and she could detect the imprint of a foot a mile away. Snipers said that she could not bear the lived-in look and that everything seemed to be wrapped in cellophane. If possible, staff members walked around the rugs rather than on them.

She was named for an Aunt Mary, but nevertheless christened Mamie, a Mary variation. It was an appealing name which the country liked, and nearly everybody liked the woman who went with it. She was pert and pretty, had the nicest complexion and bluest eyes imaginable, and a smile to match. The smile became almost as famous as the grin of her husband, Dwight David (Ike) Eisenhower, a popular President who had been extremely popular as the commanding general of World War II. "We Like Ike" was the slogan of the times and to it often was attached "And We *Love* Mamie."

All America blossomed out in pink in honor of Mamie's favorite color and even women who should not have done so began wearing their hair in bangs. She was the most feminine First Lady in many a day and was quite the youngest looking grandmother since Elizabeth Monroe. She symbolized the "new women who did not have to grow old." Before her husband entered politics she confided to friends the fear that she was much too "corny and slangy" to be First Lady and when the first political leaders came to visit she, knowing that they were inspecting her, too, maintained a reserved dignity. When she threw that stiffness overboard and became her gay, charming self, things worked much better.

She would never have chosen to add politics to her husband's careers because she had been looking forward to retirement, and ever since World War I had dreamed of a farm of their own near Gettysburg, Pennsylvania. They acquired it during Ike's Presidency and the First Lady was in seventh heaven, fixing it up and fitting in all the furniture and furnishings which she had stashed away in storage.

Mamie was like wives everywhere and that is probably what made her so loved by her vast public. She had a temper of buzz-saw velocity, or so it was written, but then other wives did, too. And she did not hold grudges. She was fluffy and frilly, but so were many of them. Her full skirts and bright colors, small flower-laden hats, matching gloves, and lots of costume jewelry were in line with the "living doll" vogue then so popular. She no doubt held back the straight skirt sack-look for quite a spell. She bought up to ten hats at a time, always asking for the ones which would photograph well, and her First Lady wardrobe of formal attire occupied two full bedrooms in the White House.

The Executive Mansion still was spanking new from its expensive overhauling which the Trumans had been able to enjoy only briefly, but Mamie saw immediately that no woman had been consulted. Why, she wondered, were the closets still so inadequate, the passenger elevator so small, and the arrangements for getting food up from the kitchens so impossible? She wanted a whole closet for her perfumes and toiletries, but it was not there, and to a woman like her it became almost tearfully embarrassing to have royal guests waiting while trays of food were rushed off the passenger lift. She solved the latter problem by sending most of the continuous stream of state visitors to live in the President's Guest House (Blair House) across the street.

At times that became confusing, too. Lillian Rogers Parks, the seamstress who wrote *My Thirty Years Backstairs at the White House* in collaboration with Frances Spatz Leighton, told of the luggage mix-up when the King and Queen of Greece came visiting. Part of the large entourage stayed at Blair House, but the luggage went everywhere: some to the Greek Embassy, some to the White House, and some to the guest house. On the night of the state dinner the Queen's maid could not locate a small bag which Her Majesty needed. A truck brought all the Greek luggage from across the street and, in the rain, White House staff members helped explore for it and found no small bag. It was found in the Queen's quarters at about the time the housekeeper from across the street telephoned, "Oh, brother! If you will send that truck back so we can get the Prime Minister's clothes, we will dress him and send him over there to dinner." It was fervently hoped that the First Lady had not been aware of the hullabaloo, for it was the type of thing which any hostess who wanted things to run perfectly would much deplore.

Mamie's jewelry and her many changes of costume were noticeable. Her sister, Mrs. Gordon ("Mike") Moore, had an amusing experience which involved it. Mrs. Moore was helping in a Washington thrift shop run for a worthy cause when a woman customer admired an antique jewelry item for which the chain alone cost more than a hundred dollars. "Oh, well," sighed the customer who had no idea who the saleslady was, "If Mamie can wear junk jewelry so can I." She bought a $1.98 item.

Some wealthy Washington hostesses, including the then Polly Guggenheim, worried so much about the First Lady having no "real" jewelry that they put forth the idea that the Smithsonian Institution should have a special collection from which Mamie and all future First Ladies could draw for state occasions, in the crown-jewels manner. It has not materialized yet, but Mamie did buy some very good jewelry before she left the White House. She continued to wear the other, however, because she liked it best and was sentimentally attached to so many of its pieces. Her charm and grandmother bracelets were part of her and not even for Karsh, the noted photographer, would she take off a watch which he thought was marring the impression he wished to create. "Ike gave it to me on our twenty-fifth anniversary and I want to be pictured in it," she said.

She was an out-and-out sentimentalist who remembered corsages she had worn in her youth, cried when songs were sad or too nostalgic or when she heard lavish praise of herself at birthday parties. She loved the anniversary-type party so much that every group in Washington wanted to give her one for her birthday each year and would gladly have given her two a year, for that matter. "It's so much fun to give a party for Mamie," club presidents said, "because she is so responsive." She held her hands up high to applaud so that all could see her enjoyment. She was the same way at her White House receptions and dinners. Her gay and warm greeting seemed just for you. Nearly anyone meeting her for the first time was apt to exclaim, "Why, I thought she was a much older woman." The truth is that Mamie left the White House looking younger than when she came to it, and that alone was record-breaking.

She was fifty-six years of age when she became First Lady and began to grow young. The reasons why she grew younger were easy to see. Right from the start she had a four-year lease on a nice house and this was renewed for another four. Meantime the President bought their dream home and she had the fun of decorating it. Husband Ike was home for good and no longer subject to military moves at a telephone call. And she was a grandmother. Prouder grandparents than the Eisenhowers never lived. Their daughter-in-law Barbara became so accustomed to it that she was not a bit embarrassed when President Ike announced at one of his press conferences that he was going to be a grandfather for the fourth time. When Mamie's only child, Major John Eisenhower, eventually was assigned to Washington, what more could the First Lady want? Except for her husband's two major illnesses and one of her own, her First Lady skies were usually unclouded.

When the President's second illness occurred in Washington, she went to Walter Reed Hospital with him. From her suite there she answered some eleven thousand letters of sympathy and concern from everywhere. Anybody who wrote at such a time deserved an answer, in her opinion.

Of course she made some changes at the White House. One of them was to change the shape of the table in the State Dining Room, as well as the seating arrangements, so that she could sit beside her husband. For her big dinners the table was E-shaped. She and the President sat side by side at the "outside middle of the longest side." Not since McKinley brought his invalid wife to sit beside him so that he could take care of her had anyone made such an innovation, but after World War II changes in protocol did not seem to be so earth-shaking any more.

Mamie received a great many delegations for her husband: from clubs and organizations meeting in Washington or official parties opening national drives for this and that. She was good at it and saved the President many hours. This was in addition to her own receptions for women's groups. She cut down on these after a time by receiving only the national officers.

Very early in the game she received more than four thousand delegates to an annual meeting. Unable to take all that handshaking in one fell swoop, she was spelled occasionally by the Vice President's wife or a Cabinet wife.

It was not exactly pleasant to hear a D.A.R. boom out, "Where's Mamie? I didn't come here to shake hands with Pat Nixon!" But First Ladies become accustomed to such things.

238

She began to receive only the officers of groups and did not promise that for every year. This did not please the outfits which lured delegates with the sure promise that the "White House will receive us." One of the banes of a First Lady's existence is always the fact that in organization-minded America, the pressure for groups to be received at the White House is every bit as great as that which lobbyists exert on Congress. The Eisenhowers had this in great measure after the Korean War ended and Americans began to travel and meet again with renewed strength and numbers. The press groups were one of the worst offenders. One year President Ike found himself dated five Saturday nights in a row for press events. So the Eisenhowers began to say, "If you do it for one you have to do it for all," and to cut the schedule. Mamie remained generous about attending lunches and "lending her name" to many groups by becoming an honorary member and, of course, the schedule was not eliminated—only shortened. Rather than shake all the hands each time, she developed a system for cheerily greeting everyone at once with a few words of welcome plus some waves and smiles.

She initiated no civic or social causes on her own but took on the special White House project of completing the china collection begun by Caroline Harrison. When she left, all Presidential families were represented and there was a complete record of her work. She took pride in having a beautiful display setting made for the collection in a ground floor room and in adding a set of plates which featured the likenesses of First Ladies.

Her mother, Mrs. John S. Doud, who visited frequently in the White House, gave the First Lady a small electric organ and there were family songfests with Mamie at the keys. "Now, Ike, don't bellow," she would tell her husband as the four grandchildren, John and Barbara, gathered around. She said that she played by ear, but she had studied music throughout her childhood. Major John inherited his mother's musical talents. She had gone to endless trouble to find a harmonica for him when he was going off to war.

Canasta was her favorite game and she played it on free afternoons with a group of old friends who became known as "Mamie's Bridge Cabinet." On Saturday afternoons she loved to watch a movie at the White House with the grandchildren. Her son and his family never lived in the White House and he bent over backward to prevent acceptance of special favors. But his family was in and out almost daily. "Mimi," as her grandchildren called the First Lady, kept an array of toys in the house for the children and Ike watched their school grades like a hawk. Grandson David was an extrovert charmer whom the public loved to watch grow up. He played golf with Ike and walked off with many a photograph. He was sent out West to camp one summer and en route told reporters that he and his buddies had sat up most of the night "learning to play poker!" His father often worried about what nearness to the White House might do to his children and when they began to go to so many birthday parties—the same trouble which their grandparents faced—he moved his family to a small house on the Gettysburg farm and commuted back and forth to his White House job.

One of Ike's real personal problems after he became President was that he had no place to cook. Nearly all his life he had cooked for fun and as a release from tension. He also liked to raid the icebox—a pleasure not provided at the White House. So he had a kitchen built for himself on the third floor and the place became more homelike. All in all, the Eisenhowers managed to enjoy many quiet and pleasant moments. The country joked about his golf games and Mamie's canasta, and there was quite a furore the first time she went out to Elizabeth Arden's health farm in Arizona. The President accompanied her in a government plane and the use of a plane for such a so-called frivolous purpose infuriated some people. Former President Truman rose to the defense of his successor on this one to declare that anything a President needed to do for the health and welfare of his family was legitimate national business. But a latent resentment against the Eisenhower vacations and forms of recreation probably continued.

What Mamie liked most about the White House, perhaps, was that her life no longer was controlled by the telephone message, "Pack a bag." That was how it was with her up to and into the days of World War II. Five days after Pearl Harbor her husband called with that message. "For how long?" she asked. "They tell me it is temporary," Ike replied. They had planned to spend that Christmas at West Point with John. Mamie went alone and returned to Fort Sam Houston to, as she said, "pack up a seventeen-room house." She attended John's graduation alone, too. The general came home a few times on secret missions and on the first one she could sense the raised eyebrows of a repairman when she heard a man's voice in her hotel apartment. When Harry Butcher wrote *My Three Years With Eisenhower* she said that she could write volumes on "My Three Years *Without* Eisenhower." She kept nine photos of the general in her apartment and several of her son. "My pin-up boys," she called them. She lost twenty-five pounds and had insomnia as she worried during World War II about both of them.

Later she was blamed for not doing war work, but that was unfair. She did wait on tables at the USO at times, but the important thing was that as the wife of the commanding general she was supposed to live quietly and to keep her mouth shut. The fewer people she saw the better the military liked it. She was not in the best of health either. She was never robust physically. She had an inner-ear imbalance problem and a heart murmur which the White House doctor said stemmed from an undiagnosed bout with rheumatic fever in her childhood. One of Ike's worries about accepting the nomination for the Presidency was what it might do to Mamie's health.

She tired easily and was subject to severe headaches in times of emotional stress. She had a severe headache at the Chicago convention which nominated her husband and had to cancel the press conference scheduled in her hotel suite immediately after the balloting. That is, if her husband won! The doctor who was called in became one of the most sought after men in Chicago that day because editors all over the country were clamoring for "Mamie's story" and every breath she drew went immediately into the public domain.

If she had been doing it deliberately, the timing could not have been worse, because one of the rumors started against Mamie had been that she drank too much. That she would have done so or even have had the chance to do so at such a time, surrounded by relatives and by almost every important Republican political leader in the country, was a fantastic idea. But no more so than the things said about other First Ladies throughout the years. The fact that a First Lady has feelings of her own rarely counts for much in the rumor mill.

Even Lillian Rogers, the writing seamstress who found Mamie a White House tyrant in many ways—but loved her, nonetheless—went out of her way to say, "I never believed that about the drinking." Nor did most other people. Mamie rallied in Chicago and within a few hours was the hit of the show. She liked people and they knew it. On the Eisenhower campaign train of nineteen cars, the longest in history, she had a marvelous time greeting crowds everywhere. "How many more stops?" she would ask, wondering how many more she could take physically, but loving them all.

Mamie was born in Boone, Iowa, in November of 1896 to a Swedish mother named Elivera Carlson and John Sheldon Doud, whose English forebears had helped found Guilford, Connecticut. The Douds moved West to Chicago in 1876 and Mamie's Grandfather Doud was on the Chicago Board of Trade. John Doud must have inherited his father's business ability, for he was so successful in his cattle and meat packing business that he was able to retire at the age of thirty-six and take his family to Colorado for his wife's health. In Denver he had a home which ranked with the best and his automobiles were always the latest and newest models. In addition, he bought his wife an electric car which was fitted up like a jewel box inside. The four Doud girls called it "Creepy" but they appreciated its showcase value. The Douds had the first basement recreation room in Denver. It was known as the "wreck room" at the time. It even had a billiard table, which some of the neighbors considered to be highflown, but the Doud girls had barrels of fun. Papa Doud seems to have been an unusual man (which all fathers are, of course!) when it came to wanting his wife and daughters to be happy. He was always there and in charge of the situation, and he went out of his way to plan special events. His lively daughter Mamie called him Pooh-bah because he was so "managing."

She, it was admitted by all, was the most popular daughter. Older sister Eleanor was the student and young "Mike" was a tomboy who threw cucumbers from the garden at anybody who tried to get her into "young lady" clothes—but Mamie was a favorite with the boys from early girlhood. (She always claimed that it was her jazzy way at the piano!) She was what was called a "good pupil but a poor student" in school, but her teachers loved her. She was obedient and gay and most entertaining, and always she wore her heart on her sleeve.

Denver had excellent theater and opera on a touring basis and Mamie went often to old Elitch's Gardens theater to weep through the tragedies and laugh through the comedies, and to enjoy the whole business. Young people congregated on the Doud steps in the dusk, just as they were doing all over America in the carefree days before World War I. One of her gay and musical Swedish uncles took her to Elitch's Gardens dancing one night and they ventured to try the new foxtrot. "Sure we can do it," Mamie said. "Here. This is the way I think it goes." Soon, to her everlasting embarrassment, there was a tap on the shoulder and the management was asking the young lady to "dance a little less sensationally!"

Sister Eleanor's health, strained by the high altitudes of Colorado, called for warmer climates. So John Doud loaded his family into the new Packard and went to San Antonio, Texas, for the winter. Mamie left behind a string of beaux who swore that they would not breathe until she returned in the spring. Mamie's mother let her have some daring new French heels for the occasion; already she was wearing her chiffon dresses down to the ankles and fixing her hair up with careful attention to the swirl which came down over her high forehead.

At old Fort Sam she met young Second Lieutenant Dwight Eisenhower—just out of West Point—on a day when he was officer of the day. He asked her to go along on his walking tour of duty and, to her surprise, she found herself going: she, Mamie, who avoided walking like the plague and who, so she said, never stood up straight if there was anything near to lean against. She was such a flirt by the standards of the day that she pretended to have dates even when she did not, lest she seem eager to see him again. Her father liked him and Ike often found himself eating supper with the family and waiting for Mamie to get back from her many actual dates.

They were married in Denver on July 1, 1916, the by-then first Lieutenant refusing to sit on his razor-sharp creases until the ceremony ended. Back at old Fort Sam they lived in his two-room quarters and took their meals at the Officers' Club at $30 a month each. Mamie was no cook and only knew how to make fudge and mayonnaise when she married. The club set-up was not the answer, though, because Ike had a malarial stomach which could not stand the food. They bought a two-burner stove, hid an icebox in the bathroom, put his books on shelves built into the fireplace (which did not work) and used the bookshelves for pots and pans. Then he proceeded to teach his bride to cook—although he continued to do much of it by preference.

He was called away on a three-months tour of duty and Mamie was alone for the first time in her life, and scared to death. He suggested leaving a gun for her, but that thought only scared her more. Next time he was away their first child, David Dwight—immediately nicknamed "Icky"—was born. Icky died at Camp Meade, Maryland, at the age of three. Daughter-in-law Barbara's first child was to wear his christening gown, every stitch of it made by Mamie, who never ceased to shed tears when Icky was mentioned. She was alone during much of World War I, but she never got used to it. She went home to Denver to have her second son, John. "I've kept house in everything except an igloo," she often said. Ike said, "Pack a bag" more frequently than did many military men, perhaps because his upward climb was so continuous and unbroken.

Perhaps their happiest assignment—before the White House—was the first time they went to Paris together a few years after the end of World War I. He was selected to write, for the Military Monuments Commission, a history of the foreign battlefields on which Americans had fought and on which many were buried. Ike and Mamie's house became a popular rendezvous for all military pals overseas and Mamie loved learning about Paris.

Her other out-of-the-country tours included Panama and the Philippines. She delayed a year going to the Philippines, however, because her son then was in junior high school and it was thought best not to transfer him. By the time that Mamie and Ike got back to Paris together, on the NATO assignment—after he resigned from the presidency of Columbia University to accept the call back to active duty—the world was much more complex and forbidding. His higher status made a "homey" life impossible. Mamie took pride in the decorating job which she did on their home, the official one for the commanding officer of the North Atlantic Treaty Alliance, and in entertaining the constant stream of world visitors. But it was not the same any more.

One of the nicest compliments a President ever paid to his wife Ike paid to Mamie from the White House on their fortieth wedding anniversary when he declared that being married to her was a treat which meant ever more enjoyment as the years passed. And Mamie still looked more like the popular girl from Denver than somebody celebrating a fortieth wedding anniversary.

JACQUELINE BOUVIER KENNEDY (1961-)

A Spectacular in Living Color

ON the snowiest inaugural night within memory (although the Tafts had it sleetier and colder) a new First Lady named Jacqueline Kennedy stepped into countless living rooms, and politics took on a new dimension in elegance for watching Americans.

There she was, floating along in all that bad weather in what appeared to be the slimmest and whitest dress ever created—and over it she wore a flowing cape of the same material. The peau d'ange of the cape, though, was covered with three layers of white chiffon. For warmth, no doubt! And the cape had a little collar with two buttons which in a jiffy could be closed up against pneumonia. Obviously the attire, designed by the new First Lady herself, was the latest thing in what fairy princesses wore when they went to a ball.

She was quite the youngest and loveliest-looking First Lady in many a generation. One wondered how many people up and down the frozen Eastern seaboard and elsewhere were exclaiming, "That child will catch her death of cold." She was thirty-one years of age and the mother of two children, but she had the airs of a little girl and her smile was so slow and timorous that one wished to pat her on the back before saying, "There, there. Everything's all right." She not only enchanted but she made one feel protective.

Washington's social arbiter, Carolyn Hagner Shaw, noted in print that the new President walked two or three paces ahead of his wife throughout the evening, and wrote that he should not do so again. "Well, then, Jackie must learn to walk a little faster," he declared when told about it.

At the *Washington Post*, where the editors were eager Kennedy fans, strict orders in mimeographed form had declared that Jackie must not under any circumstances be called Jackie. She was a home town girl, so to speak, having lived a great deal in Washington, but there was going to be no undue familiarity around here. "The wife of the President of the United States will not be referred to in our pages as 'Jackie'," the *Post* averred. She is instead Mrs. John F. Kennedy, Mrs. Kennedy, Jacqueline Kennedy, etc., (but not Jacqueline alone)!" Well, so much for good intentions—because almost everyone all over the country began calling her Jackie immediately.

Until the evening of the inaugural ball Jackie was rather lost in the midst of all those vivacious blonde Kennedy in-laws. On Capitol Hill at the noontime swearing-in ceremonies she was bundled up beyond recognition and anyway the TV cameras were busy with her husband's speech, with the fire which broke out at the rostrum while Robert Frost was reading his poetry, and with the four ecclesiastics who prayed loud and long for the Nation's salvation. The new President's crisp and exciting speech was shorter than the prayers.

On the night before there was a great pre-inaugural gala which turned out to be a free-for-all of snow and informality. Sir Laurence Olivier, only one of many theatrical stars on hand, rehearsed all afternoon and started to his hotel to change into formal attire. The streets were so impossible that by the the time he reached his room he had time to change only his tie. Ethel Merman, noted for such glad songs as "Everything's Coming Up Roses," could not leave the rehearsal hall at all and was near tears as she began to sing in her tweeds. Frank Sinatra, charged with the task of pulling the star-filled evening together, was on edge, too.

But the night of the ball belonged to Jackie, who obviously could not have cared less about the weather. She walked off with the show, and this she is capable of doing any time she puts her mind to it. Not since Eleanor Roosevelt has the public been so interested in a First Lady.

Jacqueline Kennedy is original and thorough. She likes to do things well or not at all. She ponders new ways to make the old forms and ceremonies interesting. Her first White House reception was held on a Sunday afternoon. There was no receiving line but a general mingling such as in one's own home. This worked so well that for parties with no more than ninety guests the stiffness of the receiving line was no longer used. Rather than parties and dinner for all diplomats, all judges, or all Congressmen she began to mix the guests so that instead of seeing only the people with whom one worked every day, the guest had a chance to catch up on what was going on in other circles.

She began to have meals served in odd ways: at round tables with gaily colored covers and with new flower arrangements. Two hundred women journalists had a buffet in the East Parlor where the tablecloths were yellow and the bouquets arranged in silver mugs. Each drew for her table number, as did the First Lady. When the State dining room began to overflow, tables were added in the Blue Parlor. When President Ayub of Pakistan came the first time the dinner for him was held on the grounds at Mount Vernon, the main guests cruising down the river in the July dusk. Never was there so much entertaining in so many different forms, and all of it relaxing.

She cut the menu to four excellent courses as more in line with what people eat at home—as well as to save time. One dinner for a hundred guests was finished in little more than one hour, without any feeling of hurry and with ample time for toasts. Such businesslike elegance is part of the New Frontier trademark. The State Department began to do more entertaining for the continuous stream of foreign visitors and the Cabinet began to sponsor evenings of culture with readings by literary lights such as Carl Sandburg and Thornton Wilder. Never had Americans been so conscious of the richness of their traditions. The White House gave a dinner for the Nobel prize winners of the Western Hemisphere. Pablo Casals, the great musician, came up from Puerto Rico to entertain at the White House. Shakespearean players came down from Connecticut and performed on a stage in the East Parlor. Ballet troupes performed. There was a dinner for the astronauts. Everything seemed new and different and filled with vitality. The twist was danced and a concert featured American jazz. The President gave many stag business lunches and at times stag dinners. There was a new air of activity at the White House.

The performing arts never had it so good and the artists responded by contributing their best. One of the aims of the administration is to raise funds with which to build a National Culture Center in Washington, in which the best of America's arts will be in almost continuous performance. The legislation for this was passed during the Eisenhower administration and the former President continued his interest. The work on the cultural fronts has been sensational, and everyone credits the First Lady, whose interests and knowledge are so varied and who makes her interests seem so stylish.

Whatever they may say about Jackie, she is never second rate. Her standards are so high that even the old and seemingly impossible National Guard Armory, where the biggest events of the capital city must take place, assumed a sort of elegance. No Washingtonian ever expected to witness the day when it would be possible either to see or hear in that big barn—where Republicans and Democrats alike usually stage their $100 fund-raising dinners. But the hotels, working together, staged an impressive dinner there for the kick-off of the National Culture Center and somebody finally learned how to decorate the old place and to stage things differently.

Jackie has the ability somehow to make others ashamed of the shoddy as unworthy of the country. She is not an easy person with whom to work, or so it is said. Her enthusiasm fluctuates wildly and she's stubborn as a mule about getting things exactly as she wants them—but her quality is undeniable and she has something which rallies others to do their best.

What she has done, or the interest which she has sparked, in the performing arts is as nothing compared to what she has done in the White House itself—although it is all in the same pattern. She took one look at the White House furniture and decided most of it was unworthy of the structure which housed it and that there must be far better stashed away somewhere in government storehouses. The eighteenth century is her history specialty and she knew that the early tenants of the White House had better furniture—more lovingly made, with each piece coming nearer to being an artistic accomplishment— than the factory-built pieces which came later. The government throws nothing away, but finding it is a problem. Jackie ransacked the storehouses and basements, found things of which most Americans never had heard, and began returning the White House to what one likes to believe was its former elegance. This is not entirely true, of course, because White House furnishings always have been a hodge-podge—except when James Monroe furnished the place complete after the British burning in 1814, and not even he furnished the big East Parlor. (Louisa Adams furnished it first, and Andrew Jackson was the first President to be able to use it. Jackson added several elegant spittoons; but Jackie, so far, has returned none of them to service.)

Her idea was much broader than just putting the old back. She tried to recapture the traditions but still to keep the place up-to-date. In the Green Room, for instance, she put some modern paintings by Cezanne (about the most green painter of all when he got started on landscapes) and over the mantel there she placed a great portrait of Benjamin Franklin, who never was President at all but who holds a special niche in the hearts of Americans. She made the White House a museum of American tradition and yet kept it livable.

She was too clever to do this on her own. Congress passed a law giving the old mansion a museum status so that no gift made to it could be sold at auction or lost forever. If not in immediate use at the White House, the gift would be packed away or on display at the Smithsonian Institution. The portraits of the First Ladies alone were a problem; many of them were mere copies and she could not string all of them up in a row without detracting from the appearance of the White House. The three things which she did definitely within her first two years as First Lady were:

1) She formed a Fine Arts Commission of private citizens

headed by Henry F. duPont to help her pass on what was suitable for the White House and what was not, and to work always with the National Fine Arts Commission; a joint private and government project.

2) She had the bill passed giving permanent museum status to the White House. Grace Coolidge obtained permission from Congress to accept gifts for the mansion, but there were no safeguards about what would happen to the gifts when somebody later did not want them.

3) She started the White House Historical Association, which was chartered in the District of Columbia as a nonprofit organization to publish the White House Guidebook, which sells for a dollar a copy and is a source of income for added antiques. An anonymous donor gave $40,000 to get the Guidebook started and the *National Geographic* printed it in color for nothing. (Nobody has ever been able to get more free gifts for the White House than the Kennedys!) Each donor received not only letters but often plaques, too. The White House became so much of a national treasure house that diplomatic families often appeared at the east entrance as early as 8:30 of a morning just to see it.

Jackie turned the Blue Room into blue and white, had white on white for the State Dining Room, gilded the dining room's silver chandelier which everyone has considered so unique as to be untouchable. She changed the red of the Red Room and was constantly changing portraits. She hung them up to the ceilings, one on top of the other, in what must have been the eighteenth century manner (at least they looked good!), and made the White House the most interesting house in the country. However different this may be from the contributions of other First Ladies, it is no mean accomplishment.

She had concerts for children, too, and during the remainder of her years in office she hopes to "do more for children," as well as push her promotion for the National Culture Center and to "keep an eye on Washington." The last reflects the fact that when she came into residence there, the whole of Lafayette Square across from the White House was about to be torn down for office buildings. (Washingtonians will build anywhere, without a bit of reverence, unless someone watches them!)

The story of Jackie in the White House is not finished, but it seems safe to say that her activities there never will sink into the routine and ordinary. Her reception by the public has been amazingly good. She has critics, of course, and topping the list of the criticisms seems to be her interest in sports such as fox-hunting and water skiing. "Travels too much away from her family" topped one critical list. She thinks that she and her family receive too much personal publicity.

The First Lady's background is a distinguished one and distinctly East Coast. It is of the old family, inherited income and social position variety rather than the more up-and-at-'em, politically oriented and *nouveau riche* background of the family into which she married. Compared to her exuberant and charming sisters-in-law, none of whom ever met a stranger, Mrs. Kennedy's childhood seems reminiscent of that of little girls brought up quietly in "the good old families" of California, Virginia, or the sheltered estate recesses of Long Island. The First Lady is more quiet and much more reticent than her sisters-in-law. Her personality is just as strong, however, and being surrounded by so many outgoing Kennedys has not changed it noticeably.

She was born at East Hampton, Long Island, in July of 1929. Her father was a darkly handsome and dashing sportsman named John Vernou Bouvier III, whose friends called him Jack or "The Sheik," and at times likened him in looks to Clark Gable. His oldest daughter Jacqueline was named for him and he was her attentive escort to horse shows almost from the time she was two. Of her it truly could be said that she virtually was "born in the saddle," and by the age of six she was walking away from horse shows with prizes.

The Bouviers—at least twenty-four of them—came to America to fight with their countryman Lafayette during the American Revolution. Afterward most of them returned to France, and so did Eustace, Jacqueline's forebear; but Michel, his son, brought up on tales of the bright new land, returned to live and die here. He settled in Philadelphia in the early 1800's. The Bouviers prospered, were much respected, and retained their pride in their French heritage.

Mrs. Kennedy's mother, Janet Lee, was a leading belle in her debutante year in New York City, and her marriage to Bouvier received much space in the city papers. In addition to her popularity and her stable-old-family background, she was noted as a fearless and outstanding horsewoman, about the best in the ring anywhere. Her second child, Lee, now married to Polish Prince Radziwill (whose family came to England during World War II and still lives there), was born when Jacqueline was three and a half years old. She's the First Lady's only full sister, but there are a half sister and a half brother.

The marriage of the First Lady's parents did not remain successful, and when she and her sister were still little girls there was a separation. Mother and daughters went to live in a New York apartment, but the girls never completely lost the affectionate attention of their father. In 1942 Janet Bouvier was married again, this time to Hugh D. Auchincloss, a broker with three children by two former marriages. The Bouvier girls came to live at Merrywood, his home in Virginia, and often spent their summers at Hammersmith Farm, the Auchincloss estate at Newport, Rhode Island. The future First Lady had her main debut party at Hammersmith Farm, and later cut the bridal cake there after her marriage to the future President, on September 13, 1953. The First Lady has called her stepfather about the kindest man in the world, and the large family grew up together in harmony.

From kindergarten days Jacqueline Bouvier was an individualist with a mind of her own, much less of a conformist than her sister Lee. An early headmistress said she had one of the most inquiring minds ever seen at the school, and added, "Otherwise we might not have kept her." Young Jackie's mother was horrified while out with her daughters in Central Park one day, to overhear a nearby tot say, "She (Jackie) goes to the headmistress' office more than anybody." It turned out to be true; the young miss in question freely admitted it. She went, listened most politely, evidently enjoyed the sessions, but apparently never remotely considered changing her behavior! Her regard for becoming "the perfect little girl" by the school's standards seems to have been nil.

By the time she was six or so she could write poetry—and add original touches, too, and often decorate it with her own drawings. Her mother lovingly kept many samples of Miss Bouvier's poetry and some of it she has shown to other people. It is charming as well as scanable, neatly and nicely printed with almost professional ability, and originally decorated. Always, it appears, Jacqueline could draw well just what she wanted to draw. The sign of the perfectionist with originality appeared very early. In her later paintings the facility for drawing to commemorate an event or "tell a story" clearly showed through.

While her husband was being nominated for the Presidency in Los Angeles in 1959, she stayed behind in Hyannis Port and painted a fitting welcome-home scene for him. It was completely intentional that one celebrant waving the former sailor home had six fingers. She likes a "zany" touch now and then and, supposedly, these oddities made her husband laugh. This particular picture shows her, daughter Caroline, Nurse Shaw, and the family dog on the wharf yelling and yelping their heads off, all in vivid color and done especially for the conquering hero.

The year after her mother remarried, young Jacqueline went to Miss Porter's School in Farmington, Connecticut, and was so lonely for Danseuse, her mother's prize mare, she hardly knew what to do. Other girls were permitted to have their horses, but her allowance would not cover the $25 extra a month needed for the animal's board. She wrote her

Grandfather Lee, the banker who advised her about poetry and life in general. He thought maybe he could spare the money because it was necessary for his granddaughter's growing up and happiness! This typifies the "thrifty" manner in which Jacqueline was brought up, and illustrates why today she is noted for always asking the price if a purchase is for herself, and saying that naturally she would wear her left-over maternity clothes before the birth of her third baby. Supposedly nothing about the last national election irritated her more than the furore raised about the comparative cost of her wardrobe and that of Pat Nixon, the wife of the opposing candidate.

Like most such furores before elections, this one died down in a short time—but to liken the First Lady's personal spending to that of someone else can lead only to hot water. If the Kennedys ever go broke it surely will not be due to Jacqueline. She bought her debutante party dress off a rack for $59 and took great pride in so doing. Her mother, busy with younger children, was a bit shocked when she heard about it, but the outfit was lovely and Jacqueline was named "Queen Deb of the Year" by New York columnist Cholly Knickerbocker.

Some call the penny watching the "French side" of the First Lady and, no doubt that side helps—but it came from both sides of the family and probably, just as important, has to do with her own preference for the functional, modern type of life and her innate practicality. Atoka, the home she designed on Rattlesnake Mountain in Virginia, is within easy weekend reach of Washington and it entitles her to ride with two hunt clubs. It is a starkly simple place, though it does include stalls for her horses and a swimming pool. Nobody believed she could build a three-bedroom plus servants' wing set-up in the Washington area for the price announced (about $50,000). However, maybe she did add or subtract a few things, as all homeowners have to do.

But whatever the cost of building, the thrifty side of the venture became evident when Jacqueline decided that, since the family was going to Hyannis Port for the summer of 1963, as usual, she would rent the new home. It amused the Washington reporters that the First Lady would bother to rent for a few months, furniture and all. Not too many women of even moderate means would like to have other people living, even briefly, in *their* new homes.

The future First Lady had to plan her initial trip to Europe as carefully as did most American girls in the days before there were so many international scholarships. Although she was attending Vassar, she wangled her way into a Smith College group spending their junior year at the University of Grenoble and the Sorbonne. She wanted to live in France for a while, perfect her knowledge of the language, and learn more about French history, which had always enthralled her. She lived with a French family (with whom she still corresponds), took second-class-fare trips to other parts of the Continent, and loved the whole business.

Some time before Jacqueline returned home, her mother noticed that *Vogue* magazine was running a contest which awarded the winner a half year's employment on its Paris edition. Mrs. Auchincloss sent an application to Jacqueline, who entered the contest and won, but chose not to accept the prize. She wanted a job, probably of a journalistic nature, but she wanted it in the United States—and not necessarily in fashion. She consulted Arthur Krock of *The New York Times,* who got her an interview with the editor of the now-defunct Washington *Times-Herald.*

"If I give you a job are you going to show up engaged next week, or are you serious?" the editor, Frank Waldrop, asked. She was very serious, Jacqueline assured him, and determined to have a career. All right then, he decreed, she could become the Inquiring Girl Photographer, whose job was to lug a camera around to take pictures of people she interviewed on agreed-upon topics.

Jacqueline was a fair amateur photographer, but she signed up for instructions on how to handle her reporter's Graflex professionally. The boys in the paper's darkroom were helpful, too. Her column was bright and informative, and the pictures were okay. One day she was sent to Capitol Hill to interview some new senators on what they thought about the Senate page boys and what the boys in turn thought about them. Among the lawmakers interviewed were John F. Kennedy, brand-new senator from Massachusetts, and Richard M. Nixon, the new vice president, who presided over the Senate. Later she met the busy new senator socially at the home of Charles Bartlett, who hoped the meeting would "take." Senator Kennedy, arriving late and appearing distracted, mumbled something to Jacqueline about taking her out to dance after dinner, but when they reached her car another of her admirers was already awaiting her.

Jacqueline had many dates, and the congressman was so busy one needed to grab him on his own schedule or risk not seeing him again soon. But somehow they managed to get together anyway, though they did it unobtrusively. She covered the coronation of Queen Elizabeth for her paper, doing her own sketches for her stories. When her plane touched down in Boston on her return she hoped the senator would be there to greet her—and there he was, leaning casually against a counter as if he had just run out to buy a newspaper. She had bought him a lot of books, paying about $100 of her own hard-earned money to ship them from London.

They became engaged in 1953, but the engagement could not be announced immediately. Jacqueline confided to an aunt but said not to mention it, that the *Saturday Evening Post* was soon to run a story on "The Senate's Gay Young Bachelor," and it would not be fair to the *Post*. Her aunt wondered what in the world a magazine could have to do with Jacqueline's engagement!

The marriage was at Newport and the party at Hammersmith Farm. To be married to an always-on-the-go Kennedy was exciting, to say the least. Young Mrs. Kennedy soon learned that her husband scarcely noticed when or whether he ate, and was almost equally indifferent to sleep. His office arranged his schedule, and consequently hers too. They lived in a rented furnished house, something new for her, until she became pregnant in 1955, and then they purchased Hickory Hill, a large house in the suburbs. She had a miscarriage. Later they moved back to Washington, to another rented house, so that Jacqueline would see more of her husband. The Robert Kennedys now live at Hickory Hill.

Worried about her husband's health, Jacqueline began sending digestible lunches for him to eat at his desk on Capitol Hill. She enrolled in a course in American History at nearby Georgetown University so that she would understand his work better. The numerous small dinners she gave were casual and often impromptu, but always nicely planned and elegantly served. When time for the Democratic National Convention rolled around in 1956 she, although several months pregnant, went along to Chicago for the hectic political free-for-all during which her husband almost won the nomination as vice president. After the convention her husband went to Europe for a vacation and she sought to rest and prepare for the birth of her child. But when it came, by emergency Caesarian section, it was stillborn. The future First Lady was very ill herself. It appeared that the Kennedys might never have a child if they continued to live under such pressure, although both wanted children.

When Jacqueline became pregnant the third time, she sought the help of Dr. John W. Walsh, who was noted for his handling of difficult cases. Daughter Caroline was born in November, 1957, and the Kennedys could scarcely believe their luck. Caroline is a storybook child, well worth waiting for. Rarely, has the White House had such an enchanting inhabitant, or one more quotable. For a while it almost seemed as if she were receiving more space in the papers than her father and mother combined. There is a story that claims a hardbitten editor once telephoned a reporter and snapped, "Never mind all that stuff about what's going on in Laos. Get what Caroline said today!" Her best remembered quote so far was made when she was just becoming accustomed to finding her way about the White House. She sauntered into the President's impressive offices and informed the startled staff, "Daddy's sitting upstairs with his shoes off."

Caroline had not yet celebrated her third birthday when Daddy was elected President, and her baby brother was not due until around Christmastime. After the campaign the President-elect flew to Florida for a short vacation, but had to turn back in transit because his son, John Fitzgerald Kennedy, Jr., had decided to arrive a month early. "Only a matter of minutes, luck, and a wonderful doctor saved the baby," it was said at the time. The candidate's wife, despite her pregnancy, had campaigned with her husband all over the country, and perhaps she had stood far too much in too many receiving lines.

So when it became known that the First Lady was pregnant in 1963, with a baby due in late August, the signals were changed completely and all her part of the White House schedule was cancelled. The President took on hosting alone or asking others to help out, and tried to attend to everything planned for her. He told the Congressional Club, made up of Congressional wives, when he appeared to speak in his wife's absence, that he was happy to do so while she was "adding to the gross national product."

A son, Patrick Bouvier Kennedy, was born prematurely to President and Mrs. Kennedy on August 7, 1963. The nation mourned with them when the infant died of a respiratory ailment two days after birth.

CREDITS FOR PORTRAITS

MARTHA CUSTIS WASHINGTON—By Charles Willson Peale, a miniature done about the time of the Revolution. Courtesy of The Mount Vernon Ladies' Association.

ABIGAIL SMITH ADAMS—By Ralph Earl, 1785. Presented by the New York State Historical Association. Courtesy of The White House.

DOLLEY MADISON—By Gilbert Stuart. Mrs. Madison did not like this painting of herself as she preferred those with large turban headdresses. She also thought the mouth "too prim." Courtesy of The White House, National Park Service.

ELIZABETH KORTRIGHT MONROE—By Benjamin West. Courtesy of Mrs. Gouverneur Hoes, owner, and the Frick Art Reference Library.

LOUISA CATHERINE JOHNSON ADAMS—By Gilbert Stuart. Courtesy of the Frick Art Reference Library.

RACHEL JACKSON—By Howard Chandler Christy, from old miniatures and imagination. Courtesy of The White House Collection, photo by Abbie Rowe, courtesy of National Park Service.

ANNA SYMMES HARRISON—Watercolor by an unknown artist. Courtesy of President Benjamin Harrison Memorial Home, Indianapolis, Indiana.

LETITIA TYLER—By an unknown artist. Reproduced from the collections of the Library of Congress.

JULIA GARDINER TYLER—By F. Anelli, before 1864. From The White House Collection. Photo by Abbie Rowe, courtesy of National Park Service.

SARAH CHILDRESS POLK—By Myna Avent. Courtesy of The White House.

ABIGAIL POWERS FILLMORE—Probably the earliest photograph of a First Lady, made during her residence at The White House. Later First Ladies were to stand at this South entrance column for their photographs. Courtesy of U.S. National Museum of the Smithsonian Institution. Gift of Mrs. Warren Powers Laird.

JANE APPLETON PIERCE—Engraving by J. C. Buttre. Courtesy of the Smithsonian Institution.

MARY TODD LINCOLN—Photo by Mathew B. Brady. Courtesy of Signal Corps, from the National Archives.

ELIZA McCARDLE JOHNSON—Engraving by J. C. Buttre. Library of Congress Collections.

JULIA DENT GRANT—Photographer unknown. Courtesy of the Library of Congress Collections.

LUCY WEBB HAYES—By Daniel Huntington, 1881. Presented by Ladies' Christian Temperance Union. Courtesy of The White House.

LUCRETIA RUDOLPH GARFIELD—Photographed while First Lady. Photographer unknown. Courtesy of the Library of Congress Collections.

FRANCES FOLSOM CLEVELAND—Portrait by Zorn. A copy of this is now in The White House. Courtesy of Marion Cleveland Amen.

CAROLINE LAVINIA HARRISON—Painted by Daniel Huntington. Presented by The Daughters of the American Revolution. Courtesy of The White House.

IDA SAXTON McKINLEY—Photographed in The White House hothouse. Courtesy of the Library of Congress Collections.

EDITH CAROW ROOSEVELT—Painted by Theobald Chartran, 1902. Presented by French Republic. Courtesy of The White House.

HELEN HERRON TAFT—By B. Kronstrand, 1910. Courtesy of The White House.

ELLEN AXSON WILSON—Photographer unknown. Courtesy of the Collections of the Library of Congress.

EDITH BOLLING GALT WILSON—By Adolf Felix Miller-Urey. Courtesy of Edith Bolling Wilson, from The White House Collection.

FLORENCE KLING HARDING—By Philip de Laszlo. Courtesy of the Collections of the Library of Congress.

GRACE GOODHUE COOLIDGE—By Howard Chandler Christy. Courtesy of The White House.

LOU HENRY HOOVER—Original painting by Philip de Laszlo, copied by Richard M. Brown for The White House Collection. Courtesy of The White House.

ELEANOR ROOSEVELT—Photographed during first term in The White House, under portrait of President Grant. Courtesy of Bradford Bachrach.

BESS WALLACE TRUMAN—Photographed while First Lady. Courtesy of Harris and Ewing.

MAMIE DOUD EISENHOWER—Painted by Thomas E. Stephens in her pink inaugural gown. Courtesy of The White House Collection, photo by Abbie Rowe. Courtesy of National Park Service.

JACQUELINE BOUVIER KENNEDY—Photographed by Mark Shaw. Courtesy of The White House.